Politicians, Economists and the Supreme Court at Work

To Colleen Jo Healy. How could I have been so lucky?

Politicians, Economists and the Supreme Court at Work

The Founders Betrayed

Timothy P. Roth, PhD

The University of Texas at El Paso, USA

Edward Elgar
Cheltenham, UK • Northampton, MA, USA

Published by
Edward Elgar Publishing Limited
The Lypiatts
15 Lansdown Road
Cheltenham
Glos GL50 2JA
UK

Edward Elgar Publishing, Inc.
William Pratt House
9 Dewey Court
Northampton
Massachusetts 01060
USA

A catalogue record for this book
is available from the British Library

Library of Congress Control Number: 2009940650

Mixed Sources
Product group from well-managed
forests and other controlled sources
www.fsc.org Cert no. SA-COC-1565
© 1996 Forest Stewardship Council

ISBN 978 1 84844 453 9

Printed and bound by MPG Books Group, UK

Contents

Preface   vii

1   The federal enterprise   1
2   The Founders' vision   42
3   The 'Old Court' at work   88
4   The 'New Court' at work   95
5   The politics and the economics of wants and needs   115
6   What would the Founders do?   156

References   183
Index   203

Preface

Former New Jersey Superior Court Judge Andrew P. Napolitano recently asked the third-ranking Democrat in the US House of Representatives 'where in the Constitution it authorizes the federal government to regulate the delivery of health care'. The congressman's answer encapsulates what I argue is the prevailing 'Washington attitude': 'There's nothing in the Constitution that says that the federal government has anything to do with most of the stuff we do'. To this the congressman added: 'How about [you] show me where in the Constitution it prohibits the federal government from doing this' (Napolitano, 2009).

The 'Washington attitude' finds expression in two related ideas and impulses. First, the Congress is free to tax, spend, borrow and regulate as *it* sees fit, unencumbered by constitutional or moral constraints. Second, the burgeoning federal enterprise is animated by the politics of 'wants and needs', by 'rights' defined in opposition to republican self-government, and by a determination to address perceived 'market failures' and to compensate for 'forbidden' income and wealth inequalities.

The recent paroxysm of federal activity – the Troubled Asset Relief Program, the Energy Improvement and Extension Act of 2008, the Tax Extenders and Alternative Minimum Tax Relief Act of 2008, the American Recovery and Reinvestment Act of 2009, the Omnibus Appropriations Act, 2009, the 'Cap-and-Trade' bill and the metastasizing 'health-care reform' bills – is not a manifestation of a recent emergence of the 'Washington attitude'. In fact, the 'attitude' is the product of a path-dependent process that has been influenced by a moral and political philosophy, a political economy and a constitutional jurisprudence that would be alien to the United States' Founders' imagination.

A recurring theme of the book is that their embrace of the Washington attitude has enabled politicians, economists and the Supreme Court variously to rationalize, to justify or to endorse an expansion of federal on-, off- and off-off-budget activity that ignores the federal government's enumerated powers, usurps the states' police powers, and substitutes impersonal agency rule-making for congressional accountability. If, as I argue, the resulting erosion of federalism and the separation of powers represents a threat to liberty, the body of discriminatory statutory and administrative law is irreconcilable with the Founders' prior ethical commitment to the moral equivalence of persons. For their part, the now-routine departures from 'regular order' and statutory budget process law effectively disenfranchise voters and ignore the moral imperative, embraced by the Founders, to promote the greatest possible equal political participation. Finally, the metastasization of entitlements is a reflection of the politics of wants and needs, and of a rights conception that the Founders would reject. All of this is defined in opposition to the Founders' procedurally based, consequence-detached republican self-government project. Stated differently, politicians, economists and the Supreme Court have given form and substance to Madison's greatest fear:

> what is of most importance is the high sanction given to a latitude in expounding the Constitution which seems to break down the landmarks intended by a specification of the Powers of Congress, and to substitute for a definite connection between means and ends, a Legislative discretion as to the former to which no practical limit can be assigned. (Madison [1819] 1999, p. 734)

Chapter 1, The Federal Enterprise, begins with a discussion of what I have styled the recent paroxysm of federal activity, and the Founders would likely characterize as the post-September 2008 'rage' of federal legislation. The balance of Chapter 1 provides an adumbration of the entire corpus of federal on-, off- and off-off-budget activity.

While there is a sense in which a comprehensive survey of federal activity is valuable for its own sake, the book is motivated by a thought experiment: suppose that the Founders were with us today. Suppose also that the Founders, now our notional contemporaries, are aware of the scope and reach of federal activity (Chapter 1), of the character and content of the 'Old' and 'New' Supreme Courts' constitutional jurisprudence (Chapters 3 and 4), and of the public philosophy and political economy that inform the 'Washington attitude' (Chapter 5). Suppose, finally, that the Founders engage in a critical appraisal of the federal enterprise. Informed by *their* moral and political philosophy, by *their* political economy and by *their* understanding of the Constitution and of the role of the Supreme Court (Chapter 2), the Founders would, I argue, conclude that much of what the federal government does is either unconstitutional, immoral, or both. While each chapter incorporates elements of this conceptual exercise, Chapter 6 answers the hypothetical question, 'What would the Founders do?'

1. The federal enterprise

1.1 BAILOUTS, STIMULUS AND ALL THAT

On 3 October 2008, President George W. Bush signed a three-part bill (US Congress, House Resolution 1424, 2008). Division A of the bill styled the Emergency Economic Stabilization Act of 2008 subsumes three 'Titles', the first of which is the Troubled Asset Relief Program (TARP). The second Title codifies reporting requirements imposed upon the Secretary of the Treasury, the Office of Management and Budget and the Congressional Budget Office, along with an adumbration of required TARP-related federal budgetary analyses. The third Title sets out TARP-related tax provisions including Special Rules for [the] Tax Treatment of Executive Compensation of Employers Participating in [TARP].

While they have received relatively less attention, the Energy Improvement and Extension Act of 2008 (Division B) and Division C, the Tax Extenders and Alternative Minimum Tax Relief Act of 2008, are important for their own sake. On the one hand, because they are non-germane – they are unrelated to TARP – they say much about the modern legislative process. On the other hand, the bulk of Divisions B and C consists in the institutionalization, extension or modification of discriminatory tax provisions targeting well-defined group and individual beneficiaries.

If Divisions B and C are, as I shall argue, a metaphor for the discriminatory post-constitutional politics that the United States' Founders abhorred, my immediate interest centers on TARP (Division A).

Section 2 of the Emergency Economic Stabilization Act of 2008 sets out TARP's 'Purpose':

The purposes of this Act are –
(1) to immediately provide authority and facilities that the Secretary of the Treasury can use to restore liquidity and stability to the financial system of the United States; and
(2) to ensure that such authority and such facilities are used in a manner that –
   (A) protects home values, college funds, retirement accounts, and life savings;
   (B) preserves homeownership and promotes jobs and economic growth;
   (C) maximizes overall returns to the taxpayers of the United States; and
   (D) provides public accountability for the exercise of such authority.

I emphasize, first, that Section 2 refers explicitly to 'the financial system', and that Section 3 paragraph (5) defines 'financial institution' as:

> any institution, including, but not limited to, any bank, savings association, credit union, security broker or dealer, or insurance company, established and regulated under the laws of the United States or any State, territory, or possession of the United States, the District of Columbia, Commonwealth of Puerto Rico, Commonwealth of Northern Mariana Islands, Guam, American Samoa, or the United States Virgin Islands, and having significant operations in the United States, but excluding any central bank of, or institution owned by, a foreign government.

The definition of 'financial institution' is important because Section 101 (a) (1) of TARP authorizes the Secretary of the Treasury:

> to establish the Troubled Asset Relief Program (or 'TARP') to purchase, and to make and fund commitments to purchase, troubled assets from any financial institution, on such terms and conditions as are determined by the Secretary, and in accordance with the Act and the policies and procedures developed and published by the Secretary.

'Troubled assets', in turn, are defined in Section 3 paragraph (9) as:

> (A) residential or commercial mortgages and any securities, obligations, or other instruments that are based on or related to such mortgages, that in each case was originated or issued on or before March 14, 2008, the purchase of which the Secretary determines promotes financial market stability; and
> (B) any other financial instrument that the Secretary, after consultation with the Chairman of the Board of Governors of the Federal Reserve System, determines the purchase of which is necessary to promote financial market stability, but only upon transmittal of such determination, in writing, to the appropriate committees of Congress.

Finally, Section 115 (a) (3) specifies that the Treasury Secretary's authority to purchase financial institutions' troubled assets under TARP 'shall be limited to $700,000,000,000 outstanding at any one time'. For its part, Section 121 (a) establishes 'the Office of the Special Inspector General for the Troubled Asset Relief Program' (SIGTARP). The SIGTARP is required, among other things, to issue periodic reports to 'the appropriate committees of Congress'. Each report, in turn, must include, 'for the period covered . . . a detailed statement of all purchases, obligations, expenditures, and revenues associated with any program established by the Secretary of the Treasury' (Section 121 (f)).

The SIGTARP's *Initial Report to Congress*, dated 6 February 2009 (SIGTARP, 2009a), includes a discussion of TARP's 'Legislative

Background'. Emphasis is placed on the fact that, 'By September 2008, US financial markets were in crisis', and that, in response, 'the Treasury Secretary met with the Chairmen of the Federal Reserve and the Securities and Exchange Commission . . . to develop the foundations of a relief program'. Whereas their 'initial proposal was not accepted by Congress, . . . it prompted a series of counterproposals . . . culminating in the passage of H.R. 1424, Division A – the Emergency Economic Stabilization Act of 2008, – on October 3, 2008' (p. 29).

The essential point is this: TARP authorizes the Secretary of the Treasury 'to purchase, and to make and fund commitments to purchase, troubled assets from any financial institution'. SIGTARP's 21 April 2009 *Quarterly Report to Congress* (SIGTARP, 2009b) emphasizes that 'TARP, as originally envisioned in the fall of 2008, *would have involved the purchase, management, and sale of up to $700 billion of "toxic" assets*, primarily troubled mortgages and mortgage-backed securities ("MBS")' (p. 3; emphasis mine). Despite this clear legislative mandate, the SIGTARP observes that:

> That framework was soon abandoned, however, and the program's scope, size, and complexity have dramatically increased. As of the writing of this report, TARP funds are being used, or have been announced to be used, in connection with 12 separate programs that . . . involve a total (including TARP funds, Federal Reserve loans, Federal Deposit Insurance Corporation ('FDIC') guarantees, and private money) that could reach nearly $3 trillion. (Ibid.)[1]

Against this background, I emphasize first that TARP's 'purposes' are outcomes based and procedurally-detached. While questions can and have been raised about TARP's ability to achieve its congressionally mandated goals that is not my immediate concern. Nor, for that matter, am I concerned with the possible unintended *consequences* of TARP-related federal initiatives. Instead, I focus, in the manner of the United States' Founders (Chapter 2 this volume), on TARP's morality and constitutionality. It is in this sense that my remarks gesture toward the argument developed in later chapters.

While their procedurally based, consequence-detached evaluative standards are fully developed in Chapter 2, it is sufficient for the moment to emphasize the Founders' prior ethical commitment to the moral equivalence of persons. It was this ethical commitment that accounts for the Founders' insistence that post-constitutional law must be just in the sense of impartiality, and that the Constitution, as the nation's 'fundamental law', must be respected. Indeed, for the Founders, the Constitution's 'auxiliary precautions', notably, though not exclusively, federalism and the separation of powers, were intended to be both formal, institutional restraints on discriminatory 'factious behavior' and the *deus ex machina* by which the greatest possible equal political participation would be promoted.

Recall now that TARP authorizes the Secretary of the Treasury 'to purchase, and to make and fund commitments to purchase, troubled assets from any financial institution'. Recall also that SIGTARP stresses that 'That framework was soon abandoned'. The nature and scope of what the Founders would have called Treasury's 'legislative encroachment' is made clear in Section 2 of SIGTARP's 21 April 2009 *Quarterly Report to Congress*: 'Treasury plans to support US financial institutions, *companies*, and *individual borrowers* through a combination of 12 separate TARP programs implemented or announced thus far' (p. 33; emphasis mine).

SIGTARP's 6 February, 21 April and 21 July 2009 *Reports* reveal that many of TARP's 'implemented programs' do *not* involve the purchase of 'troubled assets', and that TARP funding has *not* been restricted to 'financial institutions'. Let us be clear: nothing in Title I of the Emergency Economic Stabilization Act of 2008 authorizes the Treasury Department to abandon what I shall call the 'financial institutions–troubled assets framework'. It follows that any TARP program that departs from this framework may plausibly be regarded as a violation of the Constitution's Legislative Powers Clause (see Chapter 4 this volume). At issue, in short, is Congress's ability, under the Constitution, to delegate powers that, in Chief Justice Marshall's words, 'are strictly and exclusively legislative' to the president and to administrative agencies. While discussion of the Supreme Court's non-delegation jurisprudence is deferred to Chapter 4, the SIGTARP's 6 February (2009a) and 21 April 2009 (2009b) *Reports* bring the issue into bold relief. Of particular relevance are Section 3, 'TARP Implementation and Administration' (SIGTARP, 2009a, pp. 43–90), and Section 2 'TARP Overview' (SIGTARP, 2009b, pp. 33–126). SIGTARP's 'summaries of [the 12 programs'] announced descriptions' and the 'Projected TARP Funding' for each program are of immediate interest.[2]

The Capital Purchase Program (CPP), the Capital Assistance Program (CAP), the Systemically Significant Failing Institutions Program (SSFI) and the Targeted Investment Program (TIP) involve capital injections into the financial system using TARP funds. The Projected TARP Funding for each of these programs is, respectively, $218 billion, 'TBD', $70 billion and $40 billion.[3] The Asset Guarantee Program (AGP) has as its 'stated goal . . . to use insurance-like protections to help stabilize at-risk financial institutions'. The Projected TARP Funding for AGP is $12.5 billion. The 'stated objective of the [Automotive Industry Financing Program (AIFP)] is to "prevent a significant disruption of the American automotive industry, which would pose a systemic risk to financial market stability and have a negative effect on the economy of the United States"'. The Projected TARP Funding for AIFP is $25 billion. Understood to be 'an expansion of AIFP, the stated purpose of [the Auto Supplier Support Program (ASSP)] is to provide up to $5 billion of Government-backed financing to break the adverse credit cycle affecting the auto suppliers and the [automobile] manufacturers'. The Projected TARP Funding for ASSP is $5 billion. A related program, 'the Auto Warranty Commitment Program, was devised by the Administration with the stated intent to bolster consumer confidence in automobile warranties on GM- and Chrysler-built vehicles'. The SIGTARP adds that 'Treasury preliminarily discussed potential funding for the Auto Warranty Commitment Program for up to an estimated $1.25 billion'. Announced on 4 March 2009, the Making Home Affordable (MHA) program, 'which might expend up to $50 billion of TARP funds . . . is a foreclosure mitigation plan intended to "help bring relief to responsible homeowners struggling to make their mortgage payments"'. The Projected TARP Funding for MHA is $50 billion. Announced in November 2008, the Term Asset-Backed Securities Loan Facility (TALF) 'was originally intended to increase the credit available for consumer and small-business loans through a Federal Reserve loan program backed by TARP funds'. The essential point is that TALF provides non-recourse loans to investors buying securities backed by consumer loans such as car loans, student loans and credit card debt. Recently, 'Treasury and the Federal Reserve have announced plans to expand TALF to cover additional asset classes, including legacy mortgage-backed securities, which could bring the total facility funding up to $1 trillion'. The Projected TARP Funding for TALF is $80 billion.

Finally, two TARP programs may be compatible with the 'financial institutions-troubled assets framework'. The Public-Private Investment Program (PPIP) is a 'coordinated effort with the [Federal Deposit Insurance Corporation] in an attempt to improve the health of financial institutions holding real estate-related assets in order to increase the flow of credit throughout the economy'. The PPIP will 'involve investments in multiple Public-Private Investment Funds (PPIPs) to purchase real estate-related loans . . . and real estate-related securities . . . from financial institutions'. The PPIP, 'involving up to $1 trillion in total' contemplates Projected TARP Funding of $75 billion. The Unlocking Credit for Small Businesses Program (UCSB) is animated by the idea that the demand for securities backed by Small Business Administration (SBA) loans 'has diminished in the secondary market'. Because this has been associated with 'a reduction in the volume of new small-business loans written by banks', Treasury has announced that 'it will begin purchasing . . . securities backed by [SBA] loans'. The Projected TARP Funding for UCSB is $15 billion.

Any objective assessment of the 12 TARP programs must conclude that SIGTARP's appraisal is correct: whereas 'TARP, as originally envisioned in the Fall of 2008, would have involved the purchase, management, and sale of up to $700 billion of "toxic" assets. . . That framework was soon abandoned'. To this I would add that the framework was abandoned *in spite of* the clear language embodied in TARP's enabling legislation. Whether this is the result of Treasury's deliberate or unwitting usurpation of Congress's legislative powers, or of congressional acquiescence or neglect (or both), this much is clear: Treasury's implementation of the Troubled Asset Relief Program raises profound constitutional questions. At issue is the Constitution's Legislative Powers Clause and, therefore, the force and effect of the separation of powers. While discussion of the Legislative Powers Clause is deferred to Chapter 4, I suggest that, when Treasury abandoned the 'financial institutions-troubled assets framework' it violated the Constitution.

Other constitutional questions attend TARP and TARP-related federal initiatives. Among these are the passage by the US House of Representatives of a bill that 'would impose a 90% surtax on employees who earn more than $250,000 at companies that have received at least $5 billion from the government's financial rescue program' (Hitt and Lucchetti, 2009, p. A1). While Richard Epstein (2009, p. A.11) argues that the 'best hope of a constitutional counteroffensive relies on substantive due process and the takings clause', it is possible, among other things, to argue that such a bill, were it to become law, would constitute either a bill of attainder or an ex post facto law – either of which is unconstitutional.

If, as I shall argue (in Chapter 2) the Founders would insist that constitutional questions trump outcomes based policy appraisal, they would also question the *justice* of TARP and other policy initiatives. Informed as they were by their prior ethical commitment to the moral equivalence of persons, the United States' Founders had a clear understanding of *justice as impartiality*. Indeed, it was precisely this idea that animated the Founders' insistence that the Constitution, through its institutional restraints on discriminatory factious behavior, both reflect, and promote respect for, the equal treatment imperative. If this meant that, for the Founders, desired 'end states' or outcomes cannot be the basis of morality, it also meant that we have a duty to promote and to respect just or impartial fundamental and post-constitutional law. Finally, we know that Madison and, it should be said, Jefferson, Benjamin Rush and others of the Founding generation 'regarded *all* decisions of economic policy as implicating questions of justice and thus of private rights' (Rakove, 1997,

p. 315; emphasis in original). While these ideas are more fully developed in Chapter 2, the essential point is that the Founders regarded discriminatory economic policies as unjust and, therefore, immoral.

Consider, finally, Madison's admonition that 'Justice is the end of government. It is the end of civil society' (Carey and McClellan, 2001, p. 271). For his part, Jefferson declared that 'the moral principles on which the government is to be administered . . . [are] what is proper for all conditions of society'. To this he adds that 'justice is the fundamental law of society; . . . the majority, oppressing an individual, is guilty of a crime' ([1816b] 1984, pp. 1386–7). It was in this spirit that Madison insisted that 'This being the end of government, that alone is a *just* government, which *impartially* secures to every man, whatever is his *own*' ([1792b] 1999, p. 515; emphasis in original).

Given the Founders' insistence that justice as impartiality is the 'end of government', post-constitutional statutory law must both respect and promote the moral equivalence of persons. It is this conception that enables us, in the manner suggested by Madison (see Chapter 2 this volume), to specify which legislative means and ends are *morally permissible*.

While justice as impartiality will inform my appraisal of the morality and constitutionality of federal on-, off- and off-off budget activity generally, immediate interest centers on TARP and TARP-related policy initiatives.

It is, of course, tautological that 'bailouts' are inherently discriminatory. While some may argue that TARP's 'purposes' are laudatory, the irremediable fact is that, as the Founders understood, discriminatory economic policies are corrosive of trust and, therefore, of the legitimacy of government (Chapter 2). If, in the limit, this represents a potential existential threat to a self-governing republic, it is also clear that discriminatory policies set beneficiaries against non-beneficiaries. The reaction of community bankers is heuristic. Why is it, they ask, that having acted responsibly, the federal government should bail out financial institutions whose relaxed lending standards contributed to the financial crisis? Whatever the merits of community bankers' implicit claim that they behaved more responsibly, this much is clear: the institutionalization of federal bailout programs implicitly underwrites risk-taking behavior – the moral hazard problem – and encourages others to queue up for government largesse.

Rent seeking is, of course, endemic to majoritarian democracy. It is both reflective of, and a catalyst to, the concentrated benefit – dispersed cost phenomenon. Whatever the stated purposes of federal bailout programs, well-defined beneficiaries stand to gain, with the cost dispersed among present and, it should be said, future taxpayers. Yet, if taxpayers absorb the direct cost of bailouts, *both* the beneficiaries *and* the taxpayers absorb indirect costs. Chief among these is the metastasizing scope and reach of federal market interventions.

It is beyond dispute that the Founders' concept of 'limited government' envisioned a constitutionally constrained federal government (see Chapter 2). If this meant, as I argue, that federal bailouts would be alien to their imagination, it is also clear that, for the Founders, the federal government's enumerated powers are few and well-defined. Equally important, the Founders hoped that their constitutional 'auxiliary precautions', notably federalism and the separation of powers, would constrain the legislative and other 'encroachments' that they feared would erode liberty.

It is against this background that the Treasury Department has considered promulgating rules that 'can change compensation practices across the financial-services industry, *including at companies that did not receive federal bailout money*'. While it is true that 'Regulators have long had the power to sanction a bank for excessive pay structures, [they] have rarely used it'. That said, 'Since 2007, [the Comptroller of the Currency] has privately directed 15 banks to change their executive compensation practices'. Moreover, Sheila Bair, Chairman of the Federal Deposit Insurance Corporation, has 'said [that] regulators need to examine compensation practices in the *mortgage industry*, suggesting new limits could stretch beyond banks' (Solomon and Paletta, 2009, p. A.1; emphasis mine).

If all of this calls to mind what Hayek called the 'errors of constructivism' – broadly speaking, the conceit that government knows how best to allocate resources – that is not my immediate concern. Rather, my interest centers on the following: Section 3 of TARP says that 'Any financial institution that sells troubled assets to the [Treasury] Secretary under this Act shall be subject to the executive compensation requirements of subsections (b) and (c)'. Subsection (b) paragraph (1), in relevant part, says that 'the Secretary shall require that the financial institution meet appropriate standards for executive compensation and corporate governance'.

At issue are the following questions: given that no 'financial institution' sold 'troubled assets' to the Secretary, and given that the phrase 'appropriate standards' is inherently ambiguous, by what authority may the Secretary 'change compensation practices across the financial services industry'? Equally important, by what authority may the Secretary 'change compensation practices . . . at companies that did not receive federal bailout money'?

While these questions are not exhaustive, they are heuristic. Nothing in the enabling legislation (TARP) authorizes the promulgation of such rules. Granting this, it is plausible to argue, again, that Treasury's rule-making violates the Constitution's Legislative Power Clause (see Chapter 4). The same is true of Treasury's potential acquisition of financial institutions' preferred stock – rather than 'troubled assets' – and of the possible conversion of those preferred shares into common equity. Setting aside the economic and other questions that attend the possible 'nationalization' of financial institutions, the essential point is that, again, nothing in the enabling legislation authorizes the federal acquisition of ownership interests in those institutions.

It is by now obvious that nothing in TARP warrants the institutionalization of the Automotive Industry Financing Program, the Auto Supplier Support Program or the Auto Warranty Commitment Program. Yet, if it is clear that their creation constitutes a usurpation of Congress's legislative powers, the programs' constitutionality may be challenged on other grounds.

Consider, for example, that Article I, Section 8 of the Constitution gives Congress the power to establish 'uniform laws on the subject of Bankruptcies throughout the United States'. The constitutional imperative to promote and respect *uniform* bankruptcy laws notwithstanding, the federal government has treated the Chrysler bankruptcy asymmetrically. At least in one account:

> The Obama administration's behavior in the Chrysler bankruptcy is a profound challenge to the rule of law. Secured creditors – entitled to first priority payment under the 'absolute priority rule' – have been browbeaten by an American president into accepting only 30 cents on the dollar of their claims. Meanwhile, the United Auto Workers union, holding junior creditor claims, will get about 50 cents on the dollar. (Zywicki, 2009, p. A.19)

While much speculation has centered on the motives that animated the administration's 'behavior', that is not my immediate concern. At issue is the failure to respect the Constitution's uniformity imperative, and the injustice that attaches to unequal treatment. On either dimension of appraisal, the Founders would find the federal government's 'behavior' objectionable.

In contrast, it appears that the Making Home Affordable program *is* consistent with Section 109 of TARP's enabling legislation. That said, it is clear that the authorized 'Foreclosure Mitigation Efforts' are fundamentally discriminatory.

At the most rudimentary level, homeowners who have paid their mortgages in full and on time have reason to ask why they, as taxpayers, should be made to bail out those who have defaulted. The same is true, of course, of renters. Equally or, perhaps more vexing, is the fact that 'About half of seriously delinquent borrowers have a second mortgage'. Some of these second mortgages are, of course, home equity loans, while some are classified as 'other'. Insofar as donor taxpayers care about the recipients' consumption patterns, the breakdown as between home equity and 'other' second mortgages is a matter of considerable interest. While account may or may not have been taken of this contingency, we know that:

> Under the [Obama Administration's] revised [Loan Modification] plan, mortgage servicing companies that participate in the loan-modification program for second liens must automatically modify the second mortgage when the first mortgage is reworked. The government will share in the cost of reducing the interest rate on second mortgages for five years. As an alternative, it will pay holders of second mortgages to extinguish that debt. (Simon, 2009, p. A.4)

Finally, if the mortgage modification program violates the Founders' equal treatment imperative, the same is true of the Term Asset-Backed Securities Loan Facility (TALF) and the Unlocking Credit for Small Businesses Program (UCSB). Whereas the former underwrites car loans, student loans and credit card debt, the latter does the same for small-business loans. It is self-evident, therefore, that TALF discriminates in favor of car buyers, students and credit card users. Yet if, in a generic sense, UCSB favors 'small business', it is also clear that it discriminates *among* small businesses:

> The Obama administration's new plan . . . should help companies that rely on the [Small Business Administration] for funds and generally qualify for bank loans. But many small businesses never apply for an SBA loan. That's particularly true for high-growth technology companies that may start out with little in the way of tangible assets to use as collateral. (Covel and Spors, 2009, p. B.5)

To this point attention has centered on Title I (TARP) of the Emergency Economic Stabilization Act of 2008. Recall now that the latter is Division A of House Resolution 1424, the bill that became law on 3 October 2008. It remains now to appraise Divisions B and C.

Division B, the Energy Improvement and Extension Act of 2008 incorporates four Titles. Broadly speaking, Title IV, styled, 'Revenue Provisions', may best be characterized as raising taxes on foreign and domestic oil and gas production, and the 'primary products thereof'. In general, Titles I, II and III provide tax incentives for the production of renewable energy, for carbon mitigation, for coal gasification and for carbon dioxide sequestration.

If the United States' Founders would have found all of this to be consistent neither with their moral and political philosophy nor with their political economy, they would surely have found the following tax provisions abhorrent (emphasis mine):

Section 108	Credit for *steel* industry fuel
Section 114	Special rules for refund of the coal excise tax to *certain* coal producers and exporters
Section 116	*Certain* income and gains relating to industrial source carbon dioxide treated as qualifying income for *publicly traded partnerships*
Section 205	Credit for new qualified plug-in electric drive motor vehicles
Section 209	Extension and modification of election to expense *certain* refineries
Section 307	Qualified green building and sustainable design projects
Section 401	Limitation of deduction for income attributable to domestic production of oil, gas, or primary products thereof

Division C, Tax Extenders and Alternative Minimum Tax Relief Act of 2008, fares little better than Division B. While the patent absurdity of Section 503 – 'Exemption from excise tax for certain wooden arrows designed for use by children' – has received considerable attention, the essential point is that the Founders' impartiality imperative is systematically ignored:

Section 202	Deduction of qualified tuition and related expenses
Section 203	Deduction for certain expenses of elementary and secondary school teachers
Section 204	Additional standard deduction for real property taxes for non-itemizers
Section 206	Treatment of certain dividends of regulated investment companies
Section 301	Extension and modification of research credit
Section 302	New markets tax credit
Section 305	Extension of 15-year straight-line cost recovery for qualified leasehold improvements and qualified restaurant improvements; 15-year straight-line cost recovery for certain improvements to retail space
Section 308	Increase in limit on cover over of rum excise tax to Puerto Rico and the Virgin Islands
Section 309	Extension of economic development credit for American Samoa
Section 311	Extension of election to expense advanced mine safety equipment
Section 312	Deduction allowable with respect to income attributable to domestic production activities in Puerto Rico
Section 317	Seven-year cost recovery for motorsports racing track facility
Section 321	Enhanced deduction for qualified computer contributions
Section 322	Tax incentives for investment in the District of Columbia
Section 323	Enhanced charitable deductions for contributions of food inventory
Section 325	Extension and modification of duty suspension on wool products; wool research fund; wool duty refunds
Section 502	Provisions related to film and television productions
Section 505	Certain farming business machinery and equipment treated as five-year property

I emphasize, again, that the Founders' prior ethical commitment to the moral equivalence of persons implies a number of corollaries (see Chapter 2). Among these are the ideas that government has a duty to promote the greatest possible equal political participation, that only certain 'ends' are permissible, and that post-constitutional statutory law must be impartial. I suggest that, by each of these standards, the tax provisions outlined above would be unacceptable to the Founders. For the moment, it is sufficient to invoke Madison's admonition that, whereas 'The apportionment of taxes . . . is an act which seems to require the most exact *impartiality* . . . there is, perhaps, no legislative act in which greater opportunity and temptation are given . . . to trample on the rules of justice' (Carey and McClellan, 2001, p. 45; emphasis mine).

If the Founders would find constitutional and moral grounds on which to object to the Emergency Economic Stabilization Act of 2008 (TARP), to the Energy Improvement and Extension Act of 2008, and to the Tax Extenders and Alternative Minimum Tax Relief Act of 2008, the same is true of the so-called 'Stimulus Bill'.

The American Recovery and Reinvestment Act of 2009, hereafter the Stimulus Bill, was signed into law on 17 February 2009 (US Congress, House Resolution 1, 2009). I note first that the 781-page bill is replete with discriminatory tax provisions and targeted grants and subsidies. Beneficiaries include consumers, homebuyers, farmers, economic and community development entities, energy producers and small businesses. If the Founders would find this *morally* objectionable, they would surely regard the passage of the Stimulus Bill as a metaphor for what James Wilson called the 'rage of legislation', and Jefferson styled the 'instability of our laws' (see Chapter 2): Congressman Tom Price, a Georgia Republican, has observed that the Stimulus Bill was filed in the House of Representatives at 11:30 p.m., with the vote occurring, the following day, at 2:00 p.m.[4]

We know that Jefferson pondered the efficacy of a 'twelve-month between the ingrossing a bill and passing it'. The predicates for this revelation, in a letter to James Madison, were his observation that 'The instability of our laws is really an immense evil', and his insistence that 'I own I am not a friend to a very energetic government. *It is always oppressive*' ([1787a] 1984, pp. 917–18; emphasis mine). If, as is clear, Jefferson regarded a slow and deliberative legislative process to be a sine qua non for the defense of liberty, it is also true that he, like Madison and the other Founders, insisted that government must promote the greatest possible equal political participation (see Chapter 2). It is safe to say, therefore, that a 14.5 hour 'debate' on a 781-page bill would, from the Founders' perspective, threaten liberty and effectively disenfranchise both the members of the polity *and* their elected representatives. In short, whatever the 'means' and 'ends' that characterize proposed legislation, deliberate violations of 'regular order' are corrosive of public trust and inimical to republican self-government.

Sadly, the Stimulus Bill is not an anomaly. Its handling, like that of the 1122-page Omnibus Appropriations Act, 2009, is symptomatic of the modern legislative process: 'Procedures guaranteeing adequate time for discussion, debate, and votes – known as "regular order" – in committee, on the floor, and in conference, which are essential if congress is to play its critical deliberative role, [are] routinely ignored to advance the majority agenda' (Mann and Ornstein, 2006, p. 7).

Two nationally recognized congressional scholars, Thomas Mann and Norman Ornstein, have provided a succinct and powerful adumbration of what is, in its essentials, a *procedural* problem:

> Committee deliberation on controversial legislation has become increasingly partisan and formalistic; with the serious work being done by the committee chair, party leadership, administration officials, and lobbyists. This pattern is repeated in conference committees, often without any pretence of a full committee mark-up with members of both political parties present. The Rules Committee routinely suspends its requirement of a 48-hour notice of meetings, invoking its authority to call an emergency meeting 'at any time on any measure or matter which the [Committee] Chair determines to be of an emergency nature'. Those meetings, . . . often [are] scheduled with little advance notice between 8:00 p.m. and 7:00 a.m. And their primary purpose [is] to dispense with regular order. (Mann and Ornstein, 2006, p. 172)

Not surprisingly, procedural license is not the exclusive province of either of the United States' major political parties. If the Stimulus Bill is the creation of a Democrat majority, the 2003 Medicare prescription drug bill is the progeny of a Republican majority. The latter was filed in the House of Representatives at 1:17 a.m. on 21 November, and passed at 6:00 a.m. on 22 November 2003 (ibid.). Yet if it is clear that both parties have, as the Founders feared, routinely sought to abuse the rights of the minority, departures from regular order also impose costs on the majority:

> Preventing the House [of Representatives] from producing legislation that reflects the view of its Members requires circumventing a body of rules and procedures developed in the past 215 years.

> The House was intended to be the centerpiece of our democracy. It can again function as a democratic institution if we return to 'regular order'. When even subcommittee chairmen don't know the content of the legislation bearing their name, the role of elected representatives has been diminished to the point that *ordinary citizens can have little confidence that their views have any weight in decisions made by Congress.* (Lilly, 2004; emphasis mine)

If, as I have suggested, these remarks apply to the Stimulus Bill, they apply with equal force to the Omnibus Appropriations Act, 2009 (hereafter 'the Act'). Signed into law in March, 2009 the 1122-page bill is an 'Act making omnibus appropriations for the fiscal year ending September, 2009, and for other purposes' (US Congress, House Resolution 1105, 2009, p. 1).

The $410 billion Act is a compilation of nine spending measures (Divisions A through I) funding certain federal operations from 7 March through 30 September 2009. Originally drafted in 2008, 'the bill did not pass due to Congress's long-standing budgetary dysfunction and the frustrating delays it yields in [the Congress's] appropriations work' (Bayh, 2009, p. A.13). The 'long-standing budgetary dysfunction' to which Senator Bayh (Democrat, Indiana) refers is captured by a familiar dynamic: having passed appropriations bills for only three Executive Departments – Defense, Homeland Security and Veterans Affairs – the rest of the federal government continued to operate, at 2008 spending levels, under a Continuing Resolution (Bendavid, 2009). Given its inability to pass the remaining appropriations bills, the Congress resorted to an omnibus appropriations bill.

If congressional appeal to omnibus bills is 'now routine' and involves a departure from regular order (Mann and Ornstein, 2006, p. 173), it also ignores 'The timetable with respect to the congressional budget process for any fiscal year' (US Congress, House Resolution 7130, 1974, p. 10). While the timetable will not be reproduced here, the essential point is this: the Congressional Budget and Impoundment Control Act of 1974 sets explicit deadlines for submission of the president's current services budget (10 November), and for submission of the president's budget (the 15th day after Congress meets). While changes of administration inevitably cause difficulties, these deadlines have generally been met. It is the *congressional* deadlines that tend systematically to be ignored. While it is true that 'no Congress can bind a succeeding Congress by a simple statute' (US Senate Committee on the Judiciary, 1981, p. 42), it is also true that Congress's cavalier handling of the budget process is irreconcilable with the Founders' insistence that the greatest possible equal political participation be promoted (see Chapter 2). In principle, the budget process provides a role for the House and Senate Budget Committees, for the Ways and Means and Senate Finance Committees, and for the 13 House and Senate Appropriations Subcommittees. Indeed, the process contemplates Member debates, public hearings and Committee mark-ups, all of which are instrumentally important to the emergence of a first concurrent resolution on the budget (15 May), and 'complete[d] action on bills and resolutions providing new budget authority and new spending authority' (the seventh day after Labor Day). Then, by 15 September, 'Congress completes action on second required concurrent resolution on the budget'. Finally, with the new fiscal year beginning on 1 October, 'Congress completes action on reconciliation bill or resolution, or both, implementing second required concurrent resolution' (25 September) (US Congress, House Resolution 7130, 1974).

If it is clear that respect for these procedural rules would allow both Members of Congress and the public to participate in the budget process, it is equally clear that omnibus appropriations bills result 'in stealth legislation that has not really passed majority muster' (Mann and Ornstein, 2006, p. 173). Sadly, such 'stealth legislation' has a long history: 'In 1980, unable to pass *any* budget on time, Congress for the first time used the "reconciliation" feature of the [1974] budget act, applying it to the first budget resolution (no second resolution passed)' (Ornstein, 1981; emphasis in original).

What Mann and Ornstein (2006) have called 'the demise of regular order' is now, undeniably, a defining characteristic of the budget process and, it should be said, of all [federal] 'economic' and 'social' legislation. If the now all-but-customary appeal to omnibus appropriations bills is a metaphor for the decline of Member and public participation in the budget process, so, too, is the 'explosion of earmarks'. Whereas, 'historically appropriations bills have not explicitly targeted funds for particular programs in particular districts' (Mann and Ornstein, 2006, p. 176), targeted earmarks have become commonplace:

> Earmarking has not simply grown in volume; the distribution of earmarks has also changed dramatically. In the 1980s, earmarks were largely rewards for Members who had persevered for years on the back benches and risen to positions of significant power on key committees. Today, earmarks are much more broadly distributed among the rank and file, and this most important advantage of incumbency affects election outcomes not just in a few districts of well-connected Members but in virtually all Congressional districts. (Lilly, 2005)

There is a sense in which it is unexceptional, then, that the Omnibus Appropriations Act, 2009 contains more than 8500 earmarks.[5] That said, it is clear that the Founders would object to an 'earmarking process' that is inherently discriminatory, lacks transparency and underwrites incumbency.

Omnibus appropriations bills, continuing resolutions and earmarks are not the only means by which the congressional budget process can be abused. One of the most egregious abuses is the ad hoc use of the budget reconciliation process.

As has been emphasized, the Congressional Budget and Impoundment

Control Act of 1974 (US Congress, House Resolution 1730, 1974) codifies a 'Timetable' for the Congressional Budget Process. The *last step* in the process, if it is necessary, is the completion of congressional action on a 'reconciliation bill or resolution, or both, implementing [the] second required concurrent resolution [on the budget]'.

Section 310, subsection (c) of the 1974 Act provides an adumbration of the budget 'Reconciliation Process'. The process assumes an antecedent; namely, that 'Not later than September 15 of each year Congress shall [have] complete[d] action on the concurrent resolution on the budget' (Section 310 subsection (b)). Then, 'If a concurrent resolution is agreed to . . . containing directions to one or more committees to determine and recommend changes in laws, bills, or resolutions', the committee (committees) is (are) 'directed to determine and recommend changes'. If 'only one committee of the House or the Senate is directed [by the concurrent resolution] to determine and recommend changes', then 'that committee shall promptly make such determination and recommendations and report to its House a reconciliation bill or reconciliation resolution, or both, containing such recommendations'. If 'more than one committee of the House or Senate is directed [by the concurrent resolution] to determine and recommend changes, each such committee . . . shall promptly make such determination and recommendations, whether . . . contained in a reconciliation bill or reconciliation resolution, and submit such recommendations to the Committee on the Budget of its House'. The Budget Committee, whether of the House or the Senate, or both, shall then 'report to its House a reconciliation bill or reconciliation resolution, or both, carrying out all such recommendations without any substantive revision'.

If the language is tedious, it is nevertheless clear: the 'reconciliation process' contemplates broad and deep Member, standing committee and public involvement. And if the reconciliation *process* is clear, the 1974 Act also provides an unambiguous *definition* of a reconciliation resolution: '[A] reconciliation resolution is a concurrent resolution directing the Clerk of the House of Representatives or the Secretary of the Senate, as the case may be, *to make specified changes in bills and resolutions which have not been enrolled*' (Section 310, subsection (c), paragraph (2); emphasis mine).

Finally, Section 310, subsection (d) and subsection (e) paragraph (2) specify, respectively, that 'Congress shall complete action on any reconciliation bill or reconciliation resolution . . . not later than September 25 of each year', and that 'Debate in the Senate on any reconciliation bill or resolution reported under subsection (c), and all amendments thereto and debatable motions and appeals in connection therewith, *shall be limited to not more than 20 hours*' (emphasis mine).

Given their procedurally based, consequence-detached moral and political philosophy (see Chapter 2), all of this would be of interest to the United States' Founders. They would understand and appreciate that the budget reconciliation process, and the budget process generally, is defined independently of political 'ends' or goals. The intention, in the spirit of the Founders' republican self-government project, is to promote the greatest possible equal political participation. It follows that any deliberate attempt to 'short circuit' the process would, from the Founders' perspective, be *morally objectionable*.

It is against this background that, in mid-April 2009 'President Barack Obama and congressional leaders agreed to use "budget reconciliation" if necessary to jam a massive health-care bill through Congress' (Sununu, 2009, p. A.13). At issue is 'reforms to [the United States'] health care system'; reforms whose constitutionality is assessed in Chapter 6, Section 6.4 of this volume. While it 'sets aside a reserve fund of more than $630 billion over 10 years', the Administration asserts that, whereas this 'is not sufficient to fully fund comprehensive reform . . . this is a crucial first step in that effort, and [the president] is committed to working with the Congress to find additional resources to devote to health care reform' (Office of Management and Budget, 2009a, p. 27).

It has been suggested that the health-care reform bill will actually constitute a 'new $ trillion health-care entitlement' (Editorial, 29 April 2009, p. A.11).[6] While this is not implausible, given 'the eight principles' to which the president says he 'will adhere' (Office of Management and Budget, 2009a, p. 27), the essential point is that, as we have seen, under budget reconciliation rules Senate debate would be limited to 20 hours, with passage of the bill requiring only a simple majority:

> The power of a reconciliation bill is this: Senate rules allow only 20 hours of debate and then passage with a simple majority. . . The historic precedent of open debate, and the requirement of 60 votes to close debate, are completely short-circuited.

> Budget reconciliation . . . was created [in 1974] as a way to help a reluctant Congress curb spending, reduce deficits, and cut the debt. . . This is clearly not the appropriate process for implementing significant new policies. (Sununu, 2009, p. A.13)

Indeed, it is *not* the 'appropriate process' to consider a health-care reform proposal that, among other things, will contemplate the 'Aim of universality': 'The plan must put the United States on a clear path to cover all Americans' (Office of Management and Budget, 2009a, p. 27).

Given their prior ethical commitment to the moral equivalence of persons the Founders would regard the 'Aim of universality' as a 'permissible [generic] end' (see Chapter 2 this volume). That said, for them, the *idea* of a self-governing republic involves *both* permissible ends – ends that respect the impartial treatment imperative – and fair in the sense of impartial *procedure*. If this means that the rights of the minority must be protected, and that '[t]he alternate domination of one faction over another . . . is itself a frightful despotism' (Washington [1796a] 1997, p. 969), it also means that post-constitutional government has a duty to promote both just in the sense of impartial institutions and the greatest possible equal political participation (Chapter 2).[7]

It is safe to say that, along any of these dimensions of appraisal, exclusive reliance on the budget reconciliation process would be alien to the Founders' imagination. Stated differently, it would be inconsistent with their conception of republican self-government. That conception, in turn, regards self-government as a sine qua non for 'the security, the liberty, and the dignity' of morally equivalent persons. The views of James Wilson, one of only six signers of both the Declaration of Independence and the Constitution, are heuristic:

> In a *moral* view, self-government increases, instead of impairing, the security, the liberty, and the dignity of the *man*; in a *political* view, self-government increases, instead of impairing, the security, the liberty, and the dignity of the *citizen*. (Hall and Hall, 2007, p. 1041; emphasis in original)

The imperative to promote and to respect just in the sense of impartial institutions is a recurring theme of this book. But if the Founders insisted that post-constitutional statutory law must be impartial, they were equally clear that respect for the Constitution's 'auxiliary precautions' is both instrumentally important to republican self-government and morally exigent. The point is precisely that federalism and the separation of powers were intended to set 'ambition against ambition' and, thereby, to minimize the effects of the narrowly self-interested 'factious' impulse (see Chapter 2).

It is in this spirit that I emphasize, again, that the Troubled Asset Relief Program (TARP) violates the Constitution's Legislative Powers Clause and, therefore, the separation of powers (see also Chapter 4). That said, it seems clear that certain provisions of the American Recovery and Reinvestment Act of 2009, the Stimulus Bill, are inconsistent with the Founders' federalism enterprise. Among the most egregious examples is Section 1607, subsection (b): 'If funds provided to any State in any division of this Act are not accepted for use by the Governor, then acceptance by the State legislature, by means of the adoption of a concurrent resolution, shall be sufficient to provide funding to such State' (US Congress, House Resolution 1, 2009, p 191).[8] Whatever else is said, it is not clear that the federal government has constitutional license to intervene in the states' budget processes.

These ideas inform the discussion in later chapters. For the moment, my interest centers on a comprehensive overview of the federal enterprise.

1.2   THE REST OF IT

Presentations of the federal budget typically distinguish between on- and off-budget activity. The Office of Management and Budget defines 'on-budget' activity as 'all budgetary transactions other than those designated by statute as off-budget' (2009b, p. 414). For its part, 'off-budget' activity subsumes 'transactions of the federal government that would be treated as budgetary had congress not designated them by statute as "off-budget". Currently transactions of the Social Security trust fund and the Postal Service fund are the only sets of transactions that are so designated' (ibid.). Whereas the 'Unified Budget' combines on- and off-budget programs (ibid., p. 415), it is not an exhaustive representation of federal activity. On the logic that 'they do not involve the direct allocation of resources by the [federal] Government', some federal government activities are characterized as 'non-budgetary' (ibid., p. 359). These non-budgetary activities, sometimes called off-off-budget activity, subsume federal credit and insurance programs, federal government-sponsored enterprises, tax expenditures, federal regulation and credit market stabilization activity (ibid., pp. 359–61).[9] Credit market stabilization activity appears for the first time in the fiscal year 2010 federal budget documents. On the one hand, the 'credit market stabilization' activities of the Federal Reserve and of the government-sponsored enterprises are treated as non-budgetary. On the other hand, 'the activities of the Department of the Treasury, the [Federal Deposit Insurance Corporation] and the [National Credit Union Administration] are budgetary' (ibid., p. 361). Indeed, 'Most of these activities, including all asset acquisitions, loans, and loan guarantees under the Troubled Asset Relief Program (TARP) are reported in the budget on a credit basis' (ibid.). While my critique of TARP and of TARP-related activities will not be reprised (see Section 1.1 above), the point of immediate interest is that the rationale for the credit basis treatment of these activities is that:

> The Government's cost of purchasing a financial asset that is intended to be sold at some point in the future is not equal to the cash used to acquire the asset at the time of acquisition. Rather, the cost is equal to the present value of the cash outflows for acquiring the asset less the present value of cash inflows from holding and ultimately selling the asset. (Ibid.)

That said, 'A very limited portion of credit market stabilization activities resulted in outlays in 2008; most activities will result in outlays in 2009'.

These outlays and 'the actual and estimated impacts of credit market stabilization efforts on the debt held by the public are included in the 2010 budget' (ibid.).

Given the federal government's Unified Budget convention, Section 1.3 focuses on on- and off-budget activity. Section 1.4 concentrates on 'non-budgetary' or off-off-budget activity.

1.3   FEDERAL ON- AND OFF-BUDGET ACTIVITY

It is not an exercise in hyperbole to say that the federal budget process is 'broken' (see Section 1.1 above). The federal on-budget account has been in surplus only eight times since fiscal year (FY) 1946. Indeed, despite the fact that the off-budget account has been in surplus in all but 15 of the post-1946 fiscal years, the Unified Budget (see also Section 1.2 above) has been in deficit in all but 12 of the post-World War II fiscal years (Office of Management and Budget, 2009c, pp. 21–3). The result has been that, 'At the end of [FY] 2008, the [federal] Government owed $5,803 billion of principal to the individuals and institutions who had loaned it the money to fund past deficits' (Office of Management and Budget, 2009b, p. 223). While it is true that 'Statutory limitations have usually been placed on Federal debt', it is also true that, 'Since 1960 Congress has passed 76 separate acts to raise the [debt] limit, extend the duration of a temporary increase, or revise the definition' (ibid., p. 233). Moreover, it is clear that the rate at which statutory debt limit increases have occurred is accelerating. Whereas the debt limit was increased three times during the 1990s, it has been raised eight times since FY 2002 (ibid.). Indeed:

> Since July 2008, the debt limit has been increased three times. . . In these three instances, the increase was included in a larger piece of legislation aimed at stabilizing the financial markets and restoring economic growth. . . On July 30, 2008, the debt limit was increased by $800 billion to $10,615 billion, as part of the Housing and Economic Recovery Act of 2008. On October 3, 2008, the Emergency Economic Stabilization Act of 2008 increased the debt limit by $700 billion, to $11,315 billion. On February 17, 2009, the American Recovery and Reinvestment Act of 2009 increased the statutory limit by $789 billion, to $12,104 billion. (Ibid.)

Recall first that the Troubled Asset Relief Program (TARP) constitutes Division A of the Emergency Economic Stabilization Act of 2008 (EESA). While neither the discussion of TARP nor of the American Recovery and Reinvestment Act of 2009 (the Stimulus Bill) (see Section 1.1 above) will be reprised, it is appropriate to emphasize that the FY 2010 federal Budget provides two estimates of TARP's 'Effects on the Deficit and Debt'. The estimates, required by EESA, are expressed on a credit and a cash basis. The former, which is intended to reflect 'the net present value of estimated cash flows to and from the Government, excluding administrative costs', is required by the Federal Credit Reform Act of 1990, as amended, and by Section 123 of EESA (Office of Management and Budget, 2009b, p. 65). The credit basis estimate of TARP's effect on the FY 2010 Budget, $242.3 billion, contrasts with the corresponding cash basis estimate of $608 billion (ibid., pp. 66–8).

While it is of more than passing interest that the cash basis estimate – some $366 billion higher than the credit basis estimate – is *not* reported in the FY 2010 Budget (ibid., p. 68), the essential point is this: whether TARP's effect on the FY 2010 Budget deficit is reported on a credit or a cash basis, as it has been implemented, TARP is both unconstitutional and immoral (see Section 1.1 above).

If the Founders would find all of this objectionable, the same can be said of a statutory 'debt limit' of $12.1 trillion. At issue is the temporal character of government borrowing. As Buchanan and Congleton have emphasized, the purpose of government borrowing 'is to implement the temporal transposition of value – to postpone until later periods the burden of payment for current outlay' (1998, p. 100). This political discrimination against *future* taxpayers by in-period majorities (Buchanan [1962a] 2000, pp. 447–8) is clearly inconsistent with the Founders' prior ethical commitment to the moral equivalence of persons (see Chapter 2 this volume).

It may be objected that, because it generates intertemporal benefits as well as costs, federal 'investment' spending may justify temporal discrimination. We know, for example, that the FY 2010 Budget contemplates 'investment outlays' totaling $596.3 billion on 'Major physical capital investment', on the 'Conduct of research and development' and on the 'Conduct of education and training' (Office of Management and Budget, 2009b, p. 34). While the projected 'investment outlays' constitute 16.6 percent of FY 2010 federal outlays (Office of Management and Budget, 2009c, p. 23), and while the associated benefits and costs will accrue intertemporally, it remains true that the moral equivalence of persons demands that those who cannot agree to bear the future cost of debt-financed programs be treated impartially. If the institutional imperative is, therefore, a constitutional balanced budget constraint (see Chapter 2), debt retirement should also be informed by the generality or impartiality principle:

Why should any particular generation of taxpayers be singled out for differentially high taxation, without corresponding benefits, in order to reduce the tax obligations of all persons who will make up the membership of future generations? The generality principle emerges here as a relatively powerful argument against any policy of debt retirement. The 'sins of the past' . . . should be borne equally across all generations. (Buchanan and Congleton, 1998, p. 102)

If, as I suggest, the Founders would reject federal deficit spending on *moral* grounds, they would also object to the *composition* of federal on- and off-budget spending programs.

While the argument is more fully developed in Chapters 2 and 6, the essential point is that the Founders had a clear understanding of the constitutionally constrained role of the federal government. Madison's view, articulated in *Federalist* No. 45, is heuristic: 'The powers delegated by the proposed constitution to the federal government, are few and defined . . . [they] will be exercised principally on external objects, as war, peace, negotiation and foreign commerce; with which last the power of taxation will, for the most part, be connected' (Carey and McClellan, 2001, p. 241).

Given the Founders' emphasis on 'limited government' – on the federal government's *enumerated* powers – *what the federal government does* is a matter of considerable import. While the Supreme Court's constitutional jurisprudence has basic relevance (see Chapters 3 and 4), immediate interest centers on the composition of federal on- and off-budget outlays.

Federal on- and off-budget spending (or outlays) is broken down by 'Budget Enforcement Act Category'.[10] The key distinction is as between 'Discretionary' and 'Mandatory' outlays.[11] The former contemplates 'National Defense' and 'Non-defense' outlays, while the latter subsumes 'Social Security', 'Deposit Insurance', 'Means Tested Entitlements', 'Other' and 'Undistributed Offsetting Receipts'.

I emphasize first that, despite the Founders' insistence that the federal government's powers shall 'be exercised principally on external objects, as war, peace, negotiation and foreign commerce' (see Chapter 2), national defense outlays have declined as a percentage of federal on- and off-budget outlays, and as a percentage of Gross Domestic Product (GDP): in FY 1962, defense outlays accounted for 49.2 percent of on- and off-budget outlays, and for 9.3 percent of GDP. Comparable estimates for FY 2010 are, respectively, 19.7 and 4.8 percent (Office of Management and Budget, 2009c, pp. 138 and 140).

The point is not that it is possible, in some objective sense, to determine the 'optimal level' of national defense outlays. What is at issue is that, on the one hand, the Founders intended that the federal government exercise only its 'few and defined' powers, and that the 'numerous and indefinite' powers of the 'several states' be respected (Chapter 2). On the other hand,

Table 1.1   Outlays for discretionary programs in constant (FY 2000) dollars: 1962 and 2010 (in billions of dollars)

Category and Program	FY 1962	FY 2010 (estimate)
National Defense	317.1	517.8
Non-Defense: International Affairs	33.1	40.1
General Science, Space and Technology	10.3	24.7
Energy	3.9	17.5
National Resources and Environment	13.7	31.7
Agriculture	2.2	4.8
Commerce and Housing Credit	8.1	7.2
Transportation	8.6	72.6
Community and Regional Development	2.6	18.4
Education, Training, Employment and Social Services	5.6	91.4
Health	6.3	51.0
Medicare		4.5
Income Security: Housing Assistance	0.8	36.9
Other	2.0	17.7
Social Security	1.9	4.6
Veterans' Benefits and services	6.2	41.4
Administration of Justice	2.6	39.1
General Government	7.6	16.1
Total non-defense discretionary	115.4	519.8
Total outlays for discretionary programs	432.5	1037.60

Source: Office of Management and Budget (2009c, pp. 160 and 165).

the declining share of national defense spending has been accompanied by a mestastasization of federal programs whose constitutionality and/or morality can, and should, be called into question.

Consider first that in FY 1962 the percentage distribution of on- and off-budget outlays was National Defense (49.2), Non-defense (18.3), Social Security (13.2), Means Tested Entitlements (4.1) and Other (14.2). The corresponding estimated outlay shares for FY 2010 are, respectively, 19.7, 19.6, 19.4, 15.6 and 23.0 percent (ibid., p. 138). While these data are heuristic, it is useful to trace the intertemporal pattern of real spending by budget category. Table 1.1 compares real discretionary program outlays in FY 1962 with estimated FY 2010 outlays. Table 1.2 does the same for mandatory and related program outlays.

Tables 1.1 and 1.2 are important, less because of what they say about in-program spending growth rates, than because of what they say about

Table 1.2   Outlays for mandatory and related programs in constant (FY 2000) dollars: 1962 and 2010 (in billions of dollars)

Category and Program	FY 1962	FY 2010 (estimate)
Human Resource Programs: Education, Training, Employment and Social Services	1.9	3.5
Health: Medicaid	0.5	234.0
Other		25.5
Total health	0.5	259.5
Medicare		370.0
Income Security	40.9	386.5
Social Security	66.1	563.5
Veterans' Benefits and Services: income security for veterans	20.3	46.0
Total mandatory human resource programs	129.7	1629.0
Other mandatory programs	--1.9	21.1
Total mandatory programs	127.8	1650.1

Source: Office of Management and Budget (2009c, pp. 148 and 153).

the changing *composition* of federal on- and off-budget spending. It is clear that, today, 'Total non-defense discretionary' (Table 1.1) and 'Total mandatory human resource programs' (Table 1.2) account for the bulk of on- and off-budget federal spending. What the data do not reveal is what the changing composition of federal spending implies for the *stock* of defense and non-defense physical capital. Whereas the former contemplates federal investment spending on weapons, other defense equipment, military construction and Department of Energy defense facilities, the latter subsumes what can broadly be characterized as investment in construction projects, equipment acquisition and grants to state and local governments for infrastructure investment, for 'community and regional development', and for public housing (Office of Management and Budget, 2009b, p. 35). The essential point is that 'The real stocks of defense and nondefense capital show very different trends'. On the one hand:

Nondefense stocks have grown consistently since 1970, increasing from $470 billion in 1970 to $1,657 billion in 2008. With the investments proposed in the budget, nondefense stocks are estimated to grow to $1,727 billion in [FY] 2010. During the 1970s, the nondefense capital stock grew at an average annual rate of 5.0 percent. In the 1980s . . . the growth rate slowed to 2.9 percent annually, with growth continuing at about that rate since then. (Ibid., p. 39)

In contrast:

> Real national defense stocks began in 1970 at a relatively high level, and declined steadily throughout the decade as depreciation from investment in the Vietnam era exceeded new investment in military construction and weapons procurement. Starting in the early 1980s, a large defense buildup began to increase the stock of defense capital. By 1987, the defense stock exceeded its earlier Vietnam-era peak. In the early 1990s, however, depreciation on the increased stocks and a slower pace of defense physical capital investment began to reduce the stock. . . . The increased defense investment in the last few years has reversed this decline, increasing the stock from a low of $631 billion in 2001 to $800 billion in 2010. (Ibid.)

Given the 'publicness' of the national defense enterprise, the issue is neither the determination of the 'optimal level' of real defense spending, nor the determination of the 'optimal rate of increase' of real defense capital investment. What *is* at issue is the fact that, from FY 1960 to FY 2002, the year before the onset of the Second Gulf War, the real net stock of national defense physical capital remained essentially constant, rising from $608 billion in FY 1960 to $636 billion in FY 2002. Over the same period, real non-defense physical capital rose from $242 billion to $1,442 billion (ibid.).

Both the asymmetric pattern of real national defense and real non-defense physical capital investment and the data displayed in Tables 1.1 and 1.2 are reflective, I suggest, of the federal government's commitment to, and pursuit of, goals and policies *other than national defense*. The 'Congressional Declarations [of Policy]' codified in the Employment Act of 1946 (US Congress Joint Economic Committee, 2002) are heuristic:

> The Congress hereby declares that it is the continuing policy and responsibility of the federal government to use all practicable means, consistent with its needs and obligations and other essential national policies, and with the assistance and cooperation of both small and larger businesses, agriculture, labor, and State and local governments, to coordinate and utilize all its plans, functions, and resources for the purpose of creating and maintaining, in a manner calculated to foster and promote free competitive enterprise and the general welfare, conditions which promote useful employment opportunities, including self-employment, for those able, willing, and seeking to work, and promote full employment and production, increased real income, balanced growth, a balanced Federal budget, adequate productivity growth, proper attention to national priorities, achievement of an improved trade balance through increased exports and improvement in the international competitiveness of agriculture, business and industry, and reasonable price stability. (US Congress Joint Economic Committee, 2002, p. 3)

If it is clear that this pot-pourri of federal policy goals would have been alien to the Founders' imagination, it is equally clear that they bear little correspondence to the federal government's enumerated powers (see Chapter 2, Section 2.3 and Chapter 6, Section 6.2 this volume). I emphasize, in particular, that there is no explicit reference to national defense. And if it is clear that the exclusively outcomes based statement of federal 'policy and responsibility' finds expression in the composition of on- and off-budget spending patterns (Tables 1.1 and 1.2), it is equally clear that this policy disposition is affirmed by the FY 2010 Budget's emphasis on 'social and economic indicators' of the federal government's performance: 'There are certain broad responsibilities that are unique to the federal government. Especially important are preserving national security, fostering healthy economic conditions including sound economic growth, promoting health and social welfare, and protecting the environment' (Office of Management and Budget, 2009b, p. 203). While the passage correctly identifies the preservation of national security as a federal responsibility, emphasis is placed on what is characterized as the 'domestic portion of [the federal government's] general objectives': 'Table 13-6 offers a rough cut of information that can be useful in assessing how well the federal government has been doing in promoting the domestic portion of these general objectives' (ibid.).

The table to which the passage refers lists 'economic' and 'social indicators' that are acknowledged to be 'only a subset drawn from the vast array of available data on conditions in the United States'. While the chosen indicators reflect the 'priority . . . given to measures that are consistently available over an extended period', the claim is that the table of indicators 'can serve two functions':

> First, [the table] highlights areas where the federal government might need to modify its current practices or consider new approaches. . . Second, the table provides a context for evaluating other data on Government activities. For example, Government actions that weaken its own financial position may be appropriate when they promote a broader social objective. (Ibid.)

The essential point is that, while it is recognized that 'The individual measures . . . are influenced . . . by many Government policies and programs, as well as by external factors beyond the Government's control', they are intended to 'provide a quantitative measure of the progress or lack of progress toward some of the ultimate goals that [federal] Government policy is intended to promote' (ibid.). It is revealing, then, that the 'Economic Indicators' identified in Table 13-6 (ibid., p. 202) fall under the following rubrics: 'Living Standards', 'Income Inequality, 'Economic Security', 'Wealth Creation', '[Technological] Innovation' and 'Air and Water Quality'. For their part, the 'Social Indicators' contemplate family characteristics, various measures of 'Safe Communities', 'Health' and 'Learning' and what might be characterized as civic participation.

For present purposes, the intertemporal 'performance' of the 'economic' and 'social' indicia is less important than the fact that they are presumed to be consonant with the 'broad responsibilities that are unique to the federal government' (ibid., p. 203).

If the striking feature of Tables 1.1 and 1.2 is the displacement of defense spending by non-defense discretionary and mandatory human resource programs, its emphasis on 'economic and social indicators' affirms the federal government's commitment to 'improvement' in what might broadly be characterized as individual, family and community 'well-being'. This outcomes based, procedurally-detached understanding of the 'broad responsibilities that are unique to the federal government' is consistent with both the economist's utilitarian theory of the state and with *modern* liberalism's moral and political philosophy (see Chapter 5 this volume). That said, this understanding of the federal government's responsibilities is inconsistent with the Founders' procedurally based, consequence-detached moral and political philosophy, and with their characterization of the constitutional roles of the federal and state governments (see also Chapters 2 and 6). On the one hand, much of what the federal government does is fundamentally discriminatory and, therefore, irreconcilable with the Founders' prior ethical commitment to the moral equivalence of persons (see Section 1.1 above and Chapter 2). On the other hand, the metastasizing role of the federal government has been underwritten by expansive readings of the Constitution's General Welfare, Necessary and Proper, Commerce and Legislative Powers Clauses (see Chapter 4).

Means Tested Entitlements, Medicare, Medicaid and Social Security are the principal components of mandatory human resource programs. As we have seen, they also command an increasing share of on- and off-budget outlays. Indeed, the same is true of GDP. Whereas in FY 1962 the ratio of Means Tested Entitlements and Social Security outlays to GDP stood at 0.8 and 2.5 percent, by FY 2010 the estimated ratios will have risen to 3.8 and 4.7 percent (Office of Management and Budget, 2009c, p. 140).

I emphasize first that governments tend, other things equal, to allocate increasing shares of their outlays to transfer programs. As Buchanan and Congleton have observed, even the generality or impartiality constrained voter 'is likely to exhibit bias in favor of transfers over public goods financing', so that 'The inclusive budget will tend to be relatively small in financing of genuinely public goods and relatively large in its financing of direct transfers' (1998, p. 119).[12] While this is not my immediate concern, it is clear that the displacement of National Defense spending by Means Tested Entitlements, Social Security, Medicare and other transfer programs is clearly consistent with this prediction. It is equally clear that extant transfer programs provide incentive both to invest in efforts to qualify for transfers, and to deploy 'public interest' arguments to justify entitlements. Moreover, both a priori logic and the empirical evidence suggest that 'As the population of [transfer payment] recipients increases relative to that of non-recipients, majoritarian politics tends to shift transfer levels further from those acceptable to net taxpayers, thereby exacerbating political tension and increasing the potential for class conflict' (ibid., p. 122). Finally, I note that taxpayer-donors, those who pay for but do not receive transfer payments, may be other-regarding. They may, in short, derive utility from income and other transfers to recipients.[13]

While each of these considerations is important, the decisive point is this: given their prior ethical commitment to the moral equivalence of persons, the Founders insisted that just, in the sense of impartial, institutions be promoted (see Chapter 2). From this perspective it is not the fact that transfer programs encourage rent seeking that is of central importance. What is critically important is that, with the exception of programs that benefit the elderly, transfer programs are inherently discriminatory. Granting this, the logic of 'means testing' is unavailing: the irremediable fact is that means testing is itself discriminatory. Means testing, in short, is inconsistent with the Founders' insistence that post-constitutional statutory law be impartial.

In contrast, because all persons age, transfer programs that benefit the elderly do, in a limited sense, satisfy the Founders' impartiality constraint. While it is true that political and 'technical' considerations militate against the impartial treatment of morally equivalent retired persons,[14] it is also true that the constitutionality of Social Security can, and has, been questioned.[15] At issue is a reading of the Constitution's General Welfare and Necessary and Proper Clauses that is difficult to reconcile with the Founders' view of constitutional interpretation (see Chapter 2, Section 2.3 and Chapter 6, Section 6.4).

Setting constitutional questions aside, it is clear that 'the key drivers of the long-range deficit are the Government's major health and retirement programs' (Office of Management and Budget, 2009b, p. 190). While single-valued 'long-range' federal budget projections, whether by the Office of Management and Budget (OMB) or the Congressional Budget Office (CBO) are notoriously inaccurate, they are nevertheless heuristic. OMB maintains a 'long-range forecasting model' that 'extends the Budget policy beyond the normal 10-year budget horizon' (ibid., p. 192). The model's forecasts are, of course, sensitive to alternative policy, economic, and technical assumptions (ibid., pp. 192–6). That said, OMB's 'Long-Run Budget Projections' suggest the following: discretionary outlays will fall from 10.1 percent of GDP in FY 1980 to 6.2 percent in FY 2080, while mandatory outlays, including Social Security, Medicare, Medicaid and Other will rise from 9.6 percent of GDP in FY 1980 to 20.8 percent in FY 2080. For their part, on- and off-budget federal revenues are projected to increase from 19.0 percent of GDP in FY 1980 to 22.6 percent in FY 2080 (ibid., Table 13-2, p. 192).

While, as I have suggested, budget forecasts are sensitive to alternative policy, economic and technical assumptions, the implications of *this* forecast are clear. On the one hand, federal debt held by the public will rise from 26.1 percent of GDP in FY 1980 to 275.0 percent of GDP in FY 2080 (ibid., p. 192). On the other hand, the declining ratio of discretionary outlays to GDP implies a continuing displacement of national defense outlays by entitlement or transfer spending. Given the Founders' view of constitutional interpretation, and given that the federal government's constitutional powers are 'few and defined', this raises profound questions (see Chapters 4 and 6).

The *Catalog of Federal Domestic Assistance* (CFDA), maintained under federal statute by the US General Services Administration (GSA), provides another measure of the nature and scope of federal activity. The GSA's CFDA website 'provides access to a database of all federal programs available to state and local governments (including the District of Columbia); federally recognized Indian tribal governments; territories (and possessions) of the United States; domestic public, quasi-public, and private and non-profit organizations and institutions; specialized groups; and individuals'; and 1796 such programs are described in the *Government Assistance Almanac* (Omnigraphics, Inc., 2009) (hereafter *Almanac*). Included in the CFDA 2008 print edition and in the *Almanac* are 15 types of 'federal domestic assistance' programs broken down as between financial and non-financial resources. The former consists of direct loans, direct payments/specified use, direct payments/unrestricted use, formula grants, guaranteed/insured loans, insurance and project grants. Non-financial resources subsume advisory services/counseling, federal employment, investigation of complaints, sale, exchange, or donation of property and goods, specialized services, technical information, training and use of property and facilities and equipment. Also listed under various program classifications are block grants that are typically awarded either as 'formula' or 'project' grants (*Almanac*, pp. 3–6).

While much can be said about this, I emphasize first that 'Currently some 56 departments, commissions, agencies, bureaus, and other federal entities administer the assistance programs' (*Almanac*, p. 3). Next, because each of the 1796 programs identifies carefully delineated 'eligible applicants' and 'eligible beneficiaries', each program is inherently discriminatory. For the United States' Founders, two questions would, with respect to each program, come immediately to mind: first, is the program non-discriminatory and, therefore *morally* permissible? Second, is the program constitutional? In particular, does the program violate the Constitution's General Welfare, Necessary and Proper, Commerce Among the States, or Legislative Powers Clauses?

While a case-by-case analysis of each of the 1796 programs at issue is beyond the scope of this book, this much can be said: too often, the 'rage of legislation' and effectively unrestrained federal agency rule-making have militated against meaningful assessment of the morality and the con-stitutionality of the federal on- and off-budget enterprise.

If federal on- and off-budget spending programs are subject to in-period and intergenerational discrimination, in-period discrimination is a defin-ing characteristic of the federal Tax Code.

I acknowledge first that the functioning of majoritarian democracy 'guarantees the emergence of discrimination in treatment between those who are members of the majority coalition and those who are not members' (Buchanan and Congleton, 1998, p. 89). It is understood, moreover, that in the case of taxation, 'Adjusted for relative group size, members of the exploiting majority have more to gain from tax discrimination against the rich than against middle or low-income groups' (ibid., p. 91). Tax rate 'progressivity', a defining characteristic of the US Tax Code, is consistent with this understanding. For its part, the metastasization of preferential tax provisions may be attributed to the rent-seeking activity of the special interest groups or 'factions' that the Founders sought to constrain. Indeed, it has been suggested that 'the tax system is the single greatest source of lobbying activity in Washington' (Armey, 1996, p. A.20).

While a detailed discussion of preferential tax provisions or 'tax expen-ditures' is deferred to Section 1.4 below, I emphasize that a progressive tax rate structure violates the Founders' equal treatment or impartial-ity standard (see Chapter 2). Stated differently, tax rate discrimination is inconsistent with the external morality of the law (Ten, 1995, p. 397). Among other things, the external morality of the law demands that legisla-tors pass just, in the sense of impartial or non-discriminatory, legislation (Rawls, 1971, p. 227). For its part, the proliferation of complex tax code provisions – many of which are surreptitiously legislated – is inconsist-ent with what has been characterized as the internal morality of the law (Fuller, 1971). Significantly, the internal morality of the law demands that laws be general, be made known, be prospective, and be clear and not contradictory. Moreover, laws must not demand the impossible, they must not be frequently changed, and they should require that government action be congruent with the law.

Given the Founders' prior ethical commitment to the moral equivalence of persons (see Chapter 2), the duty to promote and to respect the external and internal morality of the law applies with equal force to *all* law. If, by this standard, the morality of much of what the federal government does may be called into question (see Sections 1.1, 1.3 and 1.4 this chapter), immediate interest centers on federal tax law.

It has been suggested that a constitutional generality or impartiality constraint (Chapter 2, Section 2.4) would 'prevent the natural tendency to use the taxing authority discriminatorily' (Buchanan and Congleton, 1998, p. 93). I do not disagree. That said, it is also clear that, while Rawls has argued that 'since the burden of taxation is to be justly shared . . . a proportional expenditure tax may be part of the best tax scheme' (1971, p. 278), a uniform or flat tax on all income and contemplating *no* exemptions or deductions would also satisfy the Founders' impartiality standard.

With all of this in mind, I turn next to federal off-off-budget activity, a category that includes fundamentally discriminatory 'tax expenditures'.

1.4   FEDERAL OFF-OFF BUDGET ACTIVITY

The federal government offers direct loans and loan guarantees 'to support a wide range of activities'. The most important of these involve housing, education, business and rural development, and international credit to support United States' exports. In addition, the federal government permits certain privately owned companies, or Government Sponsored Enterprises (GSEs) 'to operate under Federal charter for the purpose of enhancing credit availability for *targeted sectors*' (Office of Management and Budget, 2009b, p. 43; emphasis mine). The federal government also 'insures deposits at depository institutions, guarantees private defined-benefit pensions, and insures against some other risks such as flood and terrorism' (ibid.). Finally, the Office of Management and Budget (OMB) notes that 'Recently, with private credit markets barely functioning, GSEs have been playing more active roles in the secondary market, Federal credit programs have been endeavoring to accommodate more borrowers, and government guarantees and insurance have been expanded to new areas of the economy' (ibid.).

The federal government's response to the 'credit crisis' has already been addressed (Section 1.1). While more can be said about this, immediate interest centers on the arguments employed to justify federal off-off-budget activities. In the OMB's account, 'Credit and insurance markets often suffer from market imperfections and can require regulation or other government intervention to function well'. It is noteworthy that

OMB has, for the first time, gone beyond the list of 'market imperfections' standardly invoked[16] to provide additional rationales for 'federal intervention' in credit and insurance markets. Whereas what I shall characterize as the 'standard list' of market imperfections contemplates 'information failures', 'limited ability to secure resources', 'insufficient competition' and 'externalities', the new rationales are 'economic disequilibrium' and 'reducing inequality and increasing access' (ibid., pp. 43–4).

While the federal government maintains that the 'market imperfections' and 'new rationales' are justificatory of federal credit and insurance programs, there are fundamental problems. I emphasize, first, that the presence of market imperfections does not imply that the government can do better.[17] Moreover, it can be shown that the theory that animates market imperfection analysis does not take account of fundamental features of observable reality (see Chapter 5). As a result, it is not a suitable device for normative public policy appraisal. Indeed, if fundamental moral, logical, empirical and ontological questions call into question the normative use of the first fundamental theorem of social welfare theory, the same can be said of the second fundamental welfare theorem. Thus, if the first theorem cannot *legitimately* be used to justify market imperfection-based government interventions, it is also true that the second theorem cannot *legitimately* be used to justify income and wealth redistribution policies. Stated differently, government interventions motivated either by perceived 'market failures' or by the desire to 'reduce inequality' or to 'increase access' must be regarded as ad hoc (see Chapter 5, Sections 5.7 and 5.8).[18]

If all of this calls into question the efficacy of federal credit and insurance programs, my interest centers on their fundamentally discriminatory nature. With this in mind, I turn first to federal credit programs.

Federal direct loans and loan guarantees are offered under the following rubrics: Housing, Education, Business and Rural Development, and International Credit Programs (Office of Management and Budget, 2009b, pp. 44–54). What follows is a brief adumbration of the various *targeted* 'sectoral' programs.

Housing Credit Programs

The Federal Housing Administration (FHA) 'guarantees mortgage loans to provide access to homeownership for people who may have difficulty obtaining a conventional mortgage. FHA has been a primary facilitator of mortgage credit for first-time and minority buyers, . . . and enhanced the credit of many moderate and low-income households' (Office of Management and Budget, 2009b, p. 44). For its part, the Department of Veterans Affairs (VA) 'assists veterans, members of the Selected Reserve, and active duty personnel in purchasing homes as recognition of their service to the nation' (ibid., p. 46). The US Department of Agriculture's Rural Housing Service (RHS) 'offers direct and guaranteed loans and grants to help very low- to moderate-income rural residents buy and maintain adequate, affordable housing' (ibid.). Finally, the mission of the housing Government Sponsored Enterprises, the Federal Home Loan Bank System, the Federal National Mortgage Association (Fannie Mae) and the Federal Home Loan Mortgage Corporation (Freddie Mac) is to 'guarantee the timely payment of principal and interest on mortgage-backed securities', and to 'finance the purchase of [mortgage] assets held in their portfolios through debt issued to the credit markets' (ibid., p. 47).

Education Credit Programs

The Department of Education 'helps finance student loans through two major programs: the Federal Family Education Loan (FFEL) program and the William D. Ford Federal Direct Student Loan . . . program'. While 'Loans are available to students regardless of income . . . borrowers with low family incomes are eligible for loans where the federal government subsidizes loan interest costs' (ibid., p. 49).

Business and Rural Development Programs

The Small Business Administration (SBA) 'helps entrepreneurs start, sustain, and grow small businesses . . . SBA works to supplement market lending and provide access to credit where private lenders are reluctant to do so without a Government guarantee'. In addition, SBA 'helps home and business-owners, as well as renters, cover the uninsured costs of recovery from disasters through its direct loan program' (ibid., p. 50). For its part, the US Department of Agriculture (USDA) 'provides grants, loans and loan guarantees to communities for constructing facilities such as health-care clinics, day-care centers, and water systems'. In addition, 'Direct loans are available at lower interest rates for the poorest communities', and 'USDA's Rural Utilities Service . . . programs provide loans for rural electrification, telecommunications, distance learning, telemedicine, and broadband, and also provide grants for distance learning and telemedicine' (ibid., p. 51). As the 'lender of last resort', the Farm Service Agency (FSA) 'assists low-income family farmers in starting and maintaining viable farming operations. Emphasis is placed on aiding beginning and socially disadvantaged farmers' (ibid.). Finally, '[t]he Farm Credit System (FCS), including the Federal Agricultural Mortgage Corporation (Farmer Mac), is a Government Sponsored Enterprise . . . that enhances credit availability for the agricultural sector'. Whereas the FCS banks and associations 'provide production, equipment and mortgage lending to farmers and ranchers, aquatic producers, their cooperatives, related businesses, and rural homeowners, . . . Farmer Mac provides a secondary market for agricultural real estate and rural housing mortgages' (ibid., p. 52)

International Credit Programs

The federal government's international credit programs 'are intended to level the playing field for US exporters, deliver robust support for US manufactured goods, stabilize international financial markets, and promote sustainable development' (ibid., p. 53). The programs, administered by the Departments of Agriculture (USDA), Defense, State and Treasury, and by the Agency for International Development (USAID), the Export-Import Bank, and the Overseas Private Investment Corporation (OPIC) 'provide direct loans, loan guarantees, and insurance to a variety of foreign private and sovereign borrowers' (ibid., p. 53).

It is *possible* to argue that United States' contributions to the International Monetary Fund and to the Exchange Stabilization Fund are motivated by a desire to 'stabilize international financial markets' rather than to directly benefit US exporters. For its part, the Enhanced Heavily Indebted Poorest Countries Initiative is intended to promote economic reform and to reduce poverty. Finally, USAID's Development Credit Authority uses 'a variety of credit tools to support its development activities abroad' (ibid., pp. 53–4). While, in a general equilibrium sense, each of these programs may benefit US exporters, this is not an explicitly stated goal. The same cannot be said of the Export-Import Bank, of USDA's Export Credit Guarantee Programs, or of OPIC.

The Export-Import Bank 'provides export credits, in the form of direct loans or loan guarantees, to US exporters who meet basic eligibility criteria and who request the Bank's assistance'. For its part, USDA's Export Credit Guarantee Programs (or GSM programs) 'similarly help to level the playing field'. On the logic that they are 'Like programs of other agricultural exporting nations, GSM programs guarantee payment from countries and entities that want to import US agricultural products but cannot easily obtain credit' (ibid., p. 53). Finally, 'OPIC . . . supports a mix of development, employment and export goals by promoting US direct investment in developing countries'. OPIC seeks to achieve these goals through political risk insurance, direct loans, product guarantees and technology and skills transfers. These programs, in turn, 'are intended to create more efficient financial markets, eventually encouraging the private sector to supplant OPIC in developing countries' (ibid., p. 54).

The defining characteristic of federal credit programs, whether domestic or international, is in-period discrimination. It is tautological that such programs favor 'targeted sectors' and, therefore, well-defined individual beneficiaries. Moreover, there is the matter of intergenerational discrimination. During FY 2008 outstanding direct and guaranteed loans totaled $286 and $1693 billion, respectively. The estimated future cost of these direct and guaranteed loans is $123 billion. In the case of direct loans, these future costs reflect 'financing account allowance for subsidy cost and the liquidating account allowance for estimated uncollectible principal and interest'. For their part, 'Loan guarantee future costs are estimated liabilities for loan guarantees' (ibid., Table 7-7, pp. 71–2). Whatever else is said, these 'estimated future costs' are imposed, without their consent, on *future* members of the polity.

While the Founders would find both the in-period and intergenerational discriminatory components of such programs morally objectionable (see Chapter 2), it is the intergenerational component that is, in an important sense, decisive: because the agreement of future generations cannot, by definition, be secured, members of the current and future generations are not temporally equivalent. On this logic, the Founders' prior ethical commitment to the moral equivalence of persons suggests an institutional imperative: federal government credit programs should be constitutionally prohibited – whatever their avowed 'social purpose'.

As in the case of federal credit programs, the 'federal role' in the provision of insurance programs is rationalized by appeal to market imperfections, 'economic disequilibrium' and 'reducing inequality and increasing access'. While that discussion will not be reprised, I emphasize, again, that the federal government provides deposit insurance, pension guarantees and flood, crop and terrorism risk insurance (ibid., pp. 54–9).

While, as has been suggested, the presence of market imperfections does not suggest that the government can 'do better', the issue of immediate interest is that the Founders' commitment to the moral equivalence of persons (see Chapter 2) implies a moral imperative. The imperative, in short, is to manage government insurance programs impartially.

I acknowledge first that 'ex post differentiation is the nature of all true insurance programs' (Buchanan and Congleton, 1998, p. 132). This is so because insurance program benefits depend upon the occurrence of random, future events. That said, what is important from the generality or impartiality perspective is that insurance programs' benefits be uniformly distributed among members of the polity in an ex ante sense. The requirement, then, is that 'each insured contingency is equally likely, and equally valued by *all* within the polity of interest' (ibid.; emphasis mine)

It is clear that adherence to the impartiality principle is difficult in this setting. We know, for example, that majoritarian cycling is likely to center on the probabilities of occurrence of random events, insurance benefits and tax prices. Moreover, as is the case with flood and crop insurance, expected benefits are likely to be geographically concentrated. Finally, different degrees of risk aversion imply, other things equal, that 'insurance programs that are actuarially identical across individuals may, nonetheless, yield different expected net benefits for more or less risk-averse individuals' (ibid., p. 133).

While deposit insurance appears roughly, in the ex ante sense, to satisfy the impartiality principle, the same cannot be said of defined-benefit pension guarantees or of flood or crop insurance. It is safe to say that, given the increasing dominance of defined-contribution pension plans, the defined-benefit pension guarantees offered by the federal government's Pension Benefit Guaranty Corporation (PBGC) are both anachronistic and plainly discriminatory. That said, 'As a result of a flawed pension system and exposure to losses from financially troubled plan sponsors, PBGC's single-employer program incurred substantial losses from underfunded plan terminations . . . The program currently has a $10.7 billion deficit in assets necessary to satisfy all claims made through 2008' (Office of Management and Budget, 2009b, p. 56). Whatever else is said, because all members of the polity do not participate in defined-benefit pension plans – indeed, many individuals have access neither to defined-benefit nor to defined-contribution pension plans – the ex ante impartiality constraint cannot be satisfied. Given the Founders' impartiality imperative it follows that 'targeted' pension benefit guarantees cannot be morally justified.

While a phase-out of subsidized flood insurance premiums has been discussed (ibid., p. 57), the fundamentally discriminatory nature of the National Flood Insurance Program is clear. Administered by the Federal Emergency Management Agency of the Department of Homeland Security, the program 'is available to homeowners and businesses in communities that have adopted and enforced appropriate flood plain management measures'. At the end of calendar 2008, the program had over 5.6 million policies in effect in more than 20 200 communities with more than $1 trillion of insurance in force (ibid., pp. 56–7). For its part, subsidized federal crop insurance, administered by the Department of Agriculture's Risk Management Agency, 'assists farmers in managing yield and revenue shortfalls due to bad weather or other natural disasters' (ibid., p. 57). While, again, a reduction in the federal subsidy to both farmers and insurers is under consideration, it is tautological that subsidized federal crop insurance targets a group of well-defined beneficiaries. It is, therefore, inherently discriminatory and inconsistent with the Founders' impartiality imperative. Moreover, there is an important technical sense in which the impartiality standard cannot be met at the *federal* level: the expected benefits of flood and crop insurance cannot, in the crucial ex ante sense, be uniformly distributed among the *national* polity. It is nevertheless true that:

> [s]ome [government] services that fail to be sufficiently general at a more inclusive level of membership in political community may be acceptable at less inclusive levels of government or within smaller self-financing and autonomous service districts. A federalized structure of government can provide heterogeneous services while satisfying the strictures of generality. (Buchanan and Congleton 1998, p. 137)

While this discussion focuses on federal 'disaster insurance' programs, the point to be emphasized is generic: 'federal systems may be said to be a first-best institutional arrangement that produces outcomes that cannot be replicated by an idealized democratic central government' (ibid.). The essential idea is that, when ex ante benefits cannot be uniformly distributed, the moral equivalence of persons demands that the Constitution prohibit *federal* government goods or services provision. There is reason to believe moreover that, under a constitutional federal system, 'a significant fraction of local government services – or at least pivotal services such as education, transport, and police protection – [will] come to be provided in accordance with the generality principle in the long run' (ibid., p. 141).[19] The logic is that, given the constitutional constraint, when the expected benefits of credit, insurance or other programs cannot be uniformly distributed among members of the national polity, beneficiaries cannot shift provision to the federal government. Moreover, given Tiebout-type mobility, competition among political jurisdictions would seem to ensure that 'local governments should be observed widely to provide substantially uniform service packages to all their citizens' (ibid.). Whatever else is said, this conception of the role of the *states* would not be alien to the Founders' imagination (see Chapter 2).

If federal credit, insurance and other programs implicate federalism-related issues, federal regulation raises federalism *and* separation of powers issues.

It has been said that 'few subjects are now considered to be beyond the pale of federal regulation' (Uhlmann, 2005, p. 229). In the broadest sense, both the stock and the flow of federal regulations are consistent with this observation. The *Code of Federal Regulations*, a compilation of all regulations that have become law, consists of 200 bound volumes (Levy and Mellor, 2008, p. 68). For its part, Volume 79 of the *Federal Register*, a compilation of orders, rules and regulations promulgated during the 12-month period ended 31 March 2009, exceeds 80 000 pages.[20] And, finally, the *Unified Agenda of Federal Regulatory and Deregulatory Actions* has, since 1983, appeared twice a year. The November 2008 issue, like its predecessors, describes the actions that regulatory agencies 'are developing or have recently completed'. By 24 November 2008 the *Unified Agenda* totaled 71 520 pages (Regulatory Information Service Center, November 2008).

If these documents are suggestive of the rapidly expanding federal enterprise, another document is a testament to the federal government's consequence based, procedurally-detached approach to public policy appraisal. The Office of Information and Regulatory Affairs, OMB, is required by the Regulatory Right-to-Know Act of 2001 to release an annual report to Congress on regulatory benefits and costs. The *2008 Report to Congress on the Costs and Benefits of Federal Regulations and Unfunded Mandates on State, Local and Tribal Entities* 'includes a ten-year look-back of major Federal regulations reviewed by OMB to examine their quantified and monetized benefits and costs' (Office of Information and Regulatory Affairs, 2008, p. iii). Among other things, the *Report* concludes that 'The estimated benefits of major regulations issued from 1992 to 2007 exceed the estimated costs by more than four fold' (ibid.). While much can be said about this, the essential point is that the focus of the *Report,* and that of the Regulatory Right-to-Know Act is relentlessly and uniquely outcomes based and procedurally-detached. If, as I suggest, this approach is consistent both with modern liberalism and the economist's utilitarian theory of the state, it is inconsistent with the Founders' moral and political philosophy, and with their political economy (see Chapters 2 and 5 in this volume).

The Founders' moral and political philosophy informed both their political economy and the Constitution. Federalism and the separation of powers, along with other procedural 'auxiliary precautions', were intended to constrain both the federal government and the self-interested 'factious behavior' that the Founders regarded as inimical to republican self-government. Given their insistence that the Constitution's procedural restraints be respected, and given their view of constitutional interpretation (Chapter 2), the scope and reach of federal regulation would astonish the Founders. In the event, it is clear that both the Supreme Court's expansive reading of the Interstate Commerce Clause, and its accommodative Legislative Powers Clause jurisprudence (Chapter 4) have underwritten the essentially unconstrained growth of federal regulatory power. Congress has also been complicit. As we have seen, Congress has revealed a marked propensity to flout its own budget process law (see Section 1.1 above). Yet, if Congress is inclined to ignore its own statutory procedural restraints, it long ago asserted a 'right' to delegate rule-making authority to administrative agencies. Administrative agencies, in turn, are either subunits of executive departments or free-standing. The latter consist of executive agencies that are ultimately accountable to the president, or 'independent' agencies that are 'wholly accountable neither to the President nor to Congress' (Uhlmann, 2005, p. 229). For present purposes it is sufficient to emphasize that Congress's increasing reliance on administrative agencies reflects a 'desire to delegate the details of governance and retain authority at the same time' (ibid., p. 230); that the number and variety of administrative agencies is a metaphor for the growth and reach of the federal government, and that administrative agencies often exercise legislative, judicial and executive powers. Finally, I note that, as in the case of federal credit and insurance programs, administrative agencies are invariably justified by appeal to 'market failures'. Characteristically, and in spite of the fact that there can be no presumption that the government can 'do better', the presence of monopoly power, externalities, insufficient or asymmetric information, or unequal bargaining power is taken to be justificatory of federal regulatory intervention (see Chapter 5).

One component of federal off-off-budget activity remains to be considered. Section 308 paragraph (c) of the Congressional Budget and Impoundment Control Act of 1974 requires that 'The [president's] Budget ... for each fiscal year shall set forth the levels of tax expenditures under existing law for such fiscal year (the tax expenditure budget)' (US Congress, House Resolution 7130, 1974, p. 27). The law defines tax expenditures as:

> those revenue losses attributable to provisions of the federal tax laws which allow a special exclusion, exemption, or deduction from gross income or which provide a special credit, a preferential rate of tax, or a deferral of tax liability; and the term 'tax expenditures budget' means an enumeration of such tax expenditures. (Ibid., p. 3)

It is of course true that tax expenditures 'subsidize particular activities and can affect resource allocation and income distribution in ways that are similar to spending programs'. And it is precisely 'Because of this similarity [that] these provisions are referred to as "tax expenditures". Unlike spending programs, however, tax expenditures reduce receipts rather than increase outlays' (Office of Management and Budget, 2008, p. 360).

The federal government's budgetary treatment of tax expenditures may best be characterized as ambivalent. As we have seen, the revenue effects of tax expenditures are incorporated in the federal Budget. At the same time, 'tax expenditures are considered non-budgetary' (ibid.). In the Office of Management and Budget's [OMB] account, 'This is because tax expenditures are not shown *explicitly* as outlays or as negative tax receipts and because tax expenditures pose significant measurement problems' (ibid.).

The 'measurement problems' to which OMB refers center on the fact that tax expenditures 'are identified and measured by first specifying a hypothetical "baseline" tax system, which . . . can be highly subjective and technically complex' (ibid.). The logic of the 'baseline' approach is straightforward: 'A tax expenditure is an exception to baseline provisions of the tax structure that usually results in a reduction in the amount of tax owed'. Yet, whereas '[t]he 1974 Congressional Budget Act . . . mandated the tax expenditure budget, [it] did not specify the baseline provisions of tax law' (ibid., p. 296).

While the fiscal year 2010 Budget documents provide an adumbration of the 'normal tax baseline' and the 'reference tax law baseline' (Office of Management and Budget, 2009b, pp. 298 and 307), this is not my immediate concern.[21] Neither is my focus the 'economic efficiency' of the 165 tax expenditures for which revenue loss estimates are provided (ibid., Table 19-1, pp. 299–302). Rather, interest centers on 'political efficiency'; on institutional restraints on rent seeking and majoritarian exploitation.

By any objective standard 'tax expenditures' are a metaphor for the inherently discriminatory post-constitutional politics that the Founders abhorred (see Chapter 2). If, as I have noted (in Section 1.3), 'since the burden of taxation is to be justly shared . . . a proportional expenditure tax may be part of the best tax scheme' (Rawls, 1971, p. 278), then we would do well to embrace Madison's admonition that 'The apportionment of taxes . . . is an act which seems to require the most exact impartiality' (Carey and McClellan, 2001, p. 45). Simply stated, a Tax Code replete with special exclusions, exemptions, deductions from gross income, special credits and preferential tax rates is irreconcilable with the Founders' equal treatment imperative.

NOTES

1. SIGTARP's 21 July 2009 *Report* (SIGTARP, 2009c) emphasizes, again, that 'TARP, as originally envisioned . . . would have involved the purchase, management, and sale of up to $700 billion of "toxic" assets, primarily troubled mortgages and mortgage-backed securities' [but] 'That framework was soon shelved' (p. 3).
2. See also SIGTARP of 21 July 2009 (2009c, pp. 31–117).
3. See Table 1.1, 'Total Funds Subject to SIGTARP Oversight, As of March 31, 2009' (SIGTARP, 2009b, p. 4).
4. Congressman Price made this observation during a 19 March 2009 interview on FOX News.
5. Interestingly, Weisman and Hitt indicate that 'White House aides said they debated whether the president should sign an omnibus spending bill that includes more than 8,500 pet projects worth $7.7 billion' (2009, p. A.6).
6. House Resolution 3200, the health-care reform bill passed out of the House Ways and Means Committee on 17 July 2009, has been the focus of the health-care reform debate.

The 1018-page bill, whose 'Short Title' is 'America's Affordable Health Choices Act of 2009' has, in fact, been estimated to cost at least $1 trillion (Editorial, 28 July 2009). Interestingly, the House Energy and Commerce Committee's health-care reform bill has also been estimated to cost $1 trillion (Adamy and Hitt, 2009).

7. The Senate Health, Education, Labor and Pensions Committee passed an amended health-care bill on 15 July 2009. While a 790-page version of the bill is available on the Committee's website, 'it doesn't include nearly 200 amendments that passed when the committee re-drafted the bill'. As the *Wall Street Journal* has observed, it is 'Too bad the committee won't reveal [the amended bill] even to other Senators, much less to the public' (Editorial, 29–30 August 2009, p. A.12). If, as the *Journal* suggests, this means that 'the Congressional Budget Office can't score [the bill]', the larger point is that the inaccessibility of the bill ignores the imperative to promote the greatest possible equal political participation.

8. The *Wall Street Journal* observes that 'The problem for . . . Governors is that they may be forced to spend the federal money whether they want it or not' (Editorial, 23 February 2009, p. A.14).

9. See also Office of Management and Budget (2008, p. 360). Non-budgetary or off-off-budget activity also includes deposit funds, monetary policy and the indirect macroeconomic effects of federal activity. 'Deposit funds' are 'non-budgetary accounts that record amounts held by the Government temporarily until ownership is determined . . . or held by the Government as an agent for others' (Office of Management and Budget, 2009b, p. 359).

10. For more on the Budget Enforcement Act of 1990 see Office of Management and Budget (2009b, pp. 398–9).

11. Whereas 'discretionary programs' are defined as 'those whose budgetary resources (other than entitlement authority) are provided in appropriations acts', 'mandatory and related programs' are understood to 'include direct spending and offsetting receipts whose budget authority is provided by law other than appropriations acts' (Office of Management and Budget, 2009c, p. 15).

12. Here, generality or impartiality connotes flat-rate income-tax-financed equal-per-head demogrants.

13. It should also be acknowledged that some taxpayers may care about the consumption patterns of income transfer recipients. This may, in part, account for the emergence of in-kind transfer programs.

14. For more on this, see Buchanan and Congleton (1998, pp. 124–7).

15. See, for example, Levy and Mellor (2008, pp. 21–3).

16. See, for example, the 'market imperfections' discussion in Office of Management and Budget (2008, pp. 69–70).

17. See, for example, Roth (2002, Section 5.2). Indeed, OMB acknowledges that 'the presence of a market imperfection does not mean that Government intervention will always be effective. To be effective, a credit or insurance program should be carefully designed to reduce inefficiencies in the targeted area while minimizing inefficiencies elsewhere' (Office of Management and Budget, 2009b, p. 43).

18. See also Roth (1999) and Roth (2002, Chapter 6).

19. It should be noted that, in a federal system, state and local governments may themselves engage in rent seeking. See, for example, Mixon and Hobson (2001).

20. See the *Table of Federal Register Issue Pages and Dates* (US Government Printing Office, 17 May 2009).

21. For more on 'tax expenditure baselines' see Office of Management and Budget (2008, pp. 296–7). See also the 'Treasury Department's Review of the Tax Expenditure Presentation' (Appendix A, pp. 315–23).

2. The Founders' vision

2.1 INTRODUCTION

A critical assessment of the burgeoning federal enterprise can proceed in many ways, and involve numerous dimensions of appraisal. Typically, however, the assessment is outcomes based and procedurally-detached, with economic efficiency and some measure of *distributive* justice as the ultimate standards of appraisal. Here, the approach is different. Attention centers on a comparison of federal on-, off- and off-off-budget activity with the post-constitutional federal role envisioned by the United States' Founders. The comparison is informed by an appreciation of the Founders' moral and political philosophy, their political economy and their understanding of the nation's fundamental law, the Constitution.

A recurring theme of the book is that much of what the federal government does is fundamentally discriminatory; that, whereas the Founders focused on fair, in the sense of impartial procedure, on the cultivation of virtue and on the reciprocal relationship between law and morality, modern statutory and administrative law is increasingly animated by the 'politics of wants and needs', and by the impulse to 'perfect the economic market'. Modern liberalism, and the economic theory to which it is conjoined, social welfare theory, have been instrumentally important to this enterprise, as has a constitutional jurisprudence that has undermined both federalism and the separation of powers. I shall argue that, just as Madison feared, the relentless advance of the 'responsive state' has been underwritten by 'the high sanction given to a latitude in expounding the Constitution which seems to break down the landmarks intended by a specification of the Powers of Congress' (Madison [1819] 1999, p. 734).

2.2 THE FOUNDERS' MORAL AND POLITICAL PHILOSOPHY

The Founders' intellectual inheritance can be traced to many sources. It is well known, for example, that a number of Enlightenment thinkers influenced the Founders and the founding generation. Particular interest has centered on Hobbes, Locke and Montesquieu. It is generally agreed that 'the Revolutionary writers took the concept of "right to life"' from Hobbes, and 'the phrase "right to liberty" as well as to property' from Locke (Schweikart and Allen, 2004, pp. 70–71). Then, in this familiar account, the Founders relied upon Montesquieu 'to determine how best to guarantee those rights':

> In *The Spirit of Laws*, drawing largely on his admiration for the British constitutional system, Montesquieu suggested dividing the authority of the government among various branches with different functions, providing a blueprint for the future government of the United States. (Ibid.)

It is understood, of course, that the Founders and the Founding generation were familiar with, and influenced by, other thinkers. We know, for example, that Jefferson read, and recommended that others read, Bacon, Blackstone, Bollingbroke, Burke, Coke, Newton, Paine, Voltaire and, it should be emphasized, Adam Smith.[1]

While Adam Smith's influence on the Founders was profound, it is nevertheless true that, 'Despite all the recent scholarship on the impact of Scottish political thought on the American founding, curiously little attention has been paid to the influence of Adam Smith' (Fleischacker, 2002, p. 897).

I emphasize first that, while Smith's *Lectures on Jurisprudence* were never published, 'it is possible that Witherspoon, Rush, or Benjamin Franklin knew of them from their days in Scotland' (ibid., pp. 898–9). More important, however, is the fact that the Founders were familiar with, and appealed either explicitly or implicitly, to Smith's *The Theory of Moral Sentiments* (TMS) and *Wealth of Nations* (WN).

As Samuel Fleischacker (2002) has observed, John Witherspoon, Thomas Jefferson, John Adams, Benjamin Rush and James Wilson either lectured about TMS (Witherspoon and Rush), recommended it for private libraries (Thomas Jefferson), wrote about it (John Adams) or 'seemed to allude to it', as in Wilson's lectures on US law. In the case of WN, we know that Jefferson wrote to John Norvell that 'If your views of political inquiry go further, to the subjects of money and commerce, Smith's Wealth of Nations is the best book to be read' (Jefferson [1807] 1984, p. 1176). We also know that 'Jefferson, Hamilton, Wilson, Adams, Webster, Morris, and the two James Madisons were some of Smith's earliest readers and among the first to take him seriously in their own political lives' (Fleischacker, 2002, p. 905). There is, for example, a remarkable congruence between Madison's argument, developed in *Federalist* No. 10 and No. 51, that a multiplicity of factions in a large republic can render each faction less dangerous (Carey and McClellan, 2001, pp. 48 and 270–71), and Smith's argument, articulated in WN, that a multiplicity of religious sects would render 'The interested and active zeal of religious teachers' less 'dangerous and troublesome' (Smith [1759] 1976, p. 792). This passage, drawn from Madison's *Federalist* No. 10 is particularly revealing:

> a religious sect may degenerate into a political faction in a part of the confederacy; but the variety of sects dispersed over the entire face of it, must secure the national councils against any danger from that source: a rage for paper money, for an abolition of debts, for an equal division of property, or for any other improper or wicked project, will be less apt to pervade the whole body of the union, than a particular member of it; in the same proportion as such a malady is more likely to taint a particular county or district, than an entire state. (Carey and McClellan, 2001, p. 48)

If the United States' Founders had a clear understanding of the dangers of faction, they also had a clear understanding of its nature. Madison's definition is heuristic:

> By a faction, I understand a number of citizens, whether amounting to a majority or a minority of the whole, who are united and actuated by some common impulse of passion, or of interest, adverse to the rights of other citizens, or to the permanent and aggregate interest of the community. (Ibid., p. 43)

It was in this context that Madison asked a series of rhetorical questions:

> Is a law proposed concerning private debts? It is a question to which the creditors are parties on one side, and the debtors on the other. *Justice* ought to hold the balance between them. Yet the parties are, and must be, themselves the judges; and . . . the most powerful faction, must be expected to prevail. Shall domestic manufacturers be encouraged, and in what degree, by restrictions on foreign manufacturers? are questions which would be differently decided by the landed and manufacturing classes; and probably by neither with a sole regard to *justice* and the *public good*. (Ibid., pp. 44–5; emphasis mine)

To this Madison adds, 'The apportionment of taxes . . . is an act which seems to require the most exact *impartiality*'. Yet, he says, 'there is, perhaps, no legislative act in which greater opportunity and temptation are given to a predominant party, to trample on the rules of justice'. Why?: '[Because] [e]very shilling with which they over-burden the inferior number, is a shilling saved to their own pockets' (ibid., p. 45).

Consider now the observations, on the same subject, of Adam Smith:

> Merchants and manufacturers are, in this order, the two classes of people who commonly employ the largest capitals, and who by their wealth draw to themselves the greatest share of the publick consideration. . . As their thoughts, however, are commonly exercised rather about the interest of their particular

branch of business, than about that of the society, their judgement . . . is much more to be depended upon with regard to the former of those two subjects, than with regard to the latter. (Smith [1759] 1976, p. 266)

The corollary that Smith draws from this is that:

The proposal of any new law or regulation of commerce which comes from this order, ought always to be listened to with great precaution. . . It comes from an order of men, whose interest is never exactly the same with that of the publick, who have generally an interest to deceive and even to oppress the publick, and who accordingly have, upon many occasions both deceived and oppressed it. (Ibid., p. 267)

It is this understanding, shared with Smith, that led Madison to conclude that 'The inference to which we are brought, is, that the *causes* of faction cannot be removed; and that relief is only to be sought in the means of controlling its effects' (Carey and McClellan, 2001, p. 45; emphasis in original).

As we have seen, Madison argued, in a manner similar to Smith, that in a large republic, the multiplicity of factions could control their effects. He also shared with Smith the view that justice as impartiality is both intrinsically valuable and instrumentally important. Thus, whereas in TMS Smith argued that 'we must become the *impartial spectators* of our own character and conduct' ([1759] 1976, p. 114; emphasis mine), Madison insisted that:

The great desideratum in Government is such a modification of the Sovereignty as will render it sufficiently *neutral* between the different interests and factions, to controul one part of the Society from invading the rights of another, *and at the same time sufficiently controuled itself,* from setting up an interest adverse to that of the whole society. ([1787a] 1999, p. 69; emphasis mine)

While, for Madison, 'Justice is the end of government' (Carey and McClellan, 2001, p. 271), neither he nor Smith was confident that impartiality would prevail in day-to-day conflictual politics. As Smith observed:

In all great countries which are united under one uniform government, the spirit of party commonly prevails less in the remote provinces than in the centre of the empire. The distance of those provinces from the capital, from the principal seat of the great scramble of faction and ambition, makes them enter less into the views of any of the contending parties, and renders them more indifferent and impartial spectators of the conduct of all. ([1776] 1976, p. 945)

Thus, while he averred that, 'How selfish soever man be supposed, there are evidently some principles in his nature, which interest him in the fortunes of others . . . though he derives nothing from it except the pleasure of seeing it' (ibid., p. 9), Smith was nevertheless concerned that impartiality would not always inform public policy. As we shall see, the Founders agreed. That said, they shared Smith's (and Immanuel Kant's) view that the perspective of the impartial spectator can be cultivated (ibid., pp. 200–211). Presumably with all of this in mind, Madison insisted that, in a republican government:

> Ambition must be made to counteract ambition. . . It may be a reflection on human nature, that such devices should be necessary to control the abuses of government. But what is government itself, but the greatest of all reflections on human nature? If men were angels, no government would be necessary. . . In framing a government which is to be administered by men over men, the great difficulty lies in this: you must first enable the government to control the governed; and in the next place oblige it to control itself. A dependence on the people is, no doubt, the primary control on the government, but experience has taught mankind the necessity of *auxiliary precautions.* (Carey and McClellan, 2001, pp. 268–9; emphasis mine)

The 'auxiliary precautions' to which Madison referred are embedded in the Constitution. From Madison's and, it should be said, from the Founders' perspective, federalism and the separation of powers were intended simultaneously to restrain factions, and to 'oblige [government] to restrain itself'. It was in this spirit that Madison asserted that the government that was sought was 'one which should not only be founded on free principles, but in which the powers of government should be so divided and balanced among several bodies of the magistracy, as that no one could transcend their legal limits, without being effectually checked and restrained by others' (ibid., p. 258).

If the formal restraints institutionalized in the Constitution are important to the argument developed in later chapters, so too are the informal institutional restraints on government and on factional behavior to which the Founders repeatedly appealed. A recurring theme was the importance to republican self-government of virtue generally, and of civic virtue in particular. There was, moreover, general agreement that virtue ought to be promoted, and that there is a reciprocal relationship between morality and law. Writing in 1822, Madison averred that:

> The American people owe it to themselves, and to the cause of free Government, to prove by their establishments for the advancement of Knowledge, that their political Institutions . . . are as favorable to the *intellectual and moral improvement of Man* as they are conformable to his individual and social Rights. ([1822] 1999, pp. 792–3; emphasis mine)

Pressing the same theme, Benjamin Rush emphasized the efficacy of 'look[ing] up to a government that encourages Virtue – establishes justice, ensures order, [and] secures property' ([1788b] 1993, p. 256).

It is true that Hamilton urged that 'It is not safe to trust to the virtue of any people' ([1775] 2001, p. 44). Indeed, Madison insisted that only three motives, 'a prudent regard to private or partial good, . . . [and] a respect for character. . . [and] religion', could restrain a majority 'from unjust violations of the rights and interests of the minority' ([1787b] 1999, pp. 150–51; [1787a] 1999, pp. 76–8). But it is precisely because he believed these motives to be 'insufficient to restrain [a majority] from injustice', that Madison promoted the Constitution's 'auxiliary precautions'.

The essential point, however, is that the Founders, notably Madison, Rush and Melancton Smith, insisted that persons' preference and value structures are mutable, and that there is a reciprocal relationship between morality and law. Madison and the Anti-Federalists agreed, for example, that 'the value of a bill of rights was primarily educative'; that 'Bills of rights would best promote . . . republican self-government if they enabled republican citizens to govern themselves – to resist the impulses of interest and passion that were the root of factious behavior' (Rakove, 1997, p. 336).[2] In short, the cultivation of virtuous citizens *capable* of self-government was a recurring theme, both of the Founders and of many contemporary US political writers.[3] Washington's thinking is heuristic. For him, patriotism was both intrinsically valuable and instrumentally important: on the one hand, he spoke of 'using my utmost exertions to establish a national character' ([1796b] 1997, p. 952). On the other hand, he insisted that 'the name of American . . . must always exalt the just pride of Patriotism, more than any appellation derived from local discriminations' ([1796a] 1997, p. 965). In Washington's view, a 'national character' – a character that could and should be cultivated – served to mitigate the propensity toward 'Geographical discriminations' (ibid., p. 967) and factious behavior generally.

Hamilton, a confidant of Washington's, shared this view. While he acknowledged 'a strong and uniform attachment [of members of Congress] to the interests of their own state' ([1788b] 2001, p. 499),[4] he argued that 'the expedients which the partisans of Faction employ toward strengthening their influence by local discriminations' ([1796] 2001, p. 858) can be overcome. Implicitly invoking justice as impartiality, the mutability of preference and value structures, and the notion that virtue can be cultivated, Hamilton insisted that 'under the regular and gentle influence of *general* laws, these varying interests will be constantly assimilating, till they embrace each other, and assume the same complexion' ([1788b] 2001, p. 501; emphasis mine). In effect, Hamilton embraced the idea that 'law, by making visible and sometimes vivid the community values that are deemed important enough to support by law, can bolster these values' (Will, 1983, p. 86).[5]

The view that law both influences and reflects morality was a familiar theme during the founding era. While it is well known that Madison invoked Montesquieu, 'The oracle who is always consulted and cited' on the necessity of a separation of powers in a republic (Carey and McClellan, 2001, p. 250),[6] it is equally important that Federalists and Anti-Federalists embraced Montesquieu's understanding of civic or public virtue as 'a constant preference of public to private interest' and 'the love of the laws and of our country' ([1750] 1977, p. 130). Noah Webster, for example, invoked 'the learned, but visionary' Montesquieu's admonition that "'Virtue is the foundation of a republic'" ([1802] 1983, p. 1226), and embraced the Smithian/Kantian idea that '[Virtue] proceeds from early habits, and a strong attachment to the place where men are born, and to the customs, manners and *government*, in which they are educated' (ibid.; emphasis mine).

US political writing and political sermons pressed these themes. Speaking in 1784, Samuel McClintock said that 'virtue is the basis of republics, . . . and the moment that the people lose their virtue, and become venal and corrupt, they cease to be free' ([1784] 1998, p. 805).[7] He added that 'It may then justly be expected from those who are the fathers and guardians of the people . . . that they will . . . both by their authority and example, . . . encourage and promote the practice of . . . virtues among the people' (ibid., p. 807). For their part, the Tradesmen of the Town of Boston suggested that the 'constitution should be adopted' because it would '*promote* industry and morality; [and] render us respectable as a nation' ([1788] 1993, pp. 717–18; emphasis mine).[8]

If, as is clear, US political commentators endorsed the idea that there is a reciprocal relationship between law and morality, they also embraced the idea that moral philosophy is the foundation of law. The views of James Kent are both heuristic and important: 'By common accord, persons who study the development of American law seriously count Kent as one of the half-dozen jurists who have put the deepest imprint on American jurisprudence' (Hyneman and Lutz, 1983b, p. 936). In his 'Introductory Lecture to a Course of Law Lectures', Kent proffered this idea: 'The doctrines of Moral Philosophy form the foundation of Human Laws and must be deemed an essential part of Judicial Education'. To this he added, 'It is the business of this Science to examine the nature and moral character of Man. . . We are led by these inquiries to a knowledge of the nature, extent, and fitness of moral obligations . . . [and] the necessity and final end of government, the justice and harmony of obedience' ([1794] 1983, p. 945).[9]

Kent's invocation of the relationship between morality and law, of the need to 'examine the nature and moral character of Man', and of 'justice and harmony of obedience' as the 'final end of government' raises a number of questions. While the question of the Founders' view of the nature and moral character of man is momentarily deferred, I focus first on the 'end of government' and next, on the 'harmony of obedience'.

Madison's view, articulated in *Federalist* No. 51 is clear: 'Justice is the end of government. It is the end of civil society' (Carey and McClellan, 2001, p. 271).[10] Jefferson is equally clear: '[T]he moral principles on which the government is to be administered . . . [are] what is proper for all conditions of society'; whereas 'Liberty, truth, probity, honor, are declared to be the four cardinal principles of your society', 'justice is the fundamental law of society' ([1816b] 1984, pp. 1386–7). Finally, in his Third Annual Message to Congress, President Washington invoked 'the benefits of an impartial administration of justice' ([1791] 1997, p. 788).

Given that, for the Founders and for many of the founding generation, justice is the end of government, two questions remain. First, what did the Founders mean by 'justice'? Second, liberty, like justice, is an important dimension of moral appraisal and discussion. Given what Kent characterized as the need for 'harmony of obedience', the meaning of liberty, as it was understood by the founding generation, is an important question.

I emphasize first that Madison, Jefferson, Adams, Rush and others embraced what I shall later characterize as a Smithian/Kantian understanding of justice as impartiality. For the moment, it is sufficient to note that Jefferson insisted that it is 'self-evident, that all Men are created equal', that Madison averred that 'the perfect equality of mankind' is 'an absolute truth' ([1789b] 1999, p. 445) and that Benjamin Rush wrote that 'where there is no law there can be no liberty, and nothing deserves the name of law but that which is *certain*, and *universal* in its operation upon all the members of the community' ([1788a] 1993, p. 418; emphasis mine).[11]

All of this notwithstanding, it is clear that both the meaning of justice as impartiality or 'equal treatment', and the character and content of liberty are matters of considerable moment and controversy.

With this in mind, I begin by noting that Timothy Stone provides 'a good summary of what Americans during the founding era felt important for the continued success of their experiment in self-government, leadership and unity' (Hyneman and Lutz, 1983b, p. 839). In his 1792 Election Sermon, Stone said:

> That liberty consists in freedom from restraint, leaving each one to act as seemeth right to himself, is a most unwise mistaken apprehension. Civil liberty, consists in . . . such a system of laws, as doth bind all classes of men, rulers and subjects, to unite their exertions for the promotion of virtue and public happiness. . . A State of society necessarily implies reciprocal dependence in all its members; and rational government, is designed to realize and strengthen

> this dependence, and to render it, in such sense equal in all ranks . . . [so] that each one may feel himself bound to seek the good of the whole. ([1792] 1983b, p. 842)

Stone spoke for many of his generation, and for the Founders, when he noted that 'liberty' is not congruent with 'freedom from restraint'. Writing some five years before Stones's speech, Noah Webster observed that:

> in civil society, political liberty consists in acting conformably to the sense of a majority of the society. In a free government, every man binds himself to obey the public voice, or the opinions of a majority; and the whole society engages to protect each individual. In such a government a man is free and safe. ([1787] 1993, pp. 153–4)

Hamilton embraced these ideas in a 30 July 1796 letter to President Washington. The letter, a draft of the President's Farewell Address, suggested this paean to the 'lately established Constitution':

> This Government the offspring of [the people's] choice uninfluenced and unawed, completely free in its principles, in the *distribution of its powers* uniting energy with safety and containing in itself a provision for its own amendment is well entitled to your confidence and support. ([1796] 2001, p. 859; emphasis mine)

The emphasis upon the Constitution as the product of self-government is clear, as is the implicit emphasis on federalism and the separation of powers as 'uniting energy with safety'. Equally important, Hamilton codifies the connection between 'the fundamental maxims of true liberty' and its correlative duties:

> Respect for [this government's] authority, compliance with its laws, acquiescence in its measures, are duties dictated by the fundamental maxims of true Liberty. . . the constitution for the time, and until changed by an explicit and authentic act of the whole people, is sacredly binding upon all. The very idea of the right and power of the people to establish Government presupposes the duty of every individual to obey the established Government. (Ibid.)

Washington's 19 September 1796 Farewell Address, with minor editorial changes, adopted Hamilton's suggested language. Whatever else is said, it is clear that the Founders regarded federalism and the separation of powers as critical to the success of their republican self-government project. It is equally clear that, for them, liberty and freedom from restraint were not congruent. Rather, 'liberty', whose distribution is determined by rights, depends upon respect both for majority rule and for the Constitution.

Above all else, the Founders conceived of the Constitution as the guardian of ordered liberty; the 'safety' to which Hamilton referred. For Madison, its author, the Constitution's 'auxiliary precautions' were both intrinsically valuable and instrumentally important. On the one hand, the Constitution's consequence-detached procedural restraints on factious behavior reflected the Founders' prior ethical commitment to the moral equivalence of persons. Given the reciprocal relationship between law and morality, the Constitution both reflected and promoted the idea of justice as impartiality. On the other hand, the Founders agreed that controlling the *effects* of faction and, therefore, protecting rights, is contingent upon respect for federalism and the separation of powers. Madison's words are heuristic:

> In the compound republic of America, the power surrendered by the people, is first divided between the two distinct governments, and then the portion allotted to each sub-divided among distinct and separate departments. Hence a double security arises to the rights of the people. The different governments will control each other; at the same time that each will be controlled by itself. (Carey and McClellan, 2001, p. 270)

It is clear that the Founders did not regard rights as antecedent to civil society. For them, rights are the result of a path-dependent process.[12] It is well known, for example, that the English inheritance, the 'rights of Englishmen', informed Madison's work on the Bill of Rights.[13] Moreover, the Founders believed that, given the reciprocal relationship between law and morality, the Bill of Rights, like the Constitution, had educative value. In a letter to Jefferson, Madison asked a rhetorical question: 'What use then . . . can a bill of rights serve in popular Governments?' Madison's answer incorporates the Founders' view that preference and value structures are mutable, and that law, whether fundamental or statutory is, and should be, the embodiment of popular will:

> I answer [that] . . . 1. The political truths declared in that solemn manner acquire by degrees the character of fundamental maxims of free Government, and as they become incorporated with the national sentiment, counteract the impulses of interest and passion. 2. Altho' it be generally true . . . that the danger of oppression lies in the interested majorities of the people rather than in usurped acts of the Government, yet there may be occasions on which the evil may spring from the latter sources; and on such, a bill of rights will be a good ground for an appeal to the sense of the community. ([1788a] 1999, pp. 421–2)[14]

In Jack Rakove's account, the 'educative' value of a bill of rights was, for Madison, decisive:

As greater popular respect for individual and minority rights developed over time, perhaps the judiciary would eventually act as Madison very much hoped yet initially doubted it would. But the greater benefit would occur if acceptance of the principles encoded in rights acted to restrain political behavior, tempering improper popular desires before they took the form of *unjust legislation*. (Rakove, 1997, pp. 355–6; emphasis mine)[15]

Their emphasis on respect for rights and their correlative duties, and their desire to promote *just*, in the sense of impartial, legislation was derivative of the Founders' prior ethical commitment to the moral equivalence of persons. And central to their understanding of justice was the Founders' insistence that, as Jefferson wrote, 'The moral sense, or conscience, is as much a part of man as his leg or arm' ([1787d] 1984, p. 901). Significantly, this formulation is roughly congruent with Adam Smith's characterization of the 'moral sense':

> Upon whatever we suppose that our moral faculties are founded, whether upon a certain modification of reason, upon an original instinct, called a *moral sense*, or upon some other principle of our nature, it cannot be doubted, that [our moral faculties] were given us for the direction and conduct in this life . . . they were set up within us to be the supreme arbiters of all our actions, to superintend all our senses, passions, and appetites, and to judge how far each of them was either to be indulged or restrained. . . No other faculty or principle of action judges of any other. . . What is agreeable to our moral faculties, is fit, and right, and proper to be done; the contrary wrong, unfit and improper. ([1759] 1976, pp. 164–5; emphasis mine)[16]

If Smith's moral sense construal was shared by the Founders, his work is also reconcilable with their view that virtue may be cultivated:

> When custom and fashion coincide with the natural principles of right and wrong. . . Those who have been *educated* in what is really good company, . . . who have been accustomed to see nothing in the persons whom they esteemed and lived with, but *justice*, modesty, humanity and good order; are more shocked with whatever seems to be inconsistent with the rules which those virtues prescribe. (Ibid., p. 200; emphasis mine)

Smith's emphasis on the 'Influence of Custom and Fashion upon Moral Sentiments' ([1759] 1976, pp. 200–211) and on the 'Influence and Authority of Conscience' (pp. 134–56) was central to what Muller has called Smith's 'civilizing project'; the idea that 'to be virtuous is to make our conduct conform to an external model which we have internalized' (Muller, 1993, p. 190):

> The love and admiration which we naturally conceive for those whose character and conduct we approve of, necessarily dispose us to desire to become ourselves

the object of the like agreeable sentiments. . . But, in order to attain this satisfaction, we must become the *impartial spectators* of our own character and
conduct. But it greatly confirms this happiness and contentment when we find
other people, viewing [our character and conduct] with those very eyes which
we, in imagination only, were endeavouring to view them, see them precisely in
the same light in which we ourselves had seen them. Their approbation necessarily confirms our own self-approbation. (Smith [1759] 1976, p. 114; emphasis
mine)

While Smith's impartial spectator construal is important for its own
sake, two points are of immediate importance. First, the impartial spectator's perspective does not emerge *in vacuo*. It is shaped by custom, tradition, family and other 'external' influences. This conception is clearly not
reconcilable with the transcendental autonomous self of modern imagination (see Chapter 5 this volume). Second, the notional impartial spectator
is fully reconcilable with the Founder's view that man has an innate moral
sense, that virtue can be cultivated, and that there is a reciprocal relationship between morality and law. The Founders would certainly associate
themselves with Smith's insistence that 'that sense of what is due to his
fellow-creatures . . . is the basis of *justice* and of society' (Smith [1759]
1976, p. 102; emphasis mine); that 'it is only by consulting this [impartial]
judge within . . . that we can ever make any proper comparison between
our own interests and those of other people' (ibid., p. 134), and that 'As
society cannot subsist unless the laws of justice are tolerably observed,
. . . the consideration of this necessity, . . . was the ground upon which we
approved of the enforcement of the laws of justice' (ibid., p. 87).

The Founders were, in fact, inclined to appeal to the golden rule. In a
letter to Jefferson, John Adams wrote, '*Jus cuique*, the golden rule, do as
you would be done by, is all the equality that can be supported or defended
by reason or common sense' (Himmelfarb, 2004, p. 216). While this may,
in part, be attributed to Americans' religious inheritance,[17] the golden rule
– and, it should be said, Smith's impartial spectator construal – is evocative of Immanuel Kant's categorical imperative or moral law. While Kant
formulates the moral law in a number of ways, the construction that 'has
had the greatest cultural impact' (O'Neill, 1993, p. 178) is the Formula of
the End in Itself: 'So act as to treat humanity, whether in thine own person
or in that of any other, in every case as an end withal, never as means only'
(Kant [1785] 1988, p. 58). It is this formulation that is perhaps most evocative of the idea that animates it; an idea that the Founders embraced, the
moral equivalence of persons:

> The conception of free and equal persons as reasonable and rational is the *basis*
> of the [moral law] construction: unless this conception and the power of moral

personality it includes – our humanity – are animated . . . in human beings, the moral law would have no basis in the world. (Rawls [1989] 1999, p. 515)

Kant himself argues that respect for the moral law must be cultivated. In this, and every other respect, Kant's conception of the moral law is reconcilable both with Adam Smith's impartial spectator construal, and with the Founders' view that respect for the impartiality imperative must be cultivated.[18]

The essential point is that, for Smith and Kant, cultivation of respect for the moral law requires a two-person perspective. For Smith, 'When I endeavour to examine my conduct. . . I divide myself, as it were, into two persons. . . The first is the spectator. . . The second is the agent. . . The first is the judge; the second the person judged of' ([1759] 1976, p. 113).[19] For Kant, 'what makes categorical imperatives possible' ([1785] 1988, p. 86) is 'One resource [that] remains to us, namely, to inquire whether we do not occupy different points of view when . . . we think ourselves as causes efficient *a priori*, and when we form our conception of ourselves from our actions as effects' (ibid., p. 82). Thus, if for Smith, 'The love and admiration which we naturally conceive for those whose character and conduct we approve of, necessarily dispose us to become ourselves the objects of the like agreeable sentiments' ([1759] 1976, p. 114), for Kant, 'There is not one, not even the most consummate villain . . . who, when we set before him examples of honesty of purpose, of steadfastness in following good maxims, of sympathy and general benevolence . . . [who] does not wish that he might also possess these qualities' ([1785] 1988, p. 87).

The Founders understood this. Like Smith and Kant, they understood that, man's innate moral sense notwithstanding, respect for the imperative to treat others as ends rather than as means must be cultivated. They also recognized, with Montesquieu, that public virtue is essential for self-government, and for 'a self-renunciation which is always arduous and painful': [Public virtue] may be defined, as the love of the laws, and of our country. As this love requires a constant preference of public to private interest, it is the source of all the particular virtues' (Montesquieu [1750] 1977, p. 130).[20]

Jefferson's thinking embraced many of these themes. Writing in 1785, he urges that 'Whenever you are to do a thing, though it can never be known but to yourself, ask yourself how you would act were the world looking at you, and act accordingly' ([1785] 1984, p. 815). This, I suggest, is evocative both of Smith's impartial spectator and of Kant's two points of view. Just as important, Jefferson, like many of the Founders, embraced the idea of an innate moral sense, rejected self-interest as the basis of morality, emphasized that 'our relations with others constitute the boundaries of morality', and acknowledged the role of 'education, instruction or restraint' in the cultivation of respect for the moral law:

> Self-interest, or rather self-love, or *egoism* has been . . . substituted as the basis of morality. But I consider our relations with others as constituting the boundaries of morality. . . To ourselves, in strict language, we can owe no duties, obligation requiring also two parties. Self-love, therefore, is no part of morality. . . It is the sole antagonist of virtue leading us constantly by our propensities to self-gratification in violation of our moral duties to others. . . subdue those propensities by education, instruction or restraint, and virtue remains without a competitor. ([1814b] 1984, pp. 1336–7)

If the emphasis on duty and obligation to others gestures toward a Smithian/Kantian understanding of procedural justice, so too does Jefferson's rejection of self-interest as the basis of morality. Indeed, Jefferson's invocation of 'our propensities to self-gratification in violation of our moral duties to others' is reminiscent of Kant's 'heteronomy' construction. For Kant, and it should be said, for Smith, any action that is animated by desire, emotion or interest is heteronomous (Scruton, 1982, p. 65). Clearly, Jefferson, Madison and others of the founding generation understood this. It is precisely because we are subject to such impulses that the Constitution's 'auxiliary precautions' are necessary, and that respect for the moral law must be cultivated. And all of this is true, moreover, *despite* our innate moral sense. Thus, despite our heteronomous dispositions, for Jefferson, like Smith, 'The want or imperfection of the moral sense in some men, like the want or imperfection of the senses of sight and hearing in others, is no proof that it is a general characteristic of the species. When it is wanting, we endeavor to supply the defect, by appeals to reason and calculation' ([1814b] 1984, pp. 1337–8).

Jefferson stresses that he was not alone in embracing what I call the Smithian/Kantian understanding of the self and, therefore, of justice. Jefferson makes this clear in an 1823 letter to Justice William Johnson. He declares that the objective of the Anti-Federalists 'was to maintain the will of the majority of the convention, and of the people themselves. We believed, with them, that man was a rational animal endowed by nature with rights, and with an innate moral sense of justice'. Implicitly invoking the Constitution's 'auxiliary precautions', he adds that '[man] could be restrained from wrongs and protected in right by moderate powers confided to persons of his own choice' ([1823] 1984, p. 1470).

If the Founders believed that man possesses 'an innate moral sense of justice', they also had a clear understanding of the *meaning* of 'justice'. Whether informed by their 'religious inheritance' and, therefore, by the 'golden rule', by Smith's impartial spectator, or by Kant's categorical imperative, justice, for the Founders, required that morally equivalent persons be treated impartially. Madison's view is illustrative. For him, 'the perfect equality of mankind . . . is an absolute truth' ([1789b] 1999, p. 445). He insists, moreover, that 'that alone is a *just* government which *impartially* secures to every man, whatever is his own' ([1792b] 1999, p. 515). In his account, discriminatory law is unjust and, therefore, immoral:

Madison in his own words

> That is not a just government, nor is property secure under it where arbitrary restrictions, exemptions, and monopolies deny to part of its citizens that free use of their faculties, and free choice of their occupations. . . What must be the spirit of legislation where a manufacturer of linen cloth is forbidden to bury his own child in a linen shroud, in order to favour his neighbour who manufactures woolen cloth; where the manufacturer and wearer of woolen cloth are again forbidden the oeconomical use of buttons of that material, in favor of the manufacturer of buttons of other materials! (Ibid., p. 516)

Madison's concern with unjust legislation, with the role of factions in promoting discrimination, and with the 'necessary and ordinary operations of government' found expression in *Federalist* No. 10:

> The most common and durable sources of factions, has been the various and unequal distribution of property. Those who hold, and those who are without property, have ever formed distinct interests in society. Those who are creditors, and those who are debtors, fall under a like *discrimination*. A landed interest, a manufacturing interest, a mercantile interest, a monied interest, with many lesser interests, grow up of necessity in civilized nations, and divide them into different classes, actuated by different sentiments and views. The regulation of these various and interfering interests, forms the principal task of modern legislation and involves the spirit of party and faction in the necessary and ordinary operation of government. (Carey and McClellan, 2001, p. 44; emphasis mine)

The passage is important because it encapsulates the Founders' concern with faction and the associated discriminatory, and therefore unjust, impulse. The crucial point, however, is that 'The examples of regulation that Madison cited reveal that he regarded *all* decisions of economic policy as implicating questions of justice and thus of private rights' (Rakove, 1997, p. 315).

If Madison's insistence upon 'the most exact impartiality' in taxation (Carey and McClellan, 2001, p. 45) is heuristic, so, too, is Jefferson's insistence that the federal government not pay 'bounties for the encouragement of particular manufactures'. Indeed, it is clear that Jefferson questioned both the morality and the constitutionality of federal 'bounties' and other subsidies and 'encouragements'.

At issue was Hamilton's 'Report on the Subject of Manufactures'.

Hamilton seeks, among other things, to 'enumerate the principal circumstances, from which it may be inferred – That manufacturing establishments not only occasion a positive augmentation of the Produce and Revenue of the Society, but that they contribute essentially to rendering them greater than they could possibly be, without such establishments' ([1791] 2001, p. 658). With his enumeration complete, and having considered 'objections to a particular encouragement of manufacturers in the United States', Hamilton avers that:

> The greatest obstacle of all to the successful prosecution of a new branch of industry in a country, . . . consists . . . in the bounties, premiums and other aids which are granted, in a variety of cases, by the nations, in which the establishments to be imitated are previously introduced. (Ibid., p. 671)

Granting all of this, and given 'the bounties, premiums and other artificial encouragements, with which foreign nations second the exertions of their own Citizens in the branches [of manufacturing]' (ibid., p. 670), Hamilton suggests that:

> it is proper . . . to consider the means, by which ['inducements to the promotion of Manufactures in the United States'] may be affected as introductory to a Specification of the objects which . . . appear the most fit to be encouraged, and of the particular measures which it may be advisable to adopt, in respect of each. (Ibid., p. 697)

Hamilton concludes the discussion (pp. 697–734), and the report, with this thought:

> In countries where there is great private wealth much may be effected by the voluntary contributions of patriotic individuals, but in a community situated like that of the United States, the public purse must supply the deficiency of private resource. In what can it be so useful as in promoting and improving the efforts of industry? (Ibid., p. 734)

If Hamilton was convinced of the efficacy of a 'system of bounties, premiums and other artificial encouragements', he also insisted that 'this species of encouragement' is constitutional:

> A Question has been made concerning the Constitutional right of the Government of the United States to apply this species of encouragement, but there is certainly no good foundation for such a question. The *National Legislature* has express authority 'To lay and Collect taxes, duties, imports and excises, to pay the debts and provide for the Common *defense* and *general welfare*'. . . . The terms *'general welfare'* . . . [are] as comprehensive as any that

could have been used . . . because this necessarily embraces a vast variety of particulars, which are susceptible neither of specification nor of definition. (Ibid., p. 702; emphasis in original)

While Hamilton's constitutional interpretation gestures toward my discussion of the Constitution's General Welfare and Necessary and Proper Clauses (in Chapter 4), I emphasize for the moment that Jefferson rejected Hamilton's view that 'bounties, premiums and other aids' to manufactures are constitutional. In his 28 February 1792 'Conversations with the President', Jefferson observed that:

particular members of the [national] legislature . . . in order to keep the game in their hands had from time to time aided in making such legislative constructions of the constitution as made it a very different thing from what the people thought they had submitted to; that they had now brought forward a proposition, far beyond every one ever yet advanced, & to which the eyes of many were turned as the decision which was to let us know whether we live under a limited or an unlimited government. ([1792a] 1984, p. 677)

When President Washington asked him 'to what proposition [he] alluded?', Jefferson replied that:

In [Hamilton's] Report on manufactures which, under colour of giving *bounties* for the encouragement of particular manufactures, meant to establish the doctrine that the power given by the Constitution to collect taxes to provide for the *general welfare* of the U.S., permitted Congress to take everything under their management which *they* should deem for the *public welfare*, & which is susceptible of the application of money: consequently that the subsequent enumeration of their powers was not the description to which resort must be had, & did not at all constitute the limits of their authority. (Ibid.; emphasis in original)[21]

I emphasize, first, that the constitutionality of discriminatory federal policies was, from the Founders' perspective, a non-trivial matter. At issue, in short, is the force and effect of Madison's 'auxiliary precautions'. While this discussion is momentarily deferred, I emphasize, again, that economic policy was, for the Founders, a *moral* issue. In a letter to P.S. Dupont de Nemours, Jefferson makes this clear:

when we come to the moral principles on which the government is to be administered, we come to what is proper for all conditions of society. . . I believe with you that morality, compassion, generosity, are innate elements of the human constitution; that there exists a right independent of force; that a right to property is founded in our natural wants, in the means with which we are endowed to satisfy these wants, and the right to what we acquire by those means without violating the similar rights of other sensible beings; that no one has a right to obstruct another, exercising his faculties innocently for the relief of sensibilities made a part of his nature; that *justice* is the fundamental law of society. ([1816b] 1984, pp. 1386–7; emphasis mine)

Jefferson's Smithian/Kantian construction – the 'innate elements of the human constitution', and his emphasis on justice as 'the fundamental law of society' and of government – gestures toward the institutional imperatives that informed the Founders' republican self-government project.

As we have seen, the Founders' Smithian/Kantian understanding of the self is animated by their prior ethical commitment to the moral equivalence of persons: because all persons are morally equivalent, each is entitled to equal or impartial consideration. The Founders understood, however, that while persons possess an 'innate sense of justice', respect for the moral law – the imperative to treat morally equivalent persons equally – must be cultivated. A corollary of this, also understood by the Founders, is that law, whether constitutional, statutory or common, should both reflect and promote respect for the moral law.

It is clear, then, that the Founders did not embrace a consequence based, procedurally-detached moral theory. The essential point is this: whereas consequentialists start with a theory of the good and argue that that good ought to be promoted (Pettit, 1993, p. 231), the Founders started with a theory of the right, the moral equivalence of persons.[22] They were concerned, therefore, with the specification of *permissible* ends, and with the institutionalization of just, in the sense of impartial, laws.

The Founders were not, and could not be utilitarians. The imperative to treat persons as ends rather than as means is procedurally based and consequence-detached. It is not, therefore, persons' 'utility' or 'happiness' that is intrinsically valuable. On the one hand, morality cannot be grounded in 'private happiness' since 'the springs it [the principle of private happiness] provides for morality . . . undermine [morality] . . . since they put the motives to virtue and to vice in the same class, and only teach us to make a better calculation, the . . . difference between virtue and vice being entirely extinguished' (Kant [1785] 1988, p. 72).[23] On the other hand, 'a man cannot form any definite and certain conception of the sum of satisfaction of all of [his inclinations] which is called happiness' (ibid., p. 24).[24] Stated differently, 'the notion of happiness is so indefinite that although every man wishes to attain it, yet he can never say definitely and consistently what it is that he really wishes and wills' (ibid., p. 45). To this I would add that, among other things, 'utility' may derive from malign and ill-informed preferences.

The essential point is this: from the Founders' perspective, the moral law – the imperative to treat morally equivalent persons impartially – requires that man 'should promote his happiness not from inclination but from *duty*, and by this would his conduct first acquire true moral worth' (ibid., p. 24; emphasis mine). Indeed, the Smithian/Kantian concept of 'duty' informed the Founders' work on the Constitution. They understood that 'the constitution is to be a just procedure satisfying the requirements of equal liberty', and that 'it is to be framed so that of all the feasible just arrangements, it is the one more likely than any other to result in a just and effective system of legislation' (Rawls, 1971, p. 221). They understood, moreover, that the Constitution and post-constitutional government must promote the greatest possible equal political participation (ibid., pp. 221–8).

While these matters are taken up below, I emphasize that their single-minded emphasis on *procedural* justice means that the contemporary politics of 'wants and needs' and of economic growth and distributive justice found no place in the Founders' imagination.

2.3   THE FOUNDERS' CONSTITUTION

In the Founders' view, the Constitution, the new republic's 'fundamental law' (Carey and McClellan, 2001, p. 404) would be both intrinsically and instrumentally valuable: it would be instrumentally important because of the procedural restraints on factious behavior that it institutionalized. It would be valuable for its own sake because it reflects a reciprocal relationship with morality. Among other things, the Constitution could promote both a 'constant preference of public to private interest', and 'the love of the laws and of our country'. Given Madison's insistence that justice, in the sense of impartiality, is 'the end of government . . . the end of civil society' (Carey and McClellan, 2001, p. 271),[25] and given that the Founders believed that the Constitution would both institutionalize and promote acceptance of this *moral* commitment, it is not surprising that, for Washington, 'the Constitution which at any time exists, 'till changed by an explicit and authentic act of the whole people, is sacredly obligatory upon all'. That said, he emphasizes that 'the very idea of the power and the right of the People to establish Government presupposes the *duty* of every Individual to obey the established Government' ([1796a] 1997, p. 968; emphasis mine).

The juxtaposition of 'right' and 'duty' is clearly Smithian/Kantian. The essential point, however, is that, whereas in a self-governing republic the people are sovereign, the people have a duty to respect the impartiality imperative that animates the Constitution. It is in this spirit that Madison avers that 'the people can change the constitution if they please, but while the constitution exists, the people must conform themselves to its dictates' ([1789a] 1999, p. 469). Hamilton's position is equally clear: 'the present

Constitution is the standard to which we are to cling. Under its banners, *bona fide* must we combat our political foes – rejecting all changes but through the channel itself provides for amendments' ([1802] 2001, p. 989).

While the Founders recognized the possibility of constitutional amendment, they had a consistent and unqualified view of constitutional interpretation. Reduced to its essentials, 'Judicial alteration of the fundamental law ran counter to [the Founders'] belief in a "fixed Constitution"; it was altogether outside their contemplation, as Hamilton made plain' (Berger, 1997, pp. 331–2). Madison and Jefferson make this clear. In a 13 March 1830 letter, Madison writes that 'It is but too common to read the expression of a remote period thro' the modern meaning of them, & to omit guards agst. misconstruction not anticipated. . . The remark is equally applicable to the Constitution itself' ([1833] 1999, p. 865).[26] Writing some 30 years earlier, Jefferson offers a similar argument against 'misconstruction' or 'broad construction' of the Constitution:

> When an instrument admits of two constructions, the one safe, the other dangerous, the one precise, the other indefinite, I prefer that which is safe and precise. I had rather ask an enlargement of power from the nation, where it is found necessary, than to assume it by a construction which would make our powers boundless. Our peculiar security is in possession of a written Constitution. Let us not make it a blank paper by construction. ([1803] 1984, p. 1140)

(handwritten margin note: Commerce Clause?)

If Madison and Jefferson gesture toward what some today call 'original meaning' or 'textualism', Hamilton implicitly appeals to Smithian/Kantian moral philosophy to argue for the independence and 'moderation of the judiciary':

> it is not with a view to infractions of the constitution only, that the independence of the judges may be an essential safe-guard against the effects of occasional ill humors of the society. These sometimes extend no farther than to *the injury of the private rights of particular classes of citizens, by unjust and partial laws*. Here also the firmness of the judicial magistracy . . . not only serves to moderate the immediate mischiefs of those [laws] which may have been passed, but it operates as a check upon the legislative body in passing them. (Carey and McClellan, 2001, p. 406; emphasis mine)

The danger of 'unjust and partial laws' was, for the Founders, a recurring theme. In his *Lectures on Law*, James Wilson, one of only six men to sign both the Declaration of Independence and the Constitution, noted that:

> [w]hen questions – especially pecuniary questions – arise between a state and a citizen – more especially still, when those questions are, as they generally must be, submitted to the decision of those who are not only parties and judges, but

legislators also; the sacred *impartiality* of the [judge] . . . is too frequently lost in the sordid interestedness of the [party], and in the arrogant power of the [legislator]. (Hall and Hall, 2007, p. 1044; emphasis mine)

Given that he, like Madison, was 'trained in the Scottish Moral Enlightenment tradition' (ibid., pp. XIV–XV), it is not surprising that Wilson should emphasize justice as impartiality and that he, like Smith, should be wary of discriminatory law. For his part, Hamilton's implicit invocation of a Kantian-style veil of ignorance (see Section 2.4 below) is, I believe, equally apparent:

> The benefits of the integrity and moderation of the judiciary . . . though they may have displeased those whose sinister expectations they may have disappointed, must have commanded the esteem and applause of all the *virtuous and disinterested*. Considerate men . . . ought to prize whatever will tend to beget or fortify that temper in the courts; *as no man can be sure that he may not be tomorrow the victim of a spirit of injustice, by which he may be a gainer to-day*. And every man must now feel, that the inevitable tendency of such a spirit [of injustice] is to sap the foundations of public and private confidence, and to introduce in its stead universal distrust and distress. (Carey and McClellan, 2001, pp. 406–7; emphasis mine)

It is clear, then, that if the Founders insisted that post-constitutional law must be impartial, they also worried that unjust laws would 'sap . . . public and private confidence, and . . . introduce in its stead universal distrust and distress'. Plainly stated, the Founders were concerned that failure to respect the moral law – and the Constitution that sought to institutionalize it – would be corrosive of social order.

The Founders' approach to the establishment and preservation of social order reflects a recognition that, despite his innate moral sense, 'man's natural proclivity is to pursue his own interests and that different persons' interests almost inevitably come into conflict'. Granting this:

> Two broadly defined escape routes have offered hope . . . through the ages. One of them is man's capacity for moral improvement. . .

> The second . . . approach starts with the empirical realities of persons as they exist, moral warts and all. These realities . . . limit the attainable states of social harmony. But even within such constraints, hope emerges for sustainable social order through the appropriate design, construction, and maintenance of rules that set limits on the way in which each person is allowed to order his conduct toward others. (Brennan and Buchanan [1985b] 2000, p. XVI)

I acknowledge, first, that the two approaches reflect 'some substitutability between rules for behavior which reflect moral norms and [behavioral constraints] which are explicitly chosen as constraints' (Buchanan [1985] 2000, p. 491).[27] That said, we know that the Founders employed both 'escape routes'. On the one hand, they sought, through education and the Constitution and Bill of Rights to *promote* respect for the moral law. On the other hand, they sought, through the Constitution's 'auxiliary precautions', to *constrain* discriminatory factious behavior. They embraced the idea, in short, that moral and constitutional constraints on discriminatory behavior and laws are a *sine qua non* for social order generally, and for republican self-government in particular.

The problem, as Hamilton and the other Founders recognized, is that failure to respect the moral law and, it should be said, the Constitution's 'auxiliary precautions', threatens both the *legitimacy* of government and the social order:

> For precisely the same reasons applicable to law, a [post-constitutional] politics that fails to satisfy some variant of the generality-equality norm cannot be deemed to be legitimate. Such a discriminatory politics cannot pass the [procedurally based consequence-detached] contractarian test. In reflective equilibrium and behind a veil of ignorance/uncertainty, persons could not have agreed to the establishment of political institutions that are predicted to discriminate explicitly in their operation. The politics of discrimination would not meet the agreement criterion that defines justice as fairness. (Buchanan and Congleton, 1998, p. 11)[28]

It is true, of course, that the Constitution's procedural restraints on discriminatory factious behavior can be supplemented by what Hayek, informed by Montesquieu and Rousseau, called the 'democratic spirit':

> The great aim of the struggle for liberty has been equality before the law. This equality under the rules which the state enforces may be supplemented by a similar equality of the rules that men *voluntarily* obey in their relations with one another. This extension of the principle of equality to the rules of moral and social conduct is the chief expression of what is commonly called the democratic spirit – and probably that aspect of it that does most to make inoffensive the inequalities that liberty necessarily produces. (Hayek, 1960, p. 85; emphasis mine)

Hayek's characterization of the 'democratic spirit' is reminiscent of the Founders' preoccupation with the cultivation of respect for the moral law. Equally important, Hayek's formulation is congruent with the Founders' Smithian/Kantian and, I maintain, Rawlsian, understanding of the nexus between the rule of law and liberty:

> Liberty . . . is a complex of rights and duties defined by institutions. . . . The principle of legality has a firm foundation . . . in the agreement of rational persons to

establish for themselves the *greatest equal liberty*. To be confident in the possession and exercise of these freedoms, the citizens of a well-ordered society, will nor-
mally want the rule of law maintained. (Rawls, 1971, pp. 239–40; emphasis mine)

The normative basis of the principle of equal liberty, or of equal political participation when applied to the political procedure defined by the
Constitution (ibid., p. 221), is the moral equivalence of persons. The
moral law, in turn, requires that we respect the agency, independence,
self-determination and dignity of morally equivalent persons.[29] The substantive values or aims that the law ought to promote, its 'external morality', find expression in these ideas (Ten, 1995, p. 397). It follows that 'the
conception of formal justice, the regular and *impartial* administration of
public rules, becomes the rule of law when applied to the legal system'
(Rawls, 1971, p. 235; emphasis mine).

The point of immediate relevance to the Founders' republican self-
government project is that the external morality of law demands that the
greatest possible equal liberty be promoted, both at the constitutional
(ibid., p. 221–8), and at the post-constitutional stage.[30] In the case of the
former, the principle of equal liberty or equal participation when applied
to political procedure, *means* that each vote has approximately the same
weight, that members of the legislature, with one vote each, represent the
same number of electors, and that all citizens have equal access to public
office (ibid., p. 223). The *extent* of equal liberty or of equal political participation contemplates 'the degree to which the procedure of (bare) majority
rule is restricted by the mechanisms of constitutionalism'. Importantly, and
as the Founders plainly understood, majorities have 'final authority' with
respect to 'devices [that] serve to limit the scope of majority rule', subject
to the constraint that 'limits on the extent of the principle of participation
. . . fall equally upon everyone' (ibid., p. 228). On this logic, the *justification*
for such limits on the scope of majority rule as the Constitution's 'auxiliary
precautions' is that they 'protect the other freedoms' (ibid., p. 229). Thus,
'A bill of rights may remove certain liberties from majority regulation
altogether, and the separation of powers with judicial review may slow
down the pace of legislative change' (ibid., p. 228).

It is a matter of considerable moment that the Founders were, in fact,
concerned with the 'pace of legislative change'. In his celebrated *Lectures
on Law*, James Wilson noted, with some irritation, that:

a citizen under a republican government . . . is frequently pestered with a
number of frivolous, ambiguous, perplexed, and contradictory laws. The very
best constitutions are subject to some complaints. What may be called the *rage
of legislation* is a distemper prevalent and epidemical among republican governments. (Hall and Hall, 2007, p. 1045; emphasis mine)

For his part, a 'P.S.' in a letter to Madison reveals the depth of Jefferson's concern with the 'instability of our laws':

> P.S. The instability of our laws is really an immense evil. I think it would be well to provide in our constitutions that there shall always be a twelve-month between the ingrossing of a bill & passing it: that it should then be offered to its passage without changing a word: and that if circumstances should be thought to require a speedier passage, it should take two thirds of both houses instead of a bare majority. (Jefferson [1787a] 1984, p. 918; [1987b] 1993, p. 213)

While Wilson's 'rage of legislation' and Jefferson's 'instability of laws' are descriptive of today's legislative process, this is the subject matter of Chapters 1 and 6. The point of immediate interest is that both Wilson's and Jefferson's remarks underscore the need for 'ordered liberty'. Simply stated, the Constitution's 'auxiliary precautions' – notably federalism and the separation of powers – were intended to limit the *extent* of liberty.

If the Founders were aware both of the *meaning* of equal political participation and of the need to limit its *extent*, it is also clear that they were cognizant of the value or *worth* of equal political participation. The latter is understood to require that the Constitution 'underwrite a fair opportunity to take part in and to influence the political process' (Rawls, 1971, p. 224). This requires, among other things, that the Constitution protect freedom of speech, assembly, contract, thought and conscience, and that all citizens 'should have the means to be informed about political issues' (ibid., p. 225). While deliberate and frequently surreptitious restrictions on 'the means to be informed about political issues' figure prominently in the argument developed in Chapters 1 and 6, I emphasize for the moment that:

> The liberties protected by the principle of [equal] participation lose much of their value whenever those who have greater private means are permitted to use their advantages to control the course of public debate. For eventually these inequalities will enable those better situated to exercise a larger influence over the development of legislation. (Ibid., p. 225)

It follows that 'Compensating steps must . . . be taken to preserve the fair value for all of the equal political liberties' (ibid.). Whether the 'compensating steps' take the form of the Founders' 'auxiliary precautions' or of other formal or informal institutional restraints, the moral imperative is to prevent the pleadings of the 'more advantaged social and economic interests' from receiving 'excessive attention'; an outcome that 'is all the more likely when the less favored members of society, having been effectively prevented by their lack of means from exercising their fair degree of influence withdraw into apathy and resentment' (ibid., p. 226).

The Founders' republican self-government project was informed, in part, by the idea that 'democratic political process is at best regulated rivalry'; it is an environment in which 'Political power rapidly accumulates and becomes unequal; and making use of the coercive apparatus of the state and its *law*, those who gain the advantage can often assure themselves of a favored position' (ibid.; emphasis mine). It follows that promotion of the greatest possible equal liberty or, at the level of political *procedure*, the greatest possible equal political participation, may require that 'the scope of majority rule' be limited. The essential point is that limits on the *extent* of equal liberty or equal political participation may increase the *worth* or value of equal political participation. The Founders' Constitution clearly reflects this understanding: given their prior ethical commitment to the moral equivalence of persons, and given the concomitant imperative to promote just, in the sense of impartial, institutions, the Founders sought, through a system of formal constitutional restraints, to ensure what Rawls has called 'the fair value of political liberty' (ibid.). The Bill of Rights is properly understood as an attempt to protect 'other freedoms'. For their part, federalism, the separation of powers and the other constitutional 'auxiliary precautions' were intended to set 'ambition against ambition' and, thereby, to mitigate the effects of intendedly discriminating factious behavior. Simply stated, the Founders sought, through *constitutional restraints on majoritarian democracy*, to mitigate the effects of what today is characterized as rent-seeking and majoritarian cycling.

It is against this background that I emphasize, again, that an 'adaptive' or 'living' Constitution was alien to the Founders' imagination.[31] Among other things, given their procedurally based, consequence-detached moral and political philosophy, they did not, and could not embrace a 'results-oriented' or instrumentalist constitutional jurisprudence. It is true that, as we have seen, the Founders worried about the erosion of the Constitution's procedural restraints on factious behavior. That said, it is also true that, whereas some would argue that the Supreme Court should be an instrument of 'social change', Hamilton was clear that 'The courts must declare the sense of the law; and if [the courts] should be disposed to exercise WILL instead of JUDGEMENT, the consequence would equally be the substitution of their pleasure to that of the legislative body' (Carey and McClellan, 2001, p. 405; emphasis in original). Writing in support of the Founders' understanding of judicial review, Hamilton insisted that 'To avoid an arbitrary discretion in the courts, it is indispensible that [the courts] should be bound down by strict rules and precedents, which serve to define and point out their duty in every particular case that comes before them' (ibid., p. 407).

Let us be clear: from the Founders' perspective, the solution of 'social problems' is the prerogative not of the judiciary, but of legislative bodies; in particular, of *state* legislators (Madison [1792a] 1999, pp. 508–9). If, as Raoul Berger has suggested, this means that the Supreme Court is not the 'conscience of the country' (1997, p. 333),[32] it also means that, as Hamilton emphasized, 'the proposed government cannot be deemed a *national* one; since its jurisdiction extends to certain enumerated objects only, and leaves to the several states, a residuary and inviolable sovereignty over all other objects' (Carey and McClellan, 2001, p. 198; emphasis in original). As Hamilton's *Federalist* No. 82 makes clear, the federal government's authority is limited to 'one of three cases':

> The principles established in a former paper [*Federalist* No. 32] teach us that the states will retain all *pre-existing* authorities which may not be delegated to the federal head; and that this exclusive delegation can only exist in one of three cases; where an exclusive authority is, in express terms, granted to the union; or where a particular authority is granted to the union, and the exercise of a like authority is prohibited to the states; or, where an authority is granted to the union, with which a similar authority in the states would be utterly incompatible. (Carey and McClellan, 2001, p. 426; emphasis in original)

If Hamilton wrote in generic terms about the states' 'pre-existing authorities', Madison's *Federalist* No. 45 codifies the federal government's 'few and defined' powers:

> The powers delegated by the proposed constitution to the federal government, are few and defined. Those which are to remain in the *state* governments, are numerous and indefinite. The former will be exercised principally on external objects, as war, peace, negotiation and foreign commerce; with which last the power of taxation will, for the most part, be connected. The powers reserved to the several states will extend to all objects, which, in the ordinary course of affairs, concern the lives, liberties, and properties of the people; and the internal order, improvement and prosperity of the state. (Ibid., p. 241, emphasis mine)

Respect for what we today call the states' 'police powers' and of the limits of the federal government's enumerated powers is the essence of the Founders' federalism enterprise. We know, however, that Madison became increasingly concerned that the Supreme Court 'has manifested a propensity to enlarge the general authority in derogation of the local, and to amplify its own jurisdiction'. In a 27 June 1823 letter to Thomas Jefferson, Madison expressed his concern, and suggested a possible remedy:

> I am not unaware that the Judiciary career has not corresponded with what was anticipated. At one point the Judges perverted the Bench of Justice into a rostrum for partizan [sic] harangues. And latterly the Court, by some of

its decisions, still more by extrajudicial reasonings & dicta, has manifested a propensity to enlarge the general authority in derogation of the local, and to amplify its own jurisdiction, which has justly incurred the public censure. . . And if no remedy of the abuse be practicable under the forms of the Constitution, I should prefer a resort to the Nation for an amendment of the Tribunal itself. ([1823] 1999, p. 802)

Writing some four years earlier, Madison attributed 'Much of the error in expounding the Constitution' to a failure to respect what Hamilton in *Federalist* No. 78 called a 'limited constitution'. As Hamilton emphasized, a limited constitution is 'one which contains certain specified exceptions to the [federal] legislative authority; such for instance as that it shall pass no bills of attainder, no *ex post facto* laws, and the like'. To this he added that 'Limitations of this kind can be preserved in practice no other way than through the medium of the courts of justice' and, importantly, that it is the Court's 'duty . . . to declare all acts contrary to the manifest tenor of the constitution void. *Without this, all the reservations of particular rights or privileges would amount to nothing*' (Carey and McClellan, 2001, p. 403; emphasis mine). Hamilton's language is clear: both the federal legislature and the Supreme Court have a duty to respect the Constitution's 'reservations of particular rights and privileges'. While he might have added that the same is true of the federal executive, the essential point is this: in the 'limited government' contemplated by the Constitution, the preservation of rights and privileges depends upon respect for federalism, the separation of powers and the other constitutional 'auxiliary precautions'.

With this as background, it is significant that Madison, with the benefit of hindsight, wrote in 1819 that:

Much of the error in expounding the Constitution has its origin in the use made of the species of sovereignty implied in the nature of Govt. The specified powers vested in Congress, it is said, are sovereign powers, and that as such they carry with them an unlimited discretion as to the means of executing them. *It may surely be remarked that a limited Govt. may be limited in its sovereignty as well with respect to the means as to the objects of his powers; and that to give an extent to the former, superseding the limits to the latter, is in effect to convert a limited into an unlimited Govt.* ([1819] 1999, p. 736; emphasis mine).

As we shall see, Madison's words should resonate today. This is equally true of Madison's admonition that 'The very existence of . . . local sovereignties is a controul on the pleas for a constructive amplification of the powers of the General Govt.' and that:

Within a single *State* possessing the entire sovereignty, *the powers given to the Govt. by the People are understood to extend to all the Acts whether as means or*

ends required for the welfare of the Community and falling within the range of just
Govt. To withhold from such a Govt. any particular power necessary or useful
in itself, would be to deprive the people of the good dependent upon its exercise;
since the power must be there or not exist at all. *In the Govt. of the U.S. the case*
is obviously different. In establishing that Govt. the people retained other Govts.
capable of exercising such necessary and useful powers as were not to be exercised
by the General Govt. (Ibid., pp. 736–7; emphasis mine)[33]

I shall argue in later chapters that Madison's words have important implications for constitutional jurisprudence; in particular, for the interpretation of the Constitution's General Welfare, Necessary and Proper and
Commerce Clauses. For the moment, my interest centers on Madison's
view of the *source* of the states' sovereignty:

in all the co-temporary discussions and comments, which the Constitution under-
went, it was constantly justified and recommended on the ground, that the powers
not given to the [federal] government, were withheld from it; and that if any doubt
could have existed on this subject, under the original text of the Constitution, it
is removed as far as words could remove it, by the [Tenth] Amendment, now a
part of the Constitution, which expressly declares, 'that the powers not delegated
to the United States, by the Constitution, nor prohibited by it to the states, are
reserved to the states respectively, or to the people'. ([1800] 1999, p. 610)

Jefferson shared the view that the debate about the Constitution, both
in Convention and during the ratification process, was informed by the
imperative to retain the states' 'sovereignties'. Moreover, he invokes the
Tenth Amendment, and insists that it is the states' responsibility to enforce
moral duties and restrain vice 'within their own territory':

Can it be believed, that under the jealousies prevailing against the General
Government, at the adoption of the constitution, the States meant to surrender
the authority of prevailing order, of enforcing moral duties and restraining vice,
within their own territory?. . . The States supposed that by their tenth amendment, they had secured themselves against constructive powers. . . *I believe*
the States can best govern our home concerns, and the General Government our
foreign ones. I wish, therefore, to see maintained that wholesome distribution
of powers established by the constitution for the limitation of both; and never
to see all offices transferred to Washington, where, further withdrawn from the
eyes of the people, they may more secretly be bought and sold at market. ([1823]
1984, pp. 1475–6; emphasis mine)[34]

There can be no doubt that the Founders' federalism enterprise was
animated by 'the jealousies prevailing against the [Federal] Government',
and by the belief that 'the states can best govern our home concerns, and
the General Government our foreign ones'. While this is important to
the argument developed in later chapters, I emphasize for the moment

Jefferson's characterization of the Supreme Court as 'the subtle corps of sappers and miners, constantly working under ground to undermine the foundations of our confederated fabric'. In his view, the Court '[is] construing our constitution from a co-ordination of a general and special government to a general and supreme one alone' ([1820] 1984, p. 1446).

Whatever else is said, it is clear that the Founders had a clear vision of the states' and the federal roles. It was a vision that they came to believe was being undermined by a Supreme Court that, in Jefferson's words, was given to 'forcing the meaning of words, hunting after possible constructions, and hanging inference on inference, from heaven to earth, like Jacob's ladder' ([1823] 1984, p. 1475).

The Founders concern that 'the Judicial Department . . . may exercise or sanction dangerous powers beyond the grant of the constitution' (Madison [1800] 1999, p. 613) found particular expression in what Madison styled 'legislative encroachments'.[35] As we shall see, his 'means and ends' formulation gestures towards modern debate about the Constitution's General Welfare, Necessary and Proper and Commerce Clauses:

> [T]he high sanction given to a latitude in expounding the Constitution . . . seems to break down the landmarks intended by a specification of the Powers of Congress, and to substitute for a definite connection between means and ends, a Legislative discretion as to the [means] to which no practical limit can be assigned. In the great system of Political Economy having for its general object the national welfare, everything is related immediately or remotely to every other thing; and consequently a Power over any one thing, if not limited by some obvious and precise affinity, may amount to a Power over every other. *Ends & means may shift their character at the will & according to the ingenuity of the Legislative Body.* ([1819] 1999, p. 734; emphasis mine)

Madison's thought experiment is instructive. He emphasizes first that 'the [Supreme] Court are disposed to retain a guardianship of the Constitution against legislative encroachments'. The Court, he notes, has said that '"Should Congress, under the pretext of executing its Powers, pass laws for the accomplishment of objects not entrusted to the [federal] Government, it would become the painful duty of this Tribunal to say that such an act was not the law of the land"'. Given these predicates, Madison asks:

> suppose Congress should, as would doubtless happen, pass unconstitutional laws not to accomplish *objects* not specified in the Constitution, but the same laws as *means* expedient, convenient or conducive to the accomplishment of objects entrusted to the [federal] Government, by what handle could the Court take hold of the case? (Ibid., pp. 734–5; emphasis mine)

Madison gives form and substance to the hypothetical with the following example:

it was the policy of the old Government of France to grant monopolies, such as that of Tobacco, in order to create funds . . . from which loans could be made to the Public. . . Were Congress to grant a like monopoly merely to aggrandize those enjoying it, the Court might consistently say, that this not being an *object* entrusted to the [federal] Governt. the grant was unconstitutional and void. (Ibid., p. 735; emphasis mine)

Granting this, Madison worried that the Supreme Court may nevertheless sanction a 'break down [of] the landmarks intended by a specification of the Powers of Congress'. At issue is the possibility that the Supreme Court may permit a 'Legislative discretion as to [means] to which no practical limit can be assigned'. Madison feared that Congress may argue that the *means* employed are 'necessary, expedient or conducive' to an object that *is* entrusted to the federal government by the Constitution:

Should Congress . . . grant the monopoly according to the French policy *as a means judged by them to be necessary, expedient or conducive to the borrowing of money*, which is an object entrusted to them by the Constitution, it seems clear that the Court, adhering to its doctrine, could not interfere without stepping on Legislative ground, to do which they justly disclaim all pretension. (Ibid.; emphasis mine)

If it is clear that Madison regarded legislative grants of monopoly to be unconstitutional, it is also clear that he understood that Supreme Court-sanctioned legislative 'ingenuity' threatens both federalism and the separation of powers. On the one hand, his appreciation of the interdependencies inherent in 'the great system of Political Economy' gestures toward the modern Supreme Court's expansive reading of the Commerce Clause (see Chapter 4). On the other hand, his concern with untrammeled 'Legislative discretion' as to 'means judged by them to be necessary' to the achievement of constitutionally sanctioned goals is reminiscent of Jefferson's fear that Congress might 'take everything under their management which *they* should deem for the *public welfare*, and which is susceptible to the application of money' ([1792a] 1984, p. 677; emphasis in original). Both formulations should, I shall argue, inform the Supreme Court's General Welfare, Necessary and Proper and Legislative Powers Clause jurisprudence (Chapter 4).

2.4 THE FOUNDERS' POLITICAL ECONOMY

The Founders' prior ethical commitment to the moral equivalence of persons meant that their republican self-government project was informed by the idea that formal and informal institutions should both reflect, and cultivate respect for, the moral law or golden rule. Indeed, the Founders' constitutional enterprise was animated by the idea that discriminatory 'factious behavior' is irreconcilable with the equal treatment imperative. It is in this sense that the Constitution's 'auxiliary precautions' may be understood as representing an attempt to institutionalize a Kantian-style social contract. Understood from this perspective, it is 'as if' the Founders employed the 'contract device' to frame a Constitution that both respected and promoted the Kantian duty of justice. Hamilton's implicit invocation of a Kantian-style veil of ignorance, already noted above is, I believe, heuristic. The essential point is, however, that *the Founders were driven by the imperative to promote just institutions.* Stated differently, a teleological or consequence-based conception of the state was alien to their imagination. We know, moreover, that the Founders regarded 'political economy' as a branch of philosophy (Jefferson [1814a] 1984, p. 1349). From their perspective, economic deliberation necessarily contemplated questions of moral and political philosophy. And, it should be clear, the political and moral philosophy they embraced was not, and could not be, utilitarianism.

My point of departure is that 'no economic theory makes sense until conjoined to some adequate political doctrine' (Scruton, 2002, pp. 106–7). For the Founders this meant that economics must be conjoined to republican political doctrine. That doctrine, in turn, was shaped by Kantian-style contractarian moral and political philosophy. Informed by the Smithian/Kantian idea of the moral equivalence of persons, an idea that Kymlicka characterizes as 'a generalization of the golden rule' (1993, p. 192), the Founders sought, through the Constitution's 'auxiliary precautions' to minimize discriminatory 'factious behavior' and so to institutionalize a *moral political structure.* For the Founders, then, like Kantian contractarians:

> our tacit consent binds us to a *legitimate* and morally acceptable state only if the conventions which comprise it are the sort of conventions that we would agree to, were we able to impartially and fairly reappraise and recreate those conventions. (Hampton, 1995, p. 383)

Given this *procedural* imperative, it is a matter of considerable moment to know how to appraise prospective or existing constitutional orders. Whereas modern economists focus on Paretian optimality, or Pareto-efficient *outcomes* (see Chapter 5), the Founders' standard of appraisal was defined independently of desired 'end states' (Buchanan [1977] 2001, p. 179). How, then, 'are criteria for "efficiency" or "justice" to be introduced without reference to end states?' James Buchanan proffers this answer:

> It is precisely at this point that the notion of agreement, of quasi-contract, becomes critical in the argument. That rule is acceptable which is itself defined by agreement among all participants. . . We may . . . substitute *fair* for *acceptable* here, and . . . we may replace *fair* with *just*. Or, . . . we may follow John Rawls in defining justice as fairness. (Ibid., pp. 179–80)

While Rawls has been characterized as 'The best-known exponent of Kantian contractarianism' (Kymlicka, 1993, p. 191), the essential point is that Buchanan and Rawls share with Kant and the Founders a prior ethical commitment to the moral equivalence of persons. While it is well known that the 'contract device' does not *justify* this prior ethical commitment since it presupposes it (ibid., p. 193), the moral law gives rise to a duty of justice that 'requires us [both] to support and to comply with *just institutions* that exist and apply to us' and 'to further just arrangements not yet established' (Rawls, 1971, p. 115; emphasis mine). If, as seems clear, the Founders understood this procedural imperative, it is also clear that they could not embrace utilitarianism. Whereas for utilitarians and, it should be said, for proponents of orthodox economic theory, the 'good' is the maximization of utility, respect for the moral law implies a procedural imperative: 'Rather than starting from a conception of the good given independently of the right, we start with a conception of the right – of the moral law – given by pure (as opposed to empirical) practical reason'. To this Rawls adds, in a manner reminiscent of Madison's 'means and ends' formulation:

> We then specify in the light of this conception what *ends are permissible* and what social arrangements are right and just . . . a moral conception is not to revolve around the good as an independent object, but around a conception of the right . . . into which any permissible end must fit. Kant believes that once we start from the good as an independent given object, the moral conception must be heteronomous. (Rawls [1989] 1999, p. 509; emphasis mine)

If, as Kant suggests, 'acting from a certain interest' is heteronomous ([1785] 1988, p. 62) and that, therefore, desired 'end states' cannot be the basis of morality, the question becomes: how is the non-heteronomous perspective to be achieved? Stated differently, how can the push and pull of contingent circumstance be overcome so that the imperative to promote just institutions may be respected? As I have emphasized, Hamilton's formulation in *Federalist* No. 78 (Carey and McClellan, 2001, pp. 406–7) gestures toward the answer: as Buchanan suggests, 'Something like "the [Kantian/Rawlsian] original position" behind the "veil of ignorance" . . . must be introduced to make [institutional] evaluation possible' ([1977] 2001, p. 180). The 'original position', in turn, is an 'initial situation of equality' in which 'One excludes the knowledge of those contingencies which set men at odds and allows them to be guided by their prejudices. In this manner the veil of ignorance is arrived at in a natural way' (Rawls, 1971, pp. 17–22).

It is understood that no person can be deprived of knowledge of the web of attachments and 'particular inclinations and aspirations, and . . . conceptions of their good' that define his decision environment. That said, the veil of ignorance 'contract device' is intended 'simply to make vivid to ourselves the restrictions that it seems reasonable to impose on arguments for principles of justice, and therefore on these principles themselves' (ibid., p. 18).

The idea of impartial consideration implicit in the veil of ignorance construction is, of course, evocative of Adam Smith's impartial spectator and of Kant's 'two points of view'. But it is also the idea that the Founders sought both to institutionalize and to promote. In effect, the Founders understood that the original position-veil of ignorance thought experiment is both intrinsically valuable and instrumentally important:

> the idea of contracting from an original position. . . can render our judgements more determinate (contractual agreements must be explicitly and publicly formulated), render them more vivid (the veil of ignorance is a vivid way of expressing the moral requirement of putting ourselves in other people's shoes), and can dramatize our commitment to them (the veil of ignorance dramatizes the claim that we would accept a certain principle however it affected us). In these and other ways, the contract device illuminates the basic idea of morality as impartiality. (Kymlicka, 1993, p. 193)

Granting all of this, it seems clear that the Founders would associate themselves with the view that the veil of ignorance 'contract device' can be employed 'to prescribe the best, or most just, form of political society' (Hampton, 1995, p. 384). Given their commitment to *procedural* justice, it is also clear that what Sandel has called the 'political economy of growth and distributive justice' (1996, p. 294) found no expression in the Founders' political economy. Instead, they engaged in 'healthily moralistic political debate' (Will, 1983, p. 105) about which economic policies were consonant with the moral imperative to respect the moral law. For the Founders, economic judgments *were* moral judgments. As such, economic judgments were important, not because of the goals or 'ends' to be achieved, but because they implicated the imperative to treat morally equivalent persons equally.

In sharp contrast, contemporary economic policy appraisal is informed by institutionless, intendedly value-free and outcomes based social welfare theory, the economist's theory of the state.[36] While a critical assessment of the theory is developed in Chapter 5, the essential point is that welfare theorists identify 'welfare' or the 'public good' with utility (Warke, 2000, p. 374). Central to this enterprise are the theory's two 'fundamental welfare theorems'; theorems that I argue can and have been deployed to rationalize ad hoc, discriminatory government interventions. On the one hand, the first fundamental welfare theorem is employed to identify and to remediate all manner of 'market failures'. On the other hand, the second fundamental welfare theorem is invoked to rationalize income and wealth redistribution schemes (see Chapters 1 and 5). In either event, the desideratum is utility maximization. The theory is silent about procedural justice and, more generally, about the imperative to promote just, in the sense of impartial, institutions. Indeed, the theory's truncated theory of *distributive* justice has been characterized as a 'time slice theory of justice'. From this perspective, 'all that needs to be looked at, in judging the justice of a distribution, is who ends up with what', with no account taken of *how* the distribution came about, and 'any two structurally identical distributions are equally just' (Nozick, 1974, p. 154).

If the theory of *distributive* justice implicit in social welfare theory would be unacceptable to the Founders, it is also clear that institutionless, outcomes based, procedurally-detached and intendedly value-free social welfare theory has no correspondence to the Founders' explicitly normative, procedurally based, outcomes-detached contractarian approach to institutional design and appraisal.

All this notwithstanding, there is a contemporary analogue for the Founders' republican political economy project. Writing in 1972, James Buchanan observed that 'When I first encountered John Rawls' conception of "justice as fairness". . . I sensed the possible extension in the explanatory-descriptive power of models for "rules of the game", derived in accordance with some criteri[on] of "fairness"'. Continuing, Buchanan notes that:

> As readers of the *Calculus of Consent* recognize, Gordon Tullock and I employed such models in our derivation of the 'logical foundations of constitutional democracy' . . . of a political structure not grossly divergent from that envisioned by the Founding Fathers and embodied in the United States Constitution, at least in its initial conception. ([1972] 2001, p. 353)

I note first that the passage is consistent with the notion that the Founders' institutional enterprise was informed by a Smithian/Kantian/Rawlsian conception of justice as impartiality. Equally important, it is evocative of Buchanan's constitutional political economy (CPE) project:[37]

> Orthodox economic analysis . . . attempts to explain the choices of economic agents . . . within the existing legal-institutional-constitutional structure. . . Normative considerations enter through the efficiency criteria of

theoretical welfare economics, and policy options are evaluated in terms of these criteria. . .

[In contrast] constitutional economic analysis attempts to explain the working properties of alternative sets of legal-institutional-constitutional *rules that constrain the choices and activities of economic and political agents.* ([1987a] 2001, pp. 3–4; emphasis mine)[38]

It is immediately clear that the CPE approach, like the Founders' republican self-government project, does not contemplate a teleological or 'goal-based' conception of the state (Buchanan [1977] 2001, p. 178). Moreover, it is clear that the explicitly normative process of institutional appraisal embraced by CPE is precisely the approach embraced by the Founders. It follows that outcomes based, procedurally-detached Paretian optimality or 'efficiency' has no role to play in the institutional appraisal process (Buchanan [1989b] 2001, p. 271). Whereas economic efficiency is an artifact of social welfare theory, the modern economist's theory of the state, *political efficiency* 'describe[s] the efficacy of differing institutions in reducing or eliminating the incentives for participants to invest resources in rent seeking aimed to secure discriminatory advantage through majoritarian exploitation' (Buchanan and Congleton, 1998, p. 40).

If the phrases 'rent seeking' and 'majoritarian cycling' would have been alien to their imagination, it is clear that they are euphemisms for what the Founders called 'factious behavior'. Indeed, it is instructive that President Washington's language comes tolerably close to the modern understanding of 'majoritarian cycling' (Arrow, 1951; Black, 1958; Buchanan and Congleton, 1998, pp. 19–20): 'The alternate domination of one faction over another . . . is itself a frightful despotism. . . sooner or later the chief of some prevailing faction . . . turns this disposition to the purposes of his own elevation, on the ruins of Public Liberty' ([1796a] 1997, pp. 969–70).

While the Founders insisted that man possesses an innate moral sense – a predisposition to respect the moral law – they were concerned that this informal constraint on 'factious behavior' would have to be supplemented by the Constitution's 'auxiliary precautions': 'A careful reading of [*Federalist* No. 10] suggests that Madison clearly recognized that individuals and groups would try to use the processes of government to further their own differential or partisan interests' (Buchanan and Tullock [1962] 1999, p. 25). Yet it seems fair to say that, 'the genius of the Founding Fathers in the construction of the American [constitutional] system' (ibid., pp. 298–9) notwithstanding, the Founders' auxiliary precautions have been unavailing (see Chapters 1, 4 and 6 this volume).

There can be no doubt that the discriminatory impulse is a defining characteristic of post-constitutional majoritarian politics. That said, the

constitutional political economist's enterprise is 'predicated on the mainte-
nance of majoritarianism as the basic [political] decision rule, while opening
up the possibility of constraining the operation of this rule by restrictions
on the set of feasible outcomes' (Buchanan [1997b] 1999, p. 421).[39] Simply
stated, constitutional political economists share with the Founders the
understanding that constitutional restrictions on majoritarian democracy
can increase the 'worth' or value of equal political participation.

Given the imperative to promote the greatest possible equal political
participation, the constitutional political economist endorses a generality
or impartiality constraint on post-constitutional statutory law. If Rawls's
characterization of a 'just constitution' provides the basic rationale for
this additional auxiliary precaution, it also captures the essence of the
Founders' constitutional project:

> By way of summing up the account of the principle of participation, we can
> say that a *just constitution* sets up a form of fair rivalry for political office and
> authority . . . rival parties seek the citizens' approval in accordance with just
> procedural rules against a background of freedom of thought and assembly
> in which the fair value of political liberty is assured. . . Representatives are
> not . . . mere agents of their constituents, since they have a certain discretion
> and they are expected to exercise their judgement in enacting legislation. In a
> well-ordered society they must, nevertheless, represent their constituents in the
> substantive sense: *they must seek first to pass just and effective legislation, since
> this is a citizen's first interest in government, and, secondly they must further their
> constituents' other interests insofar as they are consistent with justice.* . . Since the
> constitution is the foundation of the social structure, the highest-order system
> of rules that regulates and controls other institutions, everyone has the same
> access to the political procedures that it sets up. *When the principle of [equal]
> participation is satisfied, all have the common status of equal citizen.* (1971,
> p. 227; emphasis mine)

Rawls's 'just constitution' formulation is, of course, consistent with
the Founders' view, articulated by Madison, that justice in the sense of
impartiality is 'the end of government . . . the end of civil society'. Equally
important, it affirms that 'the common status of equal citizen' requires that
legislators pass just – again, in the sense of impartial – legislation. This, it
is clear, is what the Founders intended. Their view of a 'just constitution'
was one in which, in Rawlsian terms, 'the fair value of political liberty is
assured'.

It may be said, then, that from the Founders' contractarian perspective, post-constitutional statutory law 'becomes legitimate only if all
persons affected are generally and reciprocally constrained in their
behavior' (Buchanan and Congleton, 1998, p. 8). It was this idea that
animated Madison's 'auxiliary precautions' enterprise. Given the moral
equivalence of persons, ordered liberty and the 'stability of social

cooperation' (Rawls, 1971, p. 240) *require* agreement on behavioral constraints; constraints that are mutually beneficial to all parties. These constraints must, in turn, find expression in constitutional *and* statutory law: absent generality or impartiality under and by it, law cannot be consistent with the moral equivalence of persons. It cannot, in short, be regarded as just.

If it is clear that the *idealized* rule of law embodies a generality or impartiality constraint, it is equally clear that the same cannot be said of post-constitutional, statutory law (see Chapter 1). On the one hand, the proliferation of 'bailouts', single-item spending 'earmarks', omnibus spending bills, a metastasizing, discriminatory tax code, and intergenerational discrimination suggest that the Founders' 'auxiliary precautions' have not succeeded in setting ambition against ambition. On the other hand, because of the inertial force of the economist's institutionless, consequence based and procedurally-detached theory of the state, 'romanticized politics remains monolithic; the "good" is defined uniquely by the collective agency of the state' (Buchanan and Congleton, 1998, p. XI). In obvious and persistent denial of fundamental features of post-constitutional political reality, the 'benevolent despot', informed by the omniscient economist, is assumed to act in the supraindividual interest of the majority.[40] This, despite the fact that, because 'post-constitutional politics is majoritarian, [it is] naturally discriminatory to the extent that participants promote separable interests' (ibid., p. 12).

The Founders plainly understood that majority coalitions may extract in-period benefits from, and impose costs upon, an extant minority. It is likely, moreover, that they appreciated that this in-period discrimination would be accepted on the 'implicit understanding [that] dominant coalitions rotate sequentially over electoral periods' (ibid., pp. 19–20). If, as has been emphasized, the Madisonian 'auxiliary precautions' were animated by these ideas, it is also clear that the moral equivalence of persons, the duty of justice, the external morality of law and the 'strategic choices made by competing interests in disregard of the effects on [the constitutional] political structure' (Buchanan [1989a] 1999, p. 372) argue for an *additional* 'auxiliary precaution': a generality or impartiality constraint.

While it is evident that a veil-of-ignorance/uncertainty situated agreement on a generality or impartiality constraint is not possible in the post-constitutional setting, it is possible at the constitutional stage:

> The constitutional choice of a rule is taken independently of any single specific decision or set of decisions and is quite rationally based on a long-term view embodying many separate time sequences and many separate collective acts disposing of economic resources. (Buchanan and Tullock [1962] 1999, p. 95)

On the logic that, at the *constitutional* stage, agents affect choices among constitutional rules freed, as it were, from considerations of contingent circumstance:

> *identifiable* self-interest is not present in terms of external characteristics. The self-interest of the individual participant at this level leads him to take a position as a 'representative' or 'randomly distributed' participant in the succession of collective choices anticipated. Therefore, he may tend to act, from self-interest, *as if* he were choosing the best set of rules for the social group. Here the purely selfish individual and the purely altruistic individual may be indistinguishable in their behavior. (Ibid., p. 96)

The essential point is this: the individual participant at the constitutional stage is not presumed, in the manner of the social welfare theorist's 'bifurcated man', to be narrowly self-interested in his market activity, while 'suppress[ing] these motives and bring[ing] out the more "noble" ones' in his political activity' (Buchanan [1962b] 1999, pp. 68–9). Rather, participants at the constitutional stage are taken to reflect 'the empirical realities of persons as they exist, moral warts and all' (Brennan and Buchanan [1985b] 2000, p. XVI). In effect, participants engaged in constitutional deliberation are presumed, in the manner of Hamilton, to understand that 'no man can be sure that he may not be tomorrow the victim of a spirit of injustice, by which he may be a gainer today' (Carey and McClellan, 2001, p. 405). If this means that a generality or impartiality constraint is possible at the constitutional stage, it also gestures toward the Founders' insistence that, given the moral equivalence of persons, members of the polity have a duty to promote just, in the sense of impartial, institutions. Equally important, it is consistent with one of the Founders' fundamental insights. Simply stated, they understood that ordered liberty, in the sense of constitutional restraints on majoritarian democracy, is instrumentally important to the survival of republican self-government. Indeed, it seems appropriate to suggest that the impartial treatment of morally equivalent persons provides the raison d'être for majoritarian democracy: rather than facilitating rent seeking and majoritarian cycling, generality-constrained majoritarian democracy would give full expression to impartial deliberation. Equally important, the formal institutionalization of a generality constraint would be consonant with the Founders' understanding of the self, and with their view of the reciprocal relationship between law and morality. Finally, whereas modern liberalism and its concomitant, social welfare theory, can provide only a contingent defense of democracy (see Chapter 5), a constitutional generality constraint would affirm majoritarian democracy's respect for the moral equivalence of persons. Granting this, a generality constraint would, to paraphrase Hamilton, bolster the foundations of public and private confidence and trust. It would, in short, underwrite the vitality and endurance of republican self-government.

I emphasize, again, that a generality or impartiality constraint is recognizable as a supplement to the Founders' constitutional restraints on 'factious behavior'. Understood in this way, it is clear that the work of the constitutional political economist is fully reconcilable with the Founders' procedurally based, consequence-detached constitutional project: 'Normatively, the task of the constitutional political economist is to assist . . . citizens . . . in their continuing search for those *rules of the political game* that will best serve their purposes, whatever these might be' (Buchanan, 1987b, p. 250; emphasis mine).

If the constitutional political economist's endorsement of a generality constraint is consistent with the Founders' constitutional enterprise, the same can be said of his rejection of 'results-oriented' jurisprudence, and of his concern with the national legislature's propensity to usurp the prerogatives of the states.

I emphasize first that, for both the Founders and the constitutional political economist, justice as impartiality is both a procedural concept and, as Madison said, 'the end of government'. Granting this, 'social justice', a consequentialist notion, finds no expression either in the Founders' or the constitutional political economist's non-teleological conception of the state. It is on this logic that James Buchanan observes that, in contrast to the Founders' view:

> The American judiciary views law as an instrument to promote the 'social good', as this good is defined by the judges, and it also allows the . . . legislative bodies to promote the 'social good' in those areas where the judiciary has chosen to remain aloof, and notably in so-called economic legislation. In matters of economic policy the effective American constitution is what Congress determines it to be; the judiciary adopts a hands-off attitude here . . . confusion between the constitutional stage of choice . . . and collective actions taken within the 'law' will almost necessarily arise as long as the objectives of the state are those of promoting the 'social good'. To the extent that the institutions of law and government, along with the prevailing public attitudes toward these institutions, reflect this teleological conception of the state, constitutional order is necessarily undermined. . . To argue directly or by inference that the constitution in itself embodies or should embody a 'social purpose' is to negate its very meaning. ([1977] 2001, p. 178)

Buchanan's formulation is clearly evocative of Jefferson's rejection of 'the doctrine that the power given by the Constitution to collect taxes to provide for the *general welfare* of the U.S., permitted Congress to take everything under their management which *they* should deem for the *public welfare*, & which is susceptible of the application of money' ([1792a]

1984, p. 677).[41] The same is true of Madison's insistence that, whereas the Congress is 'limited in its sovereignty as well with respect to the means as to the objects of [its] powers', the powers given to the *states* 'are understood to extend to all the Acts whether as means or ends required for the welfare of the Community, and falling within the range of *just* Govt.' ([1819] 1999, p. 736; emphasis mine).

It is clear, then, that if the work of the constitutional political economist is evocative of the Founders' concern with legislative and judicial 'encroachments', it also calls to mind their insistence that ours is a *federal* system. Thus, if the Founders asserted that a 'just government' is one that treats morally equivalent persons impartially, they also insisted that the *states* retained a 'residuary and inviolable sovereignty' (Carey and McClellan, 2001, p. 198) over 'all objects, which, in the ordinary course of affairs, concerns the lives, liberties, and properties of the people; and the internal order, improvement, and prosperity of the state' (ibid., p. 241).

These ideas also find expression in the work of the constitutional political economist. Whereas the orthodox economist's theory of the state, social welfare theory, models politics as the activity of a benevolent despot who 'seeks always and everywhere to promote "the public interest"', the constitutional political economist, like the Founders, rejects this 'romanticized image of politics'. In the constitutional political economist's view, bounded rationality, information asymmetry, positive transaction and monitoring costs, and their concomitant, opportunistic behavior, are all defining characteristics of post-constitutional conflictual politics. It follows that 'any increase in the relative size of the political sector of an economy must carry with it an increase in the potential for [discriminatory] exploitation' (Buchanan [1995] 2001, p. 68). That said, it is also true that 'The federalized structure, *through the force of interstate competition*, effectively limits the power of the separate political units to extract surplus value from its citizenry' (ibid., p. 70; emphasis mine). On this logic, Tiebout-type mobility among states would seem to ensure that, under a federal system, substantially similar service packages will emerge. The essential idea is that, from the constitutional political economist's perspective (Buchanan and Congleton, 1998, p. 142):

> Federalism clearly allows uniform services to be a consequence of competition rather than a manipulated feature of constitutional design. In this, federalism is perhaps the best real laboratory of the appeal of the generality principle. . .
>
> It may also be said that our analysis of the generality principle makes the first-best case for federalism.

If the Founders sought via the Constitution's 'auxiliary precautions' to minimize discriminatory factious behavior, they also sought, through the Constitution and Bill of Rights to promote respect for the moral law. Animated by the same prior ethical commitment to the moral equivalence of persons, the constitutional political economist seeks to promote both the generality or impartiality principle and respect for the Constitution. And, like the Founders, he regards respect for the moral law to be both intrinsically valuable, and instrumentally important to the legitimacy of, and, trust in, government:

> The effective operation of democratic government, in its fiscal as well as its nonfiscal aspects, requires the adherence of its citizens to what may be called the 'constitutional attitude'. . . Individuals, and groups, must recognize the importance of constitutional-institutional continuity. . . If this is not recognized, and *if individuals come to consider governmental processes as nothing more than available means through which separate coalitions can exploit each other, democracy cannot, and should not, survive.* (Buchanan [1967] 1999, pp. 301–2; emphasis mine)

Informed, as were the Founders, by the Smithian/Kantian/Rawlsian duty of justice, the constitutional political economist recognizes his obligation both to promote the greatest possible equal political participation and to support, comply with and promote just, in the sense of impartial, institutions. That said, while a constitutional generality constraint is both morally exigent and instrumentally important, the 'publicness' and durability of constitutional provisions militate against constitutional amendment. Given that the expected benefits of constitutional amendments are not partitionable, the question becomes, 'Who are to take upon themselves the personal burden of designing . . . proposals for basic changes in the [constitutional] rules?' (Brennan and Buchanan [1985c] 2000, p. 160). Moreover, it is clear that the present value of the expected net benefits of constitutional amendment will not be coextensive with the finite planning horizon of the participatory agent (Buchanan [1975] 2000, p. 156). On this logic, both the 'free rider' problem and the lack of congruence between ideal and finite planning horizons complicate the constitutional amendment process.

All this notwithstanding, the Founders would surely associate themselves with the constitutional political economist's procedurally based, consequence-detached approach. On the one hand, the Founders would welcome a moralistic debate about the discriminatory nature of modern US day-to-day conflictual politics (see Chapter 1). The debate would center on the reconcilability of a consequentialist politics of 'wants and needs', and of economic growth and distributive or 'social' justice with a Constitution informed by the procedural imperative to treat morally equivalent persons impartially. On the other hand, given the moral exigency, instrumental importance and 'publicness' of the impartiality principle, the Founders would agree with constitutional political economists that constitutional dialogue must be encouraged. Moreover, the Founders and constitutional political economists agree that preference and value structures are mutable, and that private and public virtue can and must be cultivated. The work of James Buchanan, is, again, heuristic:

> The methodological individualist must . . . acknowledge the relationships between individual utility functions and the socioeconomic-legal-political-cultural setting within which evaluations are made. But [this] carries with it . . . the possible productivity of investment in the promulgation of moral norms. (Buchanan [1989a] 1999, p. 369)

The logic of an effort to promulgate moral norms would not be alien to the Founders' imagination.[42] Given the duty of justice, the individual, as a member of the polity, must be encouraged to understand that he has an 'ethical responsibility of full and informed participation in a continuing constitutional convention' (ibid., p. 372).

While it is true that its 'publicness' complicates the constitutional amendment process, the efficacy of the promulgation of moral norms enterprise – and the promotion of a constitutional generality constraint – requires only that citizens 'rationally will "want others to want better wants"', or, specifically that *others* behave more cooperatively toward themselves in social intercourse' (Buchanan, 1991, p. 186; emphasis mine). Granting this, the equal treatment imperative can be fashioned into 'models amenable to public comprehension' (Buchanan [1975] 2001, p. 227). The same is true of the notion that discriminatory politics is corrosive of trust and of the legitimacy of government.

Whatever else is said, it should be clear that the Smithan/Kantian/ Rawlsian 'contract device' retains it basic relevance: the individual, self-governing citizen can, and should, be made to understand that, given rent seeking and majoritarian cycling, a constitutional impartiality constraint is in his/her self-interest. As Hamilton observed, because a member of the polity cannot foresee his future contingent circumstance, he will appreciate that current membership in a dominant majority does not ensure that he will not, in the future, be a member of an exploited minority. On this logic, it is ignorance of future contingent states that provides the incentive to agree to a generality or impartiality constraint.

While these ideas inform the discussion in the final chapter, the essential point is this: if it is clear that agreement on a constitutional impartiality constraint is possible, it is also clear that the Founders' vision of a procedurally based, consequence-detached republican political economy finds contemporary expression in the work of the constitutional political economist.

NOTES

1. See, for example, Peterson (1984, pp. 939–40, 966–8, 977–8, 1451 and 1495).
2. See also Levy (2001, pp. 30, 33 and 35) and Rakove (1997, p. 333).
3. In his 3 January 1778 *New York Journal* article, the Anti-Federalist, Brutus, insisted that 'We ought to furnish the world with an example of a great people, who in their civil institutions hold chiefly in view, the attainment of virtue, and happiness among ourselves' ([1788] 1993, p. 693). See also the Rev. Stephen Peabody's 1797 Sermon before the General Court of the State of New Hampshire ([1797] 1998, pp. 1323–38, esp. p. 1337), and Samuel Langdon's 15 June 1788 Sermon before the General Court of New Hampshire ([1788] 1998, pp. 943–67). I note, in particular, Langdon's admonition that 'you are impowered to make righteous laws for promoting public order and good morals' (p. 957). Finally, in his 1802 'An Oration on the Anniversary of the United States of America', Zephaniah Swift Moore noted that 'The fathers of America chose a different path, in which to seek the desired object. The cultivation of science, the dissemination of knowledge, and the practice of virtue, were by them pursued, as the only means of rightly forming the public mind, and perpetuating national freedom and happiness. They well knew, that civil liberty could not be preserved without these means; and that good citizens must be made, by making good men' ([1802] 1983, p. 1218).
4. For a discussion of 'certain principles in human nature', see Hamilton's 27 June 1788 'Speech in the New York Ratifying Convention on the Distribution of Powers' ([1788a] 2001, p. 509).
5. The view that law both reflects and shapes societal norms is an emerging theme in the law and economics literature. See, for example, McAdams and Rasmusen (2004) and Posner (1977).
6. Both Federalists and Anti-Federalists invoked Montesquieu's admonition that 'when the legislative and executive powers are united in the same person, or in the same body of magistracy, there can be then no liberty' ([1750] 1977, p. 202). See, for example, Madison's *Federalist* No. 47 (Carey and McClellan, 2001, p. 251) and Ketcham (2003, p. 251).
7. See also Bishop James Madison ([1795] 1998, p. 1319) and Jonathon Edwards ([1794] 1998, p. 1215).
8. While he was less sanguine about the Constitution's ability to promote virtue, David Ramsay's 5 June 1788 oration included these words: 'When the majority of our citizens become corrupt, even our well balanced constitution cannot save us from slavery and ruin. Let it therefore be the unceasing study of all who love their country, to promote virtue and dispense knowledge through the whole extent of our settlements. Without them our growing numbers will soon degenerate into barbarism' ([1788] 1993, p. 513).
9. In a 1786 sermon, Joseph Lathrop both anticipated Kent's 1794 Lecture and echoed Madison's view of the importance of electing virtuous leaders: 'We must . . . contribute our aid to carry into effect the good laws of the state, especially those which relate to virtue and morals. . . The more virtue there is among the people, the more there will be among rulers, because better men will be elected to power; and they, who are elected, will be more strongly influenced to a right use of their power' ([1786] 1998, p. 877).
10. It has been suggested that 'Madison was an objectivist in the sense that he attached meaning to such terms as "justice," "permanent and aggregate interests of the community," and the "rights of other citizens". . . For instance, justice, probably his highest end, is not to be equated with what any majority, or "the great body of the people" may

regard it to be at any given point in time; it embodies known and objective characteristics that are the measure of whether a group is factious' (Carey, 1995, p. 41).

11. For his part, Hamilton gestured toward a Rawlsian notion of equal political participation ([1792] 2001, p. 783).

12. The work of the Constitutional Convention's Committee of Detail is heuristic. In a draft of a constitution 'evidently drafted by Edmund Randolph and John Rutledge' the Committee noted that 'A preamble seems proper, but. . . [A] display of theory, howsoever proper in the first formation of state governments, is unfit here; since we are not working on the natural rights of men not yet gathered into society, but upon those rights, modified by society, and interwoven with what we call the rights of the states' (Rakove, 1997, pp. 316–17). See also Berger (1997, p. 303) and Levy (2001, pp. 15–25).

13. The essence of the 'inheritance' or the 'rights of Englishmen' has been elegantly summarized by Schweikart and Allen: 'The resemblance of [the English] Declaration and Bill of Rights to the eighteenth-century American Declaration and Bill of Rights is striking, and one could argue that the Americans were more radicalized by the Glorious Revolution than the English' (2004, p. 37). The essential point is that Madison's work on the Bill of Rights reflected the fact that 'The language of rights came naturally to the [American] colonists; it was, they thought, their native tongue. As eighteenth-century writers repeatedly argued, the original English settlers had carried all their rights with them, and passed these rights on to their descendants as a birthright and a patrimony' (Rakove, 1997, p. 290). The Anti-Federalist, the Federal Farmer, articulated a view that is consistent with this understanding. As to the source of the rights that the Bill of Rights did not create, he affirmed that the people of the states 'derived all these rights from one common source, the British systems', and that, having incorporated these rights in their state constitutions, 'discovered that their ideas relative to these rights are very similar' (Smith [1787] 2003, p. 266).

14. Jack Rakove regards the first reason as 'remarkably optimistic' by Madison's own standards, and that, as for the second, 'Madison treated even this more as a speculative possibility than as a serious threat' (1997, p. 333).

15. I emphasize, again, that the reciprocal relationship between law and morality was, for the Founders, a familiar theme. It is significant that Madison, Richard Henry Lee, Patrick Henry, Melancton Smith and others of the founding generation, some Federalists, some Anti-Federalists, expressed this view. Richard Henry Lee argued that a bill of rights 'would assist popular "education" because it taught "truths" upon which freedom depends and that the people must believe as "sacred"' (Levy, 2001, p. 30). Patrick Henry 'seemed to suppose that a bill of rights would operate as a moral restraint on Congress' (Rakove, 1997, p. 323). For the Federal Farmer, 'long thought to be Richard Henry Lee . . . but more probably the New York anti-federalist Melancton Smith' (Ketcham, 2003, pp. 256–7), a bill of rights was important, neither because it 'creat[ed] the rights it declared' nor because 'their ancestors once got together and enumerated them on paper, but because, by repeated negotiations and declarations, all parties are brought to realize them, and . . . to believe them to be sacred' (Rakove, 1997, pp. 323–4).

16. See also Smith ([1759] 1976, p. 58). See Himmelfarb (2004, pp. 200–201) for more on Smith's influence on Jefferson.

17. Hyneman and Lutz suggest that 'Americans during the founding era frequently had a deeper philosophical or theological basis for their understanding of concepts like freedom and equality than is apparent from their political writing' (1983a, p. 137). Indeed, whereas 'Locke built his theory from rationalist assumptions, . . . Americans built their institutions on biblical foundations, especially upon the notion of a covenant' (ibid., p. 158).

18. It is perhaps significant that Kant was familiar with Adam Smith's *The Theory of Moral Sentiments* (TMS): 'It seems that Kant knew and valued TMS, judging from a letter of 1771 written to him by one Markus Herz. A passage in this letter speaks of the "Englishman Smith who, Dr. Friedlander tells me, is your favorite" (Liebling), and

then goes on to compare the work of Smith with "the first part" of "Home, Kritik", no doubt meaning *Elements of Criticism* by Henry Home, Lord Kames. As Eckstein points out, the date of 1771 (too early for [*The Wealth of Nations*] and one year after the publication of the first German publication of TMS) and the comparison with Kames shows that the writer must have had TMS in mind. . . Eckstein goes on to note that there is a passage in Kant's *Reflections on Anthropology* where Kant writes of "the man who goes to the root of things" and who looks at every subject "not just from his own point of view but from that of the community" and then adds, in brackets, "the Impartial Spectator" (der Unpartheyische Zuschauer)' (Introduction to Smith [1759] 1976, p. 31).

19. See also Smith ([1759] 1976, p. 110).
20. Like the Founders, Montesquieu's particular concern was the influence, in the absence of public virtue, of 'faction' ([1750] 1977, pp. 118–19). For a more expansive definition of public or 'political' virtue, see David Wallace Carrithers' 'Introduction' to *The Spirit of Laws* (ibid., pp. 60–61). For more on 'love of country', see Adam Smith ([1759] 1976, pp. 227–34).
21. See also Jefferson's 'Letter to the President of the United States' ([1792b] 1984, pp. 994–5).
22. See Goodin (1993, p. 241) for more on ethical theories of the right and of the good.
23. For Kant, 'all moral conceptions have their seat and origin completely *a priori* in the reason . . . they cannot be obtained by abstraction from any empirical, and therefore merely contingent knowledge' ([1785] 1988, pp. 38–9). Stated differently, 'Empirical principles are incapable of serving as a foundation for moral laws' (ibid., p. 71). See also Paton (1964, p. 51).
24. See also Kant ([1785] 1988, pp. 19, 45, 52 and 74) and Rawls ([1989] 1999, p. 519).
25. See also Jefferson's letter to P.S. Dupont de Nemours ([1816b] 1984, p. 1837).
26. Raoul Berger quotes 'one of the first Founders', James Iredell as saying, "We are too apt, in estimating a law passed at a remote period, to combine in our consideration, all the subsequent events which have had an influence upon it, instead of confining ourselves (which we ought to do) to the existing circumstances at the time of its passing' (1997, p. 9).
27. See also Brennan and Buchanan ([1985b] 2000, p. XVI).
28. For more on the veil of ignorance/uncertainty see Section 2.4 of this chapter.
29. As we shall see, the Smithian/Kantian understanding of 'autonomy', an understanding embraced by the Founders, is congruent neither with modern liberalism's nor with the social welfare theorist's transcendental, autonomous self construal (see Chapter 5 this volume). James Buchanan emphasizes that, for the constitutional political economist (see Section 2.4): 'Individual autonomy . . . does not . . . imply that the individual chooses and acts as if he or she exists in isolation from and apart from the community or communities of other persons with whom he or she may be variously associated. Any form of community or association of individuals may reflect some sharing of values, and, further, any individual's formation of values may be influenced by the values of those with whom he or she is variously associated in communities' ([1990] 1999, p. 390).
30. For a discussion of 'the precepts of justice associated with the rule of law', its internal morality, see Fuller (1971) and Rawls (1971, pp. 236–40). See also Section 1.3 in Chapter 1 of this volume.
31. For more on this, see Berger (1997, Chapter 20, esp. pp. 403–5).
32. See also Berger (1997, pp. 347–57).
33. See also Madison's *The Federalist* No. 39 (Carey and McClellan, 2001, p. 198).
34. For more on Jefferson's view of the federal and states' rules, see Jefferson's 8 February 1786 letter to Madison ([1786] 1984, pp. 848–9).
35. Interestingly, in *The Federalist* No. 81, Hamilton notes that 'It may in the last place be observed, that the supposed danger of judiciary encroachments on the legislative authority, which has been upon many occasions reiterated, is, in reality, a phantom' (Carey and McClellan, 2001, p. 420).

36. The characterization of social welfare theory as the 'economist's theory of the state' may be attributed to Geoffrey Brennan. See his 'The Contribution of Economics' (1995, p. 142).
37. It has been observed that 'Buchanan literally founded the field of constitutional political economy' (Tollison, 2001, p. XI). For more on *The Calculus of Consent* (Buchanan and Tullock, 1962) as 'the first attempt to derive what [Buchanan and Tullock] called an "economic theory of political constitutions"' see Buchanan ([1983b] 2000, pp. 20 and 23–4) and Buchanan ([1978] 2000, p. 46).
38. See also Buchanan ([1989b] 2001, pp. 270–74; [1997a] 2001, pp. 225–34).
39. Buchanan's remark captures, in broad outline, the nature of his contractarian enterprise. The project is informed by a prior ethical commitment to the moral equivalence of persons, by a concomitant commitment to political equality, and by an insistence that 'the [Kantian/Rawlsian contract device] will tend to exclude from consideration decision rules that explicitly deny some persons or groups *ex ante* access to political process' (Buchanan ([1986a] 2001, p. 219).
40. For a critique of the 'omniscient, omnipotent, benevolent' government see Dixit (1996).
41. See also Jefferson's 'Letter to the President of the United States' ([1792b] 1984, pp. 994–5).
42. For more on 'preaching', see Buchanan ([1991] pp. 185–6; 1994a; 1994b, p. 80).

3.   The 'Old Court' at work

3.1   INTRODUCTION

The burgeoning federal enterprise described in Chapter 1 may be accounted for in many ways. Some may argue that it is the natural consequence of majoritarian democracy; that rent seeking and majoritarian cycling are endemic to the system, with the growth of government a natural outcome of self-interested 'factious' behavior. In fact, this appreciation of unrestrained majoritarian democracy is not new. The Founders understood that the 'limited [federal] government' that they envisioned required that man's innate moral sense, the inclination to treat others as ends rather than as means, must be supplemented by procedural restraints on post-constitutional, majoritarian democracy. This fundamental insight was informed by the Founders' moral and political philosophy. And central to their moral and political philosophy was a prior ethical commitment to the moral equivalence of persons. This commitment found expression in their procedurally based, consequence-detached political economy, and in the 'auxiliary precautions' embedded in the Constitution (see Chapter 2 in this volume).

The point is not that the Founders could not imagine the expansive and expanding role of the federal government. The point is that what they feared might happen, has happened. It has happened, I suggest, because their moral and political philosophy has been displaced by *modern* liberalism, a public philosophy to which is conjoined an outcomes based, institutionless and intendedly value-free political economy. If this means that the Founders' understanding of rights as the product of self-government has been replaced by a theory of rights as trumps against the Founders' constitutional restraints, it also means that the Founders' emphasis on procedural justice and impartial statutory law has been rejected in favor of a political economy of wants and needs and of distributive justice (see Chapter 5).

If the public philosophy and the economics of the modern United States have underwritten the scope and reach of the federal government, so, too, has the Supreme Court. The constitutional jurisprudence of what may be characterized as the 'Old' and 'New' Supreme Courts has, in different ways, and just as Madison feared, 'manifested a propensity to enlarge the general authority in derogation of the local, and to amplify [its] own jurisdiction' ([1823] 1999, p. 802). At issue, in short, is Hamilton's insistence that 'the proposed government cannot be deemed a national one; since its jurisdiction extends to certain enumerated objects only, and leaves to the several states, a residuary and inviolable sovereignty over all other objects' (Carey and McClellan, 2001, p. 198). So too, is Madison's concern with 'legislative encroachments' ([1819] 1999, pp. 734–5), and with the possibility that 'the Judicial Department . . . may exercise or sanction dangerous powers beyond the grant of the Constitution' ([1800] 1999, p. 613).

This chapter focuses on the 'Old Court' and, in particular, on the post-Civil War period. Employing the Fifth and Fourteenth Amendments, the Supreme Court (hereafter the Court) emphasized the rights of property and contract. The result was that, during a four-decade period following the Civil War, the Court 'invalidated close to two hundred laws, including attempts by state and federal governments to regulate the industrial economy through laws governing prices, wages and hours, and labor union activities' (Sandel, 1996, pp. 40–41). Among the most famous of these cases are *Lochner* v. *New York* (1905), *Adair* v. *United States* (1908) and *Coppage* v. *Kansas* (1915).

3.2   *LOCHNER* v. *NEW YORK*

In *Lochner* v. *New York* (1905) the Court held that the 1897 'labor law of the State of New York . . . interferes with the right of contract between the employer and employes [sic], concerning the number of hours in which the latter may labor in the bakery of the employer' (Opinion, p. 4). In the Court's view, 'The general right of contract in relation to his business is part of the liberty of the individual protected by the Fourteenth Amendment of the Federal Constitution' (ibid.).

The *Lochner* Court balanced the right of contract against the State of New York's police powers and found that, because the statute made 'no reference whatever to the question of health, we think that a law like the one before us involves neither the safety, the morals nor the welfare of the public, and that the interest of the public is not in the slightest degree affected by such an act' (ibid., p. 5). On this logic, the Court concluded that 'The limitation of the hours of labor does not come within the [states'] police power on that ground' (ibid.). Granting this, whereas it acknowledged that it has 'recognized the existence and upheld the exercise of the police powers of the States' (ibid., p. 4), the *Lochner* Court held that the New York statute 'is not a legitimate exercise of the police power of the State' (ibid., p. 1). Rather, the New York statute is 'an illegal interference with the rights of individuals, both employers and employes [sic], to make contracts regarding labor upon such terms as they may think best, or which they may agree' (ibid., p. 7).

While the *Lochner* Court's 'liberty of contract' holding has been applauded by many as a defense of 'economic freedom', others have argued that the Court was hostile to 'humane reforms' and that, 'Armed with the [Fourteenth Amendment's] doctrine of due process, it had defended the excesses of industrial capitalism and *frustrated progressive reforms*' (Sandel, 1996, p. 42; emphasis mine). Indeed, in his Dissent, Justice Holmes insists that 'this case is decided upon [a laissez-faire] economic theory which a large part of the country does not entertain' (p. 11).

If Holmes's Dissent gestures toward the thinking that informed the New Court (see Chapter 4), Justice Harlan's Dissent questions both the Court's reading of the Fourteenth Amendment and the constitutionality of discounting New York's and, therefore, the states' police powers:

> I take leave to say that the New York statute . . . cannot be held to be in conflict with the Fourteenth Amendment, without enlarging the scope of the Amendment far beyond its original purpose and without bringing under the supervision of this court matters which have been supposed to belong exclusively to the legislative departments of the several States when exerting their conceded power to guard the health and safety of their citizens by such regulations as they in their wisdom deem best. (p. 10)

At issue, in short, are a number of constitutional questions. While much attention has centered on the *Lochner* Court's emphasis on equal protection and the 'right of contract', it is clear that *Lochner* raises fundamental states' rights or federalism issues. These questions will be addressed in later chapters. For the moment, attention centers on the *Lochner* Court's Opinion. Writing for the majority, Justice Peckham argues that, for New York's police power to 'prevail' against the right of contract:

> The [New York] act must have a more direct relation, as a means to an end, and the end itself must be appropriate and legitimate, before an act can be held to be valid which interferes with the *general right of an individual to be free in his person* and in his power to contract in relation to his own labor. (p. 6; emphasis mine)

If this passage is evocative of Madison's 'means' and 'ends' formulation (see Chapter 2 in this volume), the invocation of the 'right of an individual to be free in his person' gestures toward modern liberalism's transcendental autonomous self-conception (Chapter 5 in this volume). This conception, I argue, is central to the New Court's constitutional jurisprudence (see Chapter 4 in this volume), and to the economic paradigm that animates contemporary economic policy (Chapter 5 in this volume).

3.3   *ADAIR* v. *UNITED STATES*

The Court's holding in *Adair* v. *United States* (1908) raises a different set of constitutional issues. At issue is the question of whether it is 'within the power of Congress to make it a criminal offense against the United States for a carrier engaged in interstate commerce, or an agent or officer thereof, to discharge an employe [sic] simply because of his membership in a labor organization' (Syllabus, p. 2).

Writing for the majority, Justice Harlan asserts that 'The first inquiry is whether [Congress's 1898 statute] . . . is repugnant to the Fifth Amendment . . . declaring that no person shall be deprived of liberty or property without due process of law' (Opinion, p. 7). On this question, Justice Harlan concludes that 'In our opinion [the tenth section of the 1898 Act] . . . is an invasion of personal liberty, as well as of the right of property, guaranteed by [the Fifth] Amendment. Such liberty and right embraces the right to make contracts for the purchase of the labor of others and equally the right to make contracts for the sale of one's own labor' (ibid.).

Harlan's second inquiry addresses the question of whether the constitutionality of the statute 'can be referred to the power of Congress to regulate interstate commerce, without regard to any question of personal liberty or right of property arising under the Fifth Amendment' (p. 9). Writing for the majority, Justice Harlan notes that:

we hold that there is no such connection between interstate commerce and membership in a labor organization as to authorize Congress to make it a crime against the United States for an agent of an interstate carrier to discharge an employe [sic] because of such membership on his part. (p. 11)

Continuing, Justice Harlan writes that:

If such a power exists in Congress it is difficult to perceive why it might not, by absolute regulation, require interstate carriers, under penalties, to employ in the conduct of its interstate business only members of labor organizations, or only those who are not members of such organizations – a power which could not be recognized as existing under the Constitution of the United States. (p. 11)

While the *Adair* majority invoked the liberty of contract 'guaranteed by [the Fifth] Amendment', and found 'no . . . connection between interstate commerce and membership in a labor organization', Justices McKenna and Holmes dissented. Justice McKenna noted, first, that the federal government's 'power to regulate commerce . . . is not confined to a regulation of the mere [interstate] movement of goods or persons' and, second, that 'there are . . . examples in [the Supreme Court's] decisions . . . of liberty of contract and liberty of forming business relations . . . which were compelled to give way to the [commerce] power of Congress'. Citing, in particular, '*United States* v. *Joint Traffic Association*, 171 US 571', Justice McKenna argued that:

> There as [in *Adair*] an opposition was asserted between the liberty of the railroads to contract with one another and the power of Congress to regulate commerce. That power was declared paramount, and it was not perceived, as it seems to be perceived now that [the Congress's Commerce Clause power] was subordinate and controlled by the provisions of the Fifth Amendment. (Dissent, p. 13)

In his Dissent, Justice Holmes wrote that 'I confess that I think that the right to make contracts at will that has been derived from the word liberty in the [Fifth and Fourteenth] amendments has been stretched to its extremes by the [Court's] decisions; but they agree that sometimes the right may be constrained' (p. 16). He concluded that 'I could not pronounce it unwarranted if Congress should decide that to foster a strong union was for the best interest, not only of men, but of the railroads and the country at large' (p. 17). For his part, Justice McKenna asserted that 'We are dealing with rights exercised in a quasi-public business and therefore subject to control in the interest of the public' (p. 16).

3.4   *COPPAGE* v. *STATE OF KANSAS*

In *Coppage* v. *State of Kansas* (1915), the Supreme Court held that a 1903 Kansas statute was 'repugnant to the "due process" clause of the Fourteenth Amendment, and therefore void' (Opinion, p. 14). Reduced to its essentials, the statute made it unlawful 'to coerce, require, demand or influence any person or persons to enter into an agreement . . . not to join or become or remain a member of any labor organization or association, as a condition of . . . employment, or continuing in the employment of such individual, firm, or corporation' (p. 5).

Justice Pitney, writing the Opinion, cites *Adair* as 'controlling upon the present controversy': '[I]f Congress is prevented from arbitrary interference with the liberty of contract because of the "due process" provision of the Fifth Amendment, it is too clear for argument that the States are prevented from the like interference by virtue of the corresponding clause of the Fourteenth Amendment' (p. 7).

Whereas Justice Pitney acknowledges that the states' police powers 'may reasonably limit the enjoyment of personal liberty, including the right of making contracts' (p. 10), he asserts that 'The mere restriction of liberty or of property rights cannot of itself be denominated "public welfare", and treated as a legitimate object of the police power; for such restriction is the very thing that is inhibited by the [Fourteenth] Amendment' (p. 11).

For Justice Holmes, in Dissent, matters are not so straightforward. For Holmes, 'there is nothing in the Constitution of the United States to prevent' a state from enacting legislation to enable a workman to 'secure a contract that shall be fair to him' (p. 14). In effect, Justice Holmes invokes an inequality of bargaining power argument in supporting his opinion that *Adair* and *Lochner* should be overruled (ibid.). This, as we shall see (Chapter 4), is a recurring theme of the 'New Court'.

Justice Day, in a separate Dissent with Justice Hughes concurring, asserts that, the majority's Opinion notwithstanding, 'nothing is better settled by the repeated decisions of this court than that the right of contract is not absolute and unyielding, but is subject to limitation and restraint in the interest of the public health, safety and welfare, and such limitations may be declared in legislation of the State' (p. 15). In Day's account, the Kansas statute was passed:

> in the exercise of that particular authority called the *police power*, the limitations of which no court has yet undertaken precisely to define, has for its avowed purpose the protection of the exercise of a legal right [to join labor unions], by preventing an employer from depriving the employe [sic] of [that right] as a condition of obtaining employment. I see no reason why a State may not, if it chooses, protect this right, as well as other legal rights. (Ibid.; emphasis mine)

3.5 WHAT DOES ALL THIS MEAN?

Whereas some have characterized the Old Court, roughly the post-Civil War to 1937 period, as one in which laissez-faire economics enjoyed a 'privileged constitutional place' (Sandel, 1996, p. 42), more is at issue. What is clear is that the *Lochner*, *Adair*, and *Coppage* Opinions and Dissents gesture toward the constitutional issues that find expression in the work of the New Court. Of particular interest is the interpretation of the Constitution's General Welfare, Necessary and Proper and Commerce Clauses. At issue is the Supreme Court's interpretation of the federal government's *enumerated* powers versus the states' 'numerous and indefinite' police powers; powers that, in Madison's account, 'extend to all objects, which, in the ordinary course of affairs, concern the lives, liberties, and properties of the people; and the internal order, improvement, and prosperity of the state' (see Chapter 2).

While it is true that the Old Court emphasized contract and property rights it is also true that:

> For the first time in American history, rights functioned as trumps. Liberty no longer depended on dispersed power alone, but found direct protection from the courts. Where fundamental rights were seen to be at stake, *even the principles of federalism and state sovereignty no longer impeded judicial intervention.* (Sandel, 1996, p. 42; emphasis mine)

4. The 'New Court' at work

4.1 THE PROGRESSIVE AGENDA

The constitutional jurisprudence of the 'New Court' was, in many ways, a reflection of the Progressive view of social progress. While, as we shall see (in Chapter 5), an emergent conception of the transcendental autonomous self is itself partially responsible for the growth of the federal enterprise, immediate interest centers on two 'progressive' ideas. Simply stated, Progressives questioned both the structure of US federalism and the conception of individual liberty that animated much of the Old Court's constitutional jurisprudence; in particular, the liberty of contract (Epstein, 2006, pp. 7–8).

Characteristically, Progressives espoused an economic nationalism whose central principle is that the 'extensive interconnection of all aspects of the American economy crie[s] out for federal regulation' (ibid., p. 8). On this logic, they insisted upon what I argue is an expansive understanding of the federal role. Interestingly, James Madison reacted in 1819 to an early expression of the 'extensive interconnection' mantra:

> In the great system of Political Economy having for its general object the national welfare, everything is related immediately or remotely to every other thing; and consequently a Power over any one thing, if not limited by some obvious and precise affinity, may amount to a power over every other. Ends and means may shift their character at will & according to the ingenuity of the [federal] Legislative Body. ([1819] 1999, p. 734)

For present purposes, the essential point is that, in Progressive hands, the 'extensive interconnection of all aspects of the American economy' was, along with increasingly unrestrained readings of the Constitution's General Welfare, Necessary and Proper, Commerce and Legislative Powers Clauses, justificatory of a powerful regulatory impulse. So, too, was the Progressives' insistence that 'ever greater inequalities of wealth justified overriding constitutionally protected rights of liberty, property and contract' (Epstein, 2006, p. 8). Thus, if for the Old Court, contract and property rights trumped the states' police powers (see Chapter 3), for the New Court, 'inequalities of wealth' trumped the same 'economic' rights and, along with the 'extensive interconnections of all aspects of the

American economy', justified the relentless expansion of federal power. As we shall see, this 'Progressive' impulse was underwritten by a public philosophy and a political economy that would be alien to the Founders' imagination (see also Chapter 5).

While an extended discussion of the Constitution's General Welfare, Necessary and Proper, Commerce and Legislative Powers Clauses is momentarily deferred, some preliminary remarks are appropriate.

4.2   THE NEW COURT: AN OVERVIEW

I emphasize, first, that Madison argued against an expansive reading of the General Welfare Clause. Indeed, both the Constitution's author and Jefferson insisted that 'the power to tax and spend did not authorize the Congress to do whatever it thought to be in the best interest of the nation' (Eastman, 2005, p. 93). Rather, the Congress is constrained to use permissible means to achieve permissible ends; ends that are limited by the federal government's enumerated powers (see Chapter 2, Section 2.3 and Chapter 6, Section 6.2). Importantly, the historical record shows that, whereas Hamilton and other Federalist leaders argued for a broader reading of the General Welfare Clause (Chapter 2), 'their reading was, on the whole, rejected both by Congress and, after the election of 1800, by the executive'. Moreover, this 'more restrictive interpretation of the spending power was adopted by every President until the Civil War' (Eastman, 2005, p. 94).

The New Court's General Welfare Clause jurisprudence begins with *United States* v. *Butler* (1936) and *Helvering* v. *Davis* (1937). It is true that, in *Butler*, the Supreme Court held that 'the tax and regulatory program at issue . . . was unconstitutional because its purpose was to regulate and control agricultural production, "a matter beyond the powers delegated to the federal government"' (ibid., p. 95). But it is also true that, whereas *Butler* struck down the Agricultural Adjustment Act (AAA), 'a 1933 statute that taxed food processors and used the proceeds to pay farmers for reducing their production' (Levy and Mellor, 2008, p. 24), Justice Roberts, writing for the *Butler* Court, concluded that 'the power of Congress to authorize expenditure of public moneys for public purposes is not limited by the direct grants of legislative power found in the Constitution' (Opinion, p. 66). On the one hand, therefore, the Court's reading of the Commerce Clause and of the Tenth Amendment led it to conclude that the federal government does not have the power to regulate agricultural production, and that, because '[t]hat power was reserved to the states under the Tenth Amendment . . . the AAA had "invaded the reserved rights of the states"' (Levy and Mellor, 2008, p. 24). On the other hand, because it found that the federal government's taxing and spending power extended beyond its enumerated powers, it seems clear that *'Butler* opened the door to the redistributive state' (ibid., p. 25).

In contrast, while it held in *Butler* that the 1933 AAA 'invaded the rights reserved to the states', the Court found that the Social Security Act did not violate the Tenth Amendment. At issue in *Helvering* v. *Davis* was the fact that the wage-based taxes imposed on employers and employees were not specifically earmarked for the payment of Old Age Benefits. Writing for the Court's 7-2 majority, Justice Benjamin Cardozo held that the Tenth Amendment was inapplicable, and that, under the General Welfare Clause, the Congress had the power to spend the non-earmarked tax proceeds for the public good (Congressional Research Service, 2004, p. 167). More generally, while Justice Cardozo acknowledged that 'The line must still be drawn between one welfare and another, between particular and general . . . The discretion belongs to Congress, unless the choice is clearly wrong, a display of arbitrary power' (Opinion, p. 640).

[handwritten margin note: opened the door to Ponzi scheme]

If the Supreme Court's General Welfare Clause jurisprudence has been deferential to Congress's discretion, the same may be said of its interpretation of the Necessary and Proper Clause. At the December 1787 Pennsylvania Ratifying Convention, James Wilson, the author of the Necessary and Proper Clause, observed that:

> It is urged, as a general objection [to the Constitution], that 'the powers of Congress are unlimited and undefined, and that [the Congress] will be the judges, in all cases, of what is necessary and proper for them to do'. To bring this subject to your view, I need do no more than point to the words in the Constitution . . . the concluding clause [of Article 1, Section 8], with which so much fault has been found, gives no more power or other powers; nor does it, in any degree, go beyond the particular enumeration; for, *when it is said that Congress shall have power to make all laws which shall be necessary and proper, those words are limited and defined by the following, 'for carrying into execution the foregoing powers'. It is saying no more than that the powers we have already particularly given, shall be effectively carried into execution.* (Kurland and Lerner, 1987c, p. 241; emphasis mine)

Simply stated, the Necessary and Proper Clause authorizes the federal government to do what is 'necessary to render effectual the particular [enumerated] powers that are granted' by the Constitution (Engdahl, 2005, p. 147). Indeed, this means-to-ends formulation, often articulated by Madison (see Chapter 2), was confirmed in *McCulloch* v. *Maryland* (1819). That said, *'McCulloch* countenanced "any means calculated to produce the end", giving Congress "the capacity to avail itself of experience, to exercise its reason, and to accommodate its legislation to circumstances"' (ibid.).

I argue that this formulation has invited all manner of casuistry; that it ignores the Necessary and Proper Clause; that it has encouraged an all-encompassing notion of the General Welfare and Commerce Clauses, and that it has, therefore, contributed to the expansion of the reach and scope of federal power. I associate myself, in particular, with the view that: 'Often the Supreme Court has not articulated [the] Necessary and Proper Clause basis for its so-called affecting commerce doctrine. This has led to one of the most confused areas of all constitutional law' (ibid., p. 149). As the passage just quoted suggests, the New Court's Commerce Clause jurisprudence has been characterized as confused. It is also, I argue, corrosive of the structure of US federalism, and congenial to a metastasization of federal regulatory activity.

At issue is the tension, already noted, between the federal power to 'regulate commerce . . . among the several states' and the states' police powers. Inevitably, the debate has, since the Founding, centered on the definitions of 'to regulate', 'commerce' and 'among the several states'. While a brief adumbration of the Court's evolving understanding of these words and phrases is provided below, immediate interest centers on the relationship between the advent of national economic legislation, itself a reflection of the Progressive movement, and the relentless expansion of the federal regulatory enterprise. In broad outline, the Court's increasingly expansive understanding of the Commerce power advanced from its restrictive holding in *United States* v. *E. C. Knight Co.* (1895) that declared that the Commerce power did not reach manufacturing, to a series of cases that asserted that Congress may regulate a *local* activity, if the activity has a 'substantial effect' on interstate commerce. Thus, by 1937, the Court held in *NLRB* v. *Jones and Laughlin Steel Corporation* that the National Labor Relations Act's regulation of factory working conditions fell within the Congress's power to regulate interstate commerce. Five years later, the Court held in *Wickard* v. *Filburn* (1942) that Congress, under the Interstate Commerce Clause, can regulate the purely local production of wheat. In response to the defendant Filburn's insistence that his crop was not sold in interstate commerce, and that most of the crop was consumed on his farm, the Court held that:

> [We have] no doubt that Congress may properly have considered that wheat consumed on the farm where grown, if wholly outside the scheme of regulation, would have a substantial effect in defeating and obstructing [the Amended 1938 Agricultural Adjustment Act's] purpose to stimulate trade therein at *increased prices*. (Opinion, pp. 128–9; emphasis mine)

The upshot is that, in a series of holdings, the Supreme Court has gradually 'turned the commerce power into the equivalent of a general regulatory power and undid the Framers' original structure of limited and delegated powers' (Forte, 2005, p. 104). Indeed, we know that: 'For more than 50 years following *Wickard*, no law was ever struck down for exceeding Congress's power under the Commerce Clause. The Interstate Commerce Clause became, and remains, the primary source of federal power' (Levy and Mellor, 2008, p. 45). *—> until now — it's la power to levy taxes*

While it is true that, in *United States* v. *Lopez* (1995), *United States* v. *Morrison* (2000) and *Gonzalez* v. *Oregon* (2006), the Court limited Congress's Commerce Clause powers, it is also true that, in *Gonzalez* v. *Raich* (2005), the Court held that 'Congress' Commerce Clause authority includes the power to prohibit the *local* cultivation and use of marijuana in compliance with California law' (Syllabus, p. 1; emphasis mine).[1]

Thus, while *Lopez*, *Morrison* and *Oregon* limited the Congress's Commerce Clause powers for the first time since the 1930s, these holdings are difficult to reconcile with *Raich*. What is clear is that the Supreme Court's holding in *Raich* affirmed the Congress's authority under the federal Controlled Substances Act to trench upon California's and, therefore, the states' police powers.[2] In this respect, the *Raich* holding is consistent with earlier decisions that upheld the constitutionality, under the Commerce Clause, of federal criminal and social reform legislation (Forte, 2005, p. 104). Yet, if *Raich* is irreconcilable with the Court's holdings in *Lopez, Morrison* and *Oregon*, Justice Thomas's Dissent in *Raich* is significant because of its emphasis upon the Necessary and Proper Clause (see Section 4.3 below and Chapter 6, Section 6.5). In rejecting the federal government's contention 'that banning Monson and Raich's intrastate drug activity is "necessary and proper for carrying into Execution" its regulation of interstate drug trafficking' (Dissent, p. 4), Justice Thomas calls to mind Madison's 'means' and 'ends' formulation (see Chapter 2, Section 2.3), and Justice Cardozo's admonition in *A.L.A. Schechter Poultry Corp.* v. *United States* (1935) that 'Activities local in their immediacy do not become interstate and national because of distant repercussions' (Forte, 2005, p. 103).[3] I argue, in short, that the New Court has ignored both Madison and Cardozo.

Finally, I return to a theme introduced in Chapter 1. At issue is Article 1, Section 1 of the Constitution. The Legislative Powers Clause is straightforward: 'All legislative Powers herein granted shall be vested in a Congress of the United States, which shall consist of a Senate and House of Representatives'.

The point of departure is that expansive readings of the General Welfare, Necessary and Proper, Interstate Commerce and Legislative Powers Clauses have had as their corollary the emergence of what some have called the modern regulatory state and its concomitant, the proliferation of federal administrative agencies. Whereas in *United States* v. *Shreveport Grain and Elevator Co.* (1932) the Supreme Court declared that 'the legislative power of Congress cannot be delegated' to the president or to administrative agencies (Opinion, p. 85), 'the Court has consistently upheld grants of authority that have been challenged as invalid delegations of legislative power' (Congressional Research Service, 2004, p. 74). Indeed: 'Since 1935, the Court has not struck down a delegation to an administrative agency. Rather, the Court has approved "without deviation, Congress' ability to delegate [legislative] power *under broad standards*"'(ibid., pp. 75–6; emphasis mine). The reference to 'broad standards' is of particular importance. The essential point is that constitutional separation of powers objections have fallen to the Supreme Court's theory, first articulated in *Wayman* v. *Southard* (1825), that Congress may, under a general legislative provision, delegate the power to 'fill up the details' (ibid., pp. 78–9). According to the Court's theory, it is sufficient 'that Congress set forth "intelligible principles" or "standards" to guide as well as limit the agency or official in the performance of its assigned task' (ibid., p. 81). A second theory advanced by the Court holds that Congress may 'legislate contingently'.

While the Court's second delegation theory will be taken up below, I emphasize for the moment that there have been only two instances in which the Court found grants of discretion to be 'unbounded, hence standardless' and, therefore, unconstitutional. That said, it is revealing that the Court has found the following 'standards' to be constitutionally adequate: 'excessive profits', 'unfair and inequitable distribution of voting power', 'fair and equitable commodities prices', 'just and reasonable rates', 'public interest', 'public convenience, interest or necessity', 'unfair methods of competition' and 'requisite to protect the public health [with] an adequate margin of safety' (ibid., pp. 76 and 82–3). If, as I suggest, these 'standards' are inherently subjective, it follows that the associated grants of discretion are, in fact, unbounded and standardless. And if, in turn, this implies that the Supreme Court has permitted unconstitutional grants of legislative power, there is an additional problem: the Court's holdings suggest that 'there is no general prohibition on delegating authority that includes the exercise of *policy judgment*' (ibid., p. 84; emphasis mine).

These and related ideas are discussed in more detail below. In anticipation of that more detailed account, I suggest that the Supreme Court's expansive reading of the Legislative Powers Clause accounts, in large measure, for the relentless expansion of the regulatory state. The regulatory state, in turn, has substituted 'government by experts' for political accountability, and enhanced the power of the 'factious interests' that the Founders sought to constrain.

With all of this as background I turn now to a more detailed discussion of the Constitution's General Welfare, Necessary and Proper, Commerce and Legislative Powers Clauses.

4.3   THE GENERAL WELFARE AND NECESSARY AND PROPER CLAUSES

The General Welfare Clause, Article 1, Section 8, Clause 1 of the Constitution, reads as follows: 'The Congress shall have Power to lay and collect Taxes, Duties, Imposts and Excises, to pay the Debts and provide for the common Defense and general welfare of the United States'.

I emphasize, first, that the General Welfare Clause limits Congress's *taxing* power. If it is clear that the Clause contemplates tax levies for the purposes of debt payment and the provision of the *common* defense and the *general* welfare of the United States, it is equally clear that it does not authorize special exclusions, exemptions, deductions or other 'targeted', special-interest tax provisions (Levy and Mellor, 2008, p. 31).[4] For its part, the last clause of Article 1, Section 8, the Necessary and Proper Clause: 'authorizes Congress to enact laws that are "appropriate" and plainly adapted for carrying into execution Congress's *enumerated powers*; it does not authorize Congress to enact any law that Congress thinks is "reasonable"' (Engdahl, 2005, p. 149; emphasis mine). Stated differently, the Clause 'does not confer general authority over a matter simply because . . . in some respects [it] *might* serve an enumerated-power end' (ibid.; emphasis mine).

While the General Welfare and Necessary and Proper Clauses are, in effect, two sides of the same coin, neither of the seminal New Court holdings, *United States* v. *Butler* (1936) and *Helvering* v. *Davis* (1937) (see Section 4.2 above) mentions the Necessary and Proper Clause.

While the contemporary view is that 'Congress's power to provide for the "general welfare" is a power to spend for virtually anything that Congress itself views as helpful' (Eastman, 2005, p. 93), this was not the view at the Founding. It is true that, in his *Report on the Subject of Manufactures* (1791), Hamilton promoted an expansive reading of the General Welfare Clause (see Chapter 2). But it is also true that Madison, Jefferson and James Wilson insisted that the power to tax and spend did not confer upon Congress the right to do whatever *it* thinks to be in the national interest. In this interpretation, federal spending and taxation must be for the 'general' or *national* welfare. It was left to the states, under what we now call the states' police powers, to attend to 'local' welfare (see Chapters 2 and 6). We know, for example, that Jefferson and Madison rejected Hamilton's 'artificial encouragements' (Chapter 2); that, on the logic that it would be unconstitutional, the First Congress refused to make a loan to a glass manufacturer, and that the Fourth Congress did not believe it had the power to provide disaster relief to the city of Savannah, Georgia (Eastman, 2005, p. 93). Indeed, at least in one account: 'while there were clearly voices urging for an expansive spending power before the Civil War, the interpretation held by Jefferson, Madison and [President] Monroe is the one that prevailed for most of the first seventy years after adoption of the Constitution' (ibid., p. 95).

wow!

A recurring theme, perhaps best articulated by President Polk, was that congressional efforts to fund 'internal improvements' within the states would not only be unconstitutional; they would enable 'combinations of individual and local interests [that would be] strong enough to control legislation, absorb the revenues of the country, and plunge the [federal] government into a hopeless indebtedness' (ibid.). President Polk, like his predecessors, worried that special or 'factious' interests would, through an expansive reading of the General Welfare Clause, overcome the Founders' 'auxiliary precautions'. In fact, what Polk understood and feared has, since 1936, found full expression in Supreme Court holdings that, effectively, leave it to Congress to determine what constitutes the 'general welfare'. Since 1933, the Court has 'accord[ed] great deference to Congress's decision that a spending program advances the general welfare, ✳ and has even questioned whether [a restriction on the spending power] is judicially enforceable' (Congressional Research Service, 2004, pp. 163–4). In this view, whatever spending limitation the General Welfare Clause might impose is a *political* decision. Equally important, 'Dispute, such as it is, turns on the conditioning of funds' (ibid., p. 164). Rather than concentrating on the constitutionality of federal *spending* programs, the Supreme Court has focused 'on whether various conditions imposed on the receipt of federal funds – conditions designed to achieve ends concededly not within Congress's enumerated powers – were constitutionally permissible' (Eastman, 2005, pp. 95–6).

great...

Might be a good counter-point

Even if one were to grant that the Congress has complete discretion with respect to what constitutes the 'general [or national] welfare', a view with which Madison, Jefferson and Wilson would surely not be associated, the Necessary and Proper Clause retains its basic relevance. Whatever else is said, the constitutionality of the conditions imposed on the receipt of federal funds implicates the Necessary and Proper Clause. The question, in short, is whether the conditions are designed to achieve ends that are 'necessary and proper for carrying into Execution' constitutionally enumerated powers (Levy and Mellor, 2008, p. 31).

As I have emphasized, the New Court's General Welfare Clause

✳ *I wonder if the program got the name "welfare" to invoke this clause intentionally.*

jurisprudence begins with *United States* v. *Butler* (1936) and *Helvering* v. *Davis* (1937) (see Section 4.2 above). If the Supreme Court's holdings in *Butler* and *Helvering* evinced a deference to congressional discretion that Madison and Jefferson would reject (Chapter 2), the same can be said of the Court's decision in *South Dakota* v. *Dole* (1987).

At issue in *Dole* was the fact that Congress conditioned states' access to certain highway funds on the adoption of a 21-year-old minimum drinking age. The stated purpose of both the highway funds and the minimum drinking age condition was safe interstate travel. Writing for the Court's 7-2 majority, Chief Justice Rehnquist focused on the 'conditioning of [the federal highway] funds'. With this in mind, the Chief Justice adopted a four-part test: (1) the federal spending program must be in pursuit of the 'general welfare', a matter left to Congress's discretion since 'the concept of welfare . . . is shaped by Congress'; (2) any conditions imposed on the receipt of funds must be 'unambiguous'; (3) any conditions imposed must be related to the program being funded and (4) the conditions imposed must not violate other constitutional provisions (Opinion, pp. 207–8). Applying this four-part test, the Court held that the 21-year-old minimum drinking age *was* sufficiently related to the federal highway funding program. The result is that, while the Court's decision did not reach the constitutionality of the federal *spending* program, it affirmed that states' access to federal highway funds can be conditioned upon their acceptance of a *federal* minimum drinking age. Whatever else is said, it can be argued that a minimum drinking age is, under their police powers, a prerogative of the individual states.

I emphasize, first, that the Supreme Court has never found a federal spending condition to be unrelated to the 'federal interest for which the funds are expended' (Congressional Research Service, 2004, p. 166). Second, while it 'has suggested that in some circumstances the financial inducement offered by Congress might be so coercive as to pass the point at which "pressure turns into compulsion"', the Court 'has never found a congressional condition to be coercive in this sense' (ibid.). Finally, the Court's relentless focus on the 'conditioning of funds' is a reflection of its 'great deference to Congress's decision that a spending program advances the general welfare' (ibid., p. 163).[5] It is precisely this judicial deference that animated Justice O'Connor's Dissent in *Dole*:

> If the spending power is limited only by Congress' notion of the general welfare, the reality . . . is that the Spending [or General Welfare] Clause gives 'power to the Congress to tear down the barriers, to invade states' jurisdiction and to become a parliament of the whole people, subject to no restrictions save such as are self-imposed'. This . . . was not the Framers' plan and it is not the meaning of the Spending Clause. (p. 217)

Justice O'Connor's Dissent in *Dole* elegantly and straightforwardly describes the problem with the New Court's General Welfare Clause jurisprudence. On the one hand, it has given Congress carte blanche to determine what constitutes the 'general welfare'. On the other hand, it has enabled the Congress to expand the scope and reach of federal on-, off-, and off-off-budget activity (see Chapter 1). If, as I suggest, this has rendered meaningless the Founders' *permissible* 'ends' and 'means' formulation, it has also underwritten the relentless expansion of the federal enterprise. Unfortunately, the same can be said of the New Court's Commerce Clause jurisprudence.

4.4   THE COMMERCE CLAUSE

The Commerce Clause, Article 1, Section 8, Clause 3 of the Constitution reads as follows: 'The Congress shall have Power . . . . To regulate Commerce with foreign Nations, and among the several States, and with the Indian Tribes'.

It is generally agreed that the Commerce Clause serves two purposes. First, it is 'the direct source of the most important powers that the Federal Government exercises in peacetime' and, second, 'except for the due process and equal protection clauses of the Fourteenth Amendment, it is the most important limitation . . . on the exercise of state [police] power' (Congressional Research Service, 2004, p. 169). I acknowledge first that, 'of the approximately 1,400 [Commerce Clause] cases which reached the Supreme Court prior to 1900, the overwhelming proportion stemmed from state legislation' (ibid.). In general, the question at issue was whether state laws interfered with the flow of interstate commerce. As a result, 'the word "commerce" came to dominate the clause while the word "regulate" remained in the background' (ibid.).

The Supreme Court's understanding of the Commerce Clause was, for a long period in its history, informed by Chief Justice Marshall's holding in *Gibbons* v. *Ogden* (1824). Of particular importance has been his interpretation of the words 'commerce' and 'regulate' and the phrase 'among the several states'. In the case of 'commerce', Marshall held that it comprehended more than 'traffic . . . buying and selling, or the interchange of commodities'. For Marshall, the term also contemplates navigation and 'intercourse' (Opinion, p. 189). In the case of 'regulation', the Chief Justice asserted that: 'the sovereignty of congress, though limited to specified objects, is plenary as to those objects, the power over commerce with foreign nations, and among the several states, is vested in congress' (pp. 196–7). Finally, for Marshall, the phrase 'among the several states' was:

not one which would probably have been selected to indicate the completely interior traffic of a state. . . The genius and character of the whole government seem to be, that its action is to be applied to all the *external concerns of the nation*, and to those *internal concerns which affect the states generally*; but not to those which are completely within a particular state, which do not affect other states, and with which it is not *necessary to interfere, for the purpose of executing some of the general powers of the [federal] government.* (pp. 194–5; emphasis mine)

Note first that Marshall's formulation includes the phrase 'affect the states generally'. As we shall see, subsequent interpretations of the phrase have been congenial to the rationalization of all manner of federal regulatory interventions. That said, it is clear that, for Marshall, purely local activities are outside the reach of Congress's Commerce Clause power. For its part, the phrase 'necessary to interfere' is clearly evocative of the Necessary and Proper Clause. Whatever else is said, it is clear that Justice Marshall's formulation is consistent with the view that *all* congressional claims of power must be evaluated in conjunction with the Necessary and Proper Clause (see Section 4.3 above). The essential point, however, is that: 'After *Gibbons* v. *Ogden*, there was little occasion for the Supreme Court to investigate the breadth of federal commerce power until the late nineteenth century and the advent of *national economic legislation*' (Forte, 2005, p. 102; emphasis mine).

Simply stated, we know that, for a long period in its history, the Court held that, if activities were either not interstate commerce, or 'bore no sufficient nexus to interstate commerce', they were not encompassed by the Commerce Clause. Thus, the Court held that, neither mining nor manufacturing, whether or not the product moved in interstate commerce, was not reachable under the Commerce Clause (Congressional Research Service, 2004, p. 170). While it is true that, 'From 1895 on, the Court experimented with differing notions of the commerce power until 1938', it is also true that, in 1938, 'it signaled that it was abdicating any serious role in monitoring Congress's exercise of this delegated power' (Forte, 2005, p. 102).

The 'constitutional revolution' of the late 1930s bore little relation either to Marshall's *Gibbons* holding, or to the Court's pre-1938 Commerce Clause jurisprudence. Just as Madison feared (see Chapter 2), in a series of cases, the Court held that activities 'which are antecedent to or subsequent to a move across state lines are conceived to be part of an integrated commercial whole and therefore subject to the reach of [Congress's] commerce power' (Congressional Research Service, 2004, pp. 171–2). This was true, for example, of manufacturing (*NLRB* v. *Jones & Laughlin Steel Corp.* (1937)) and of mining (*Sunshine Anthracite Coal Co.* v. *Adkins* (1940)).

Moreover, if the Court stressed the interrelationships among industrial production and interstate commerce, it also emphasized that minor transactions have an effect on interstate commerce (*Wickard* v. *Filburn* (1942); *NLRB* v. *Fainblatt* (1939), and others), and that the 'cumulative effect of many minor transactions, [each] with no separate effect on interstate commerce' may, when '*viewed as a class* . . . be sufficient to merit congressional regulation' (ibid., p. 173; emphasis mine).[6]

These expansive readings of the Commerce Clause informed a series of cases involving New Deal, Depression Era federal laws. The cases of immediate interest involve the National Labor Relations Act of 1935, the Fair Labor Standards Act of 1938 and the Agricultural Marketing Agreement Act of 1937.

In broad outline, the cases (*NLRB* v. *Jones & Laughlin Steel Corp.* (1937), *United States* v. *Darby* (1941) and *United States* v. *Wrightwood Dairy Co.* (1942)) expanded the reach, under the Commerce Clause, of federal regulatory power. In *Jones & Laughlin*, the Court 'reduced the distinction between "direct" and "indirect" effects [on interstate commerce] to the vanishing point and thereby placed Congress in the position to regulate productive industry and labor relations in these industries' (Congressional Research Service, 2004, p. 199). Equally important, Chief Justice Hughes, writing for the Court, argued that 'The close and intimate effect which brings the subject within the reach of federal power may be due to activities in relation to productive industry although the industry when separately viewed is *local*' (Opinion, pp. 41–2; emphasis mine). In *Darby* the Court upheld a statute that 'prohibited [both] the *shipment* in interstate commerce of goods manufactured by employees whose wages are less than the prescribed maximum [and] the *employment* of workmen in the production of goods for such commerce at other than the prescribed wages and hours' (Congressional Research Service, 2004, p. 201; emphasis mine). Chief Justice Stone, writing for a unanimous Court, averred that:

> The motive and purpose of the present regulation are plainly to make effective the congressional conception of public policy that interstate commerce should not be made the instrument of competition in the distribution of goods produced under substandard labor conditions, which competition is injurious to the commerce and to the States from and to which the commerce flows. (Opinion, p. 115)

Finally, in *Wrightwood Dairy Co.* the Court sustained an agricultural marketing order of the Secretary of Agriculture, setting the minimum prices to be paid to producers of milk in the Chicago 'marketing area'. The Court held that:

Congress plainly has power to regulate the price of milk distributed through the medium of interstate commerce. . . The commerce power is not confined in its exercise to the regulation of commerce among the States. It extends to those activities *intrastate* which so *affect* interstate commerce, or the exertion of the power of Congress over it, as to make regulation of them appropriate means to the attainment of a legitimate end, the effective execution of the granted power to regulate interstate commerce. . . It follows that *no form of State activity can constitutionally thwart the regulatory power granted by the commerce clause to Congress. Hence the reach of that power extends to those intrastate activities which in a substantial way interfere with or obstruct the granted power.* (Opinion, pp. 118–19; emphasis mine)

In light of all of this, I emphasize again (see Section 4.2), that in *Wickard* v. *Filburn* (1942), the Court held that the commerce power extends to agricultural production not intended for interstate commerce. On the logic that it might have a 'substantial effect' on interstate commerce, the Court sustained Commerce Clause regulation of wheat intended for use on the producer's farm.

At issue was the Agricultural Adjustment Act of 1938. As amended, the Act regulated agricultural production, even when that production was intended for the producer's consumption, rather than for intra- or interstate commerce. In *Wickard*, the Court noted that the purpose of the Act was to increase wheat prices. With this in mind, the Court held that:

It can hardly be denied that a factor of such volume and variability as home-consumed wheat would have a substantial influence on price and market conditions. This may arise because being in marketable condition such wheat overhangs the market and, if induced by rising prices, tends to flow into the market and check price increases. But if we assume that it is never marketed, it supplies a need of the man who grew it which would otherwise be reflected by purchases in the open market. . . *This record leaves us in no doubt that Congress may properly have considered that wheat consumed on the farm grown, if wholly outside the scheme of regulation, would have a substantial effect in defeating and obstructing its purpose to stimulate trade therein at increased prices.* (Opinion, pp. 128–9; emphasis mine)

At the heart of the Court's 'affecting commerce' jurisprudence is the so-called 'rational basis' test; a test that is itself derivative of Justice Holmes's Dissent in *Lochner* v. *New York* (1905) (Epstein, 2006, p. 11).[7] The test found expression in a series of cases in which the Court held that Congress had a 'rational basis' for determining either that a regulated activity 'affects' interstate commerce, or that there is a reasonable connection between the regulatory means and the asserted ends (Congressional Research Service, 2004, p. 214).

If, as I argue, the rational basis test manifests an excessive deference to congressional action, it is also, by definition, inconsistent with the 'strict

[handwritten margin note: how does this not conflict w/ individual freedom, ie. pursuit of happiness?]

scrutiny' standard. The latter says that a law is unconstitutional unless the *end* it promotes rises to the level of a 'compelling state interest', and the *means* employed are '"narrowly tailored" to achieve that well-defined objective' (Epstein, 2006, p. 11). Insofar as it contemplates ends that are subsumed by the federal government's enumerated powers, and the means are 'necessary and proper' to the achievement of those ends, 'strict scrutiny' is broadly consistent with the level of scrutiny envisioned by the Founders (see Chapter 2).

Finally, I associate myself with the view that, if the 'rational basis' test has been a powerful catalyst to federal regulatory activity, 'a still more potent engine of regulation has been the expansion of the class-of-activities standard, which began in the "affecting" [interstate commerce] cases' (Congressional Research Service, 2004, p. 214). Two relatively recent cases are heuristic.

In *Russell* v. *United States* (1985), the Court held that a *federal* arson statute applied to an attempted 'torching' of a two-unit apartment building. In its holding the Court simply asserted that real estate rental 'unquestionably' *affects* interstate commerce, and that 'the *local* rental of an apartment unit is merely an element of a much broader commercial market in real estate' (Opinion, pp. 858 and 862; emphasis mine). The 'class-of-activities' or aggregation of local activities test also found expression in an antitrust case. In *Summit Health, Ltd.* v. *Pinhas* (1991), the Court allowed the continuation of an antitrust suit challenging a denial of hospital privileges to a surgeon. The Court's holding asserted that establishing the necessary jurisdictional connection to interstate commerce does not require that the Court focus on the *actual* effects of the alleged conspiracy. Rather, the appropriate test is 'the *possible consequences* for the *affected* market if the conspiracy is successful'. In the Court's view, the required nexus between the denial of one surgeon's hospital privileges and interstate commerce is to be measured by the *potential impact* of the denial on extant and potential participants in the market from which the surgeon was excluded (Opinion, pp. 330–32; emphasis mine).

As has been emphasized (in Section 4.2), the result of these expansive readings of the Commerce Clause and, it should be said, of the General Welfare and Necessary and Proper Clauses, has been that, for 53 years following *Wickard* v. *Filburn* (1942), no federal law was found to be unconstitutional because it exceeded Congress's Commerce Clause power. While it is true that, in *United States* v. *Lopez* (1995), the Court struck down a law making it a federal offense to possess a firearm within 1000 feet of a school, it is also true that its holding in *Gonzalez* v. *Raich* (2005) is difficult to reconcile with *Lopez*, with *United States* v. *Morrison* (2000), or with *Gonzalez* v. *Oregon* (2006).[8] What *is* clear is that the Court's expansive readings of the Commerce Clause have underwritten 'the massive federalization of traditional *state* functions, particularly in the area of criminal law – absurdly characterized as regulation of interstate commerce' (Levy and Mellor, 2008, p. 45; emphasis mine).

In sum, I argue that, in its Commerce Clause jurisprudence, as in its General Welfare and Necessary and Proper Clause jurisprudence, the Supreme Court has ignored Madison's 1823 observation that 'the [Supreme] court, by some of its decisions, still more by extrajudicial reasonings and dicta, has manifested a propensity to enlarge the [federal] authority in derogation of the local, and to amplify [the Supreme Court's] own jurisdiction' (see Chapter 2). Unfortunately, the same can be said of the Court's Legislative Powers Clause jurisprudence.

4.5 THE LEGISLATIVE POWERS CLAUSE

The Legislative Powers Clause, Article 1, Section 1 of the Constitution says simply that: 'All legislative Powers herein granted shall be vested in a Congress of the United States, which shall consist of a Senate and House of Representatives'.

Writing in 1825, in *Wayman* v. *Southard*, Chief Justice Marshall asserted that, whereas Congress may not delegate powers that 'are strictly and exclusively legislative', it may delegate 'power which [it] may rightfully exercise itself' (Opinion, p. 25).

Whatever else is said, it is clear that Marshall's language does not provide 'bright line' guidance as to the interpretation of the Constitution's Legislative Powers or Non-delegation Clause. It is safe to say, moreover, that the Supreme Court has accepted as constitutional the delegation of vast powers to the president and to administrative agencies. Administrative agencies, in turn, appear in many forms:

> Some [administrative] agencies are subunits of executive departments; others are free-standing. The latter, in turn, fall into two categories: executive agencies (so-called because they are ultimately accountable to the President) and 'independent' agencies (which are wholly accountable neither to the President nor to Congress). (Uhlmann, 2005, p. 229)

The development of the Court's non-delegation jurisprudence has involved two constitutional principles. On the one hand, a strict application of separation of powers would mean that the Congress could not confer any of its powers on either the executive or the judicial branches. Application of the separation of powers principle has been complicated, however, by the Court's insistence, in *Loving* v. *United States* (1996) that delegation, 'another branch of our separation of powers jurisdiction', is informed solely by the provision of standards (Opinion, pp. 758–9). On the other hand, the second constitutional principle underlying delegation law 'is a due process conception that undergirds the delegation of *rule-making authority* to administrative agencies' (Congressional Research Service, 2004, p. 78; emphasis mine).

It is clear that, the separation of powers notwithstanding, administrative agencies exercise legislative, executive and judicial powers: '[Administrative agencies] can issue regulations having the same force and effect as statutes, impose fines and penalties for violations of their regulations, and conduct trial-type proceedings that affect the rights and interests of particular parties' (Uhlmann, 2005, p. 229).

While Congress has evinced a marked propensity to delegate rule-making authority to administrative agencies, it has been sensitive to the constitutional due process imperative. Thus, 'Unless otherwise specified in their enabling acts or subsequent legislation, agency operations are governed by the 1946 Administrative Procedures Act (APA)'. The APA authorizes various administrative proceedings, codifies rules for each proceeding, and 'establishes criteria for obtaining judicial review following final agency action' (ibid.).

The provision of 'standards' and due process have been central to the two theories that animate the Supreme Court's delegation jurisprudence. The standards theory, advanced by Chief Justice Marshall in *Wayman* v. *Southard* (1825), distinguishes between 'important' subjects 'which must be entirely regulated by the legislature itself', and subjects 'of less interest, in which a general provision may be made, and power given to those who are to act under such general provisions, to *fill up the details*' (Opinion, p. 41; emphasis mine). The second theory, first articulated in the *Brig Aurora* (1813), is that Congress may *legislate contingently*. Here, rather than directing that a general statute be applied, or that it be supplemented by detailed regulation, 'Congress commands that a previously enacted statute be revived, suspended, or modified, or that a new rule be put into effect, *upon the finding of certain facts by an executive or administrative officer*' (Congressional Research Service, 2004, p. 80; emphasis mine).

Implicit in the 'fill up the details' construct is the requirement that, in delegating rule-making authority, Congress provide an 'intelligible principle' or 'standard' to be applied by the rule-making administrative agency. In *Arizona* v. *California* (1963), Justice Harlan, writing in Dissent, outlined the logic of the Court's 'standards' requirement:

> [The standards requirement] insures that the fundamental policy decisions in our society will be made not by an appointed official but by the body immediately

responsible to the people, [and] it prevents judicial review from becoming merely an exercise at large by providing the courts with some measure against which to judge the official action that has been challenged. (Dissent, p. 626)

Justice Harlan's wording gives clear lexical priority to the idea that the standards requirement 'insures' that fundamental policy decisions will be made by elected rather than appointed officials. Implicit in this formulation is, of course, that such decisions *should* be made by elected officials; that is, by Members of Congress.

With this in mind, I emphasize that, whereas it generally requires that Congress provide standards that indicate broad policy objectives, the Court has sustained the delegation of congressional authority to express *policy judgment*. This, I argue, is deeply corrosive of the separation of powers. Writing in 1819 James Madison invoked the Founders' understanding that a 'limited constitution' is one in which, among other things, congressional 'sovereignty' is 'limited . . . as well with respect to the *means* as to the *objects* of [its] powers; and that to give an extent to the former, superseding the limits to the latter, is in effect to convert a limited into an unlimited Govt.' ([1819] 1999, p. 736).[9]

It seems clear that the Founders' limited government construal is irreconcilable with congressional delegation of 'policy judgment'. While the following examples are not exhaustive, they clearly illustrate that the Supreme Court has, in fact, sanctioned *policymaking* delegations that the Founders would find unacceptable:

- In *Mistretta* v. *United States* (1989), the Court ruled that Congress's 'creation of the U.S. Sentencing Commission – an entity in which federal judges are authorized to act in an executive policymaking capacity – did not violate the independent authority of the judiciary' (Ring, 2004, p. 43). The Court's holding authorized the Commission to develop and promulgate guidelines binding federal judges and limiting their discretion in sentencing criminal defendants. Significantly, the Court stated that delegations may carry with them 'the need to exercise judgment on matters of policy' (Opinion, p. 378).
- The Court has upheld economic regulations of industries in which the administrative agencies acted without the congressional guidance they had requested (*Permian Basin Area Rate Cases* (1968) and *American Trucking Association* v. *Atchison, Topeka & Santa Fe Railroad* (1967)).
- The Court held in *Chevron U.S.A. Inc.* v. *Natural Resources Defense Council, Inc.* (1984) that '[A]n agency to which Congress has delegated *policymaking* responsibilities may, within the limits of that delegation,

properly rely upon the incumbent administration's views of wise policy to inform its judgments' (Opinion, p. 865; emphasis mine).

Whether the *Chevron* Court's substitution of 'policymaking' for 'policy judgment' was meant to suggest a congruence between the two concepts cannot be known with certainty. What *is* clear is that the Founders' understanding of the separation of powers did not contemplate congressional delegation of Congress's legislative or 'policymaking' powers.

If the Supreme Court's 'policy judgment' and 'legislate contingently' conceptions have eroded the separation of powers, the same is true of its 'fill up the details' construction. While, as I have noted, it has insisted that an 'intelligible principle' or 'standard' is a *sine qua non* for 'fill[ing] up the details', the court has consistently found *ambiguous* standards to be constitutionally adequate (see Section 4.2 above).

The constitutional adequacy of ambiguous 'standards' found what may be its most robust expression in *Chevron U.S.A. Inc.* v. *Natural Resources Defense Council, Inc.* (1984). In *Chevron*, the Court advanced a two-part test for reviewing an administrative agency's interpretation of statutes. First, the Court determines whether the statute's provisions speak directly and unambiguously to the question at issue. Second, if the statute is 'silent or ambiguous', the Court determines whether the agency's regulations are 'based on a permissible construction of the statute' (Opinion, p. 843). In Richard Epstein's account:

> It was *Chevron* that inaugurated the principle of high judicial deference to administrative agencies on practically all questions of law. Those agencies – which are nowhere to be found in the original assignment of powers to the legislative, executive, or judicial branches – were allowed to push the law to its limits and beyond. (Levy and Mellor, Foreword, 2008, p. XV)

The judicial deference to which Epstein refers has been so pervasive that 'The only *two* instances in which the Court has found an unconstitutional delegation . . . have involved grants of discretion that the Court found to be unbounded, hence standardless' (Congressional Research Service, 2004, p. 81; emphasis mine).[10] Given the history of the Supreme Court's Legislative Powers or non-delegation jurisprudence I associate myself with the view that '[i]t seems therefore reasonably clear that the Court does not really require much in the way of standards from Congress' (ibid., p. 85).

Finally, I note that, if the Court's deference to Congress's rule-making delegations is congenial to the metastasization of federal regulation the same is true of the justifications proffered for the *existence* of administrative agencies. First, it is recognized that administrative agencies are typically justified by appeal to 'their ability to redress perceived or actual *market failures*: for example, controlling monopoly power, "windfall" profits, or "excessive" competition; or compensating for externalities, inadequate information, or unequal bargaining power' (Uhlmann, 2005, p. 229; emphasis mine). While the reference to 'unequal bargaining power' is evocative of the Progressive movement (see Section 4.1 above), the essential point is that many of the justificatory 'market failures' are either inherently subjective, or invite the application of the economist's decidedly problematic, consequence based, procedurally-detached theory of the state. Given the inherent ambiguities, and given that the economist's theory of the state, social welfare theory, can be used to rationalize all manner of ad hoc market interventions, I argue that 'market failures' cannot, its questionable constitutionality aside, justify the delegation of legislative or judicial powers to administrative agencies.

As we have seen, the need to 'fill up the details' has also been invoked to justify congressional delegation of rule-making authority. The rationale, in turn, is that 'In a complex society, Congress cannot specify every detail of legislative policy. Room must be left for the exercise of discretionary judgment, which means that legislative delegation is inevitable if Congress decides to regulate many subjects extensively' (Uhlmann, 2005, p. 230).

While the growing 'complexity' of society is, in a sense, not in dispute, societal complexity does not have as its corollary that Congress must 'decide to regulate many subjects extensively'. If, given the federal government's limited, enumerated powers, extensive federal regulation is not what the Founders intended (see Chapter 2), it is also clear that it is the *pace of legislation* (Chapter 1), along with the desire simultaneously to receive credit and to shift responsibility, that accounts for Congress's legislative lacunae.

The upshot of all of this is that the Constitution's Legislative Powers or Non-delegation Clause has, over time, been interpreted to mean that virtually any delegation of legislative or judicial power is constitutionally permissible. Thus, if the Supreme Court's General Welfare, Necessary and Proper and Commerce Clause jurisprudence is corrosive of the Constitution's federalism structure, its non-delegation doctrine has eroded the separation of powers.

While it is clear that the growth in the number and variety of administrative agencies would have been alien to the Founder's imagination, the essential point is that the Founders' 'auxiliary precautions' (see Chapter 2) have, over time, become less effective constraints on the narrowly self-interested 'factious behavior' that the Founders sought to restrain. Add to this the roughly concurrent emergence of a politics and an economics of wants and needs (Chapter 5), and the expansion of federal on-, off- and off-off-budget activity (Chapter 1) was all-but-assured.

NOTES

1. See also Section 4.4 below, and Roth (2007, Chapter 8).
2. At issue in *Raich* was California's Compassionate Use Act, voted in by ballot initiative in 1996. While the Supreme Court stipulated that the Act 'authorizes limited marijuana use for medical purposes' (Syllabus, p. 1), Justice Stevens, writing for the 6-3 majority, held that 'It is beyond peradventure that federal power over commerce is "superior to that of the States to provide for the welfare or necessities of their inhabitants", however legitimate or dire the necessities may be' (Opinion, p. 26).
3. In his Dissent Justice Thomas pointed out that 'This Court . . . has casually allowed the Federal Government to strip States of their ability to regulate intrastate commerce – not to mention a host of local activities like mere drug possession, that are not commercial' (p. 14). In Justice Thomas's account, interstate commerce does not contemplate activities like the medicinal use of marijuana: 'Throughout founding-era dictionaries, Madison's notes from the Constitutional Convention, *The Federalist Papers*, and the ratification debates, the term "commerce" is consistently used to mean trade or exchange – not all economic or gainful activity that has some attenuated connection to trade or exchange' (p. 2).
   In her Dissent in *Raich*, Justice O'Connor rejects Justice Stevens' claim 'that congress had a rational basis for believing that failure to regulate the *intrastate* manufacture and possession of marijuana would leave a gaping hole in the [federal] Controlled Substances Act' (p. 19; emphasis mine). In Justice O'Connor's account: 'because . . . medical marijuana users may be limited in number and California's Compassionate Use Act and similar state legislation may well isolate activities relating to medicinal marijuana from the illicit market, the effect of those activities on interstate drug traffic is not self-evidently substantial' (p. 12).
   Equally important, citing James Madison's *Federalist* No. 45, Justice O'Connor emphasizes that 'The powers reserved to the several states will extend to all those objects which, in the ordinary course of affairs, concern the lives, liberties, and properties of the people, and the internal order, improvement, and prosperity of the State' (p. 16). With this in mind, Justice 'O'Connor observes that: 'We enforce the "outer limits" of the Congress' Commerce Clause authority not for their own sake, but to protect historic spheres of state sovereignty from excessive federal encroachments and thereby to maintain the distribution of power fundamental to our federalist system of government' (p. 1).
4. See also Chapter 1. For more on the General Welfare Clause and Congress's taxing power, see Kurland and Lerner (1987b), pp. 407–70.
5. For more on this, see Eastman (2005, pp. 95–6).
6. Other cases include *United States* v. *Wrightwood Dairy Co.* (1942), *NLRB* v. *Reliance Fuel Oil Co.* (1963) and *Hodel* v. *Virginia Surface Mining & Reclamation Association* (1981).
7. See also Chapter 3.
8. For more on *Lopez, Morrison* and *Oregon*, see Roth (2007, Chapter 8).
9. In his *Federalist* No. 78, Hamilton wrote that: 'By a limited constitution I understand one which contains certain specified exceptions to the legislative authority; such for instance as that it shall pass no bills of attainder, no *ex post facto* laws, and the like. Limitations of this kind can be preserved in practice no other way than through the medium of the courts of justice; whose duty it must be to declare all acts contrary to the manifest tenor of the constitution void. Without this, all the reservations of particular rights or privileges would amount to nothing' (Carey and McClellan, 2001, p. 403). For more on this, see Chapter 2 this volume.
10. The two cases are *Panama Refining Co.* v. *Ryan* (1935) and *A.L.A. Schechter Poultry Corp.* v. *United States* (1935).

5. The politics and the economics of wants and needs

5.1 AN OVERVIEW

During the early years of the republic, the United States' political economy, and the public philosophy to which it was conjoined, were reflective of the Founders' vision. Today, that vision has been lost. Sadly, the trajectory of change has been both inconsistent with the Founders' prior ethical commitment to the moral equivalence of persons, and corrosive of their constitutional restraints on self-interested factious behavior. This, in turn, has underwritten an expansion of the scope and reach of federal power and activity that would have found no place in the Founders' imagination (see Chapter 1).

As we saw in Chapter 2, the Founders embraced a theory of the right, the moral equivalence of persons. With this in mind, they emphasized the moral imperative to promote just, in the sense of impartial, institutions. Given their prior ethical commitment, the Founders sought, through a system of constitutional 'auxiliary precautions', to insure what has been called the fair value of political liberty (see Chapter 2). Federalism, the separation of powers and the other constitutional restraints on majoritarian democracy were intended both to constrain discriminatory behavior and to promote respect for the moral law. *Nothing* in the Founders' republican self-government project contemplated either the satisfaction of 'wants and needs' or the achievement of 'distributive' or 'social' justice. What mattered to the Founders was a Constitution that sought to institutionalize impartial procedure, and a post-constitutional politics characterized by impartial, in the sense of non-discriminatory, statutory law.

The Founders' procedurally based, consequence-detached moral and political philosophy was gradually displaced by the embrace of a theory of the good. In this consequence based, procedurally-detached formulation, a political economy animated by the imperative to maximize utility or satisfaction is conjoined to a moral and political philosophy whose focal point is the prerogatives, rights and preferences of a 'transcendental, autonomous self'; a person with no social attachments save those that he has chosen. While a discussion of the logical, empirical and other difficulties that attend this formulation is momentarily deferred, the essential point is this: the Founders codified a Constitution and Bill of Rights whose animating principles included the idea that:

> The enjoyment of rights is inseparable from self-governance, and that means actual representation of those being governed. Those rights might be abridged or qualified in a number of ways, but the only legitimate manner of so doing would be to secure the consent of the holders of those rights. (Kurland and Lerner, 1987a, p. 424)

The rights and self-governance nexus contrasts with the modern view in which freedom, and the rights that determine its distribution, are defined in opposition to self-government. In this formulation rights are antecedent to civil society, and constitute the individual's guarantee against majority rule. A corollary of this is that federalism and the separation of powers '[fade] as a constitutional concern, and freedom comes to depend on rights that enable persons to choose and pursue their own ends'. Precisely because of 'its reliance on rights secured by the government, the [modern] liberal conception of freedom does not depend on dispersed power' (Sandel, 1996, p. 28).[1]

How, then, did we arrive at a paradigm that is irreconcilable with the Founders' republican self-government project, and inimical to the constitutional restraints on narrowly self-interested factious behavior? As we know, the Founders' theory of the right found expression in many ways, including Madison's insistence that 'The apportionment of taxes . . . require[s] the most exact impartiality' (Carey and McClellan, 2001, p. 45), and in the Hamilton–Jefferson debate about the morality and constitutionality of Hamilton's proposal to subsidize domestic manufacturers (see Chapter 2). These and related ideas were embraced during the Jacksonian era. On the one hand, President Jackson shared the Jeffersonian view that justice as impartiality does not require that government address the inequalities that arise from disparate human capital endowments.[2] In his 10 July 1832 Veto Message, Jackson noted that 'Distinctions in society will always exist under every *just* government. Equality of talents, of education, or of wealth cannot be produced by human institutions' (Jackson [1832] 1896, p. 590; emphasis mine). Moreover, Jackson opposed federal support for commerce and industry. Like the Founders, he recognized the danger to republican self-government of factious behavior and embraced the impartial treatment imperative: 'It is to be regretted that the rich and powerful too often bend the acts of government to their selfish purposes. . . If [government] would confine itself to equal protection, and, . . . shower its favors alike on the high and the low, the rich and the poor, it would be an unqualified blessing' (ibid.). Finally, like the Founders, Jackson was sensitive to the impact of economic policies on the moral character of citizens.

The essential point is that, for most of the first half of the nineteenth century, Americans embraced these ideas, along with the notion, often articulated by the Anti-Federalists, that economic arrangements should promote civic virtue.[3] In this Jeffersonian account, small producer-owners were 'free', not only in the sense that they voluntarily engaged in the production of goods and services, but in the sense that they acquired the 'habits and dispositions' that 'equipped them to think as independent citizens capable of sharing in self-government' (Sandel, 1996, p. 169.[4] It was, however, the emergence of 'factory life' and its concomitant, wage labor, that raised the question: is working for a wage consistent with freedom? (ibid., p. 168).

Broadly speaking, during the post-Civil War period, many of its defenders began to argue that wage labor is consistent with freedom, not because it promotes civic virtue, but because it is voluntary. As we have seen, this view found its ultimate expression in the Supreme Court's *Lochner*, *Adair* and *Coppage* holdings (see Chapter 3).

The '*Lochner* Era' is important for at least two reasons. First, as we have seen, the Court's holdings had profound implications for the states' police powers. The Court's expansive reading of the Fourteenth Amendment meant that liberty did not depend, as Madison insisted, on the Constitution's 'auxiliary precautions'. Whereas, from the Founders' perspective, liberty depends upon dispersed power, on federalism and the separation of powers, the *Lochner-Adair-Coppage* holdings asserted, for the first time in US history, that contract and other rights trump the states' police powers. A corollary of this has been that, 'as Madison glimpsed, national power and individual rights would expand together, at the expense of the sovereignty of the states' (Sandel, 1996, p. 39). Second, the Court's holdings served both as a reflection of, and an important catalyst to, the Progressive movement (see Chapter 4). While, in general, Progressive reformers embraced the 'freedom of contract' that the *Lochner* Court affirmed, they insisted that 'true' freedom of contract required both equality of bargaining power and the 'exercise of genuine consent'. Echoing the Dissents to *Lochner* Era holdings (see Chapter 3), Progressives defended legislation 'designed to give laborers some measure of practical independence, and which, if allowed to operate, would put them in a position of reasonable equality with their [employer] masters' (Pound, 1909, pp. 471–2). For its part, the notion of 'genuine consent' was animated by the idea that 'Necessitous men are not, truly speaking, free men, but, to answer a present exigency, will submit to any terms that the crafty may impose upon them' (ibid.). On this logic, the first President of the American Economic Association, Richard Ely, averred that 'While free contract must be the rule, liberty demands the social regulation of many contracts. Regulation of contract conditions means establishing the "rules of the game" for competition' (1914, pp. 731–2). Whatever else is said, it is clear that these ideas informed the work of the 'New Court' (see Chapter 4).

If the 'genuine consent' idea gave rise to the notion that 'liberty demands the social regulation of many classes of contracts', it was also the catalyst to a new understanding of the self. Whereas the Founders imagined that respect for the moral law could be cultivated, and that self-governing individuals could, as Jefferson wrote, overcome 'our propensities to self-gratification in violation of our duties to others' ([1814b] 1984, pp. 1336–7), the *modern* liberal insists that 'government must be neutral on what might be called the question of the good life' (R. Dworkin, 1985, p. 191).[5] In this view:

> Since the citizens of a society differ in their conceptions [of the good life], the government does not treat them as equals if [the government] prefers one conception to another, either because the officials believe that one is intrinsically superior, or because one is held by the more numerous or more powerful group. (Ibid.)

From this perspective, 'equal treatment' requires that government be neutral toward the values its citizens embrace, and that it respect each person's capacity to choose their own ends. This is modern liberalism's 'constitutive political position'; a position that is 'valued for its own sake' (ibid., pp. 184 and 188). As it happens, both the constitutive political position and the positions that are instrumentally important to its achievement, modern liberalism's 'derivative' political positions (ibid., p. 184), involve the 'perfection' of majoritarian democracy and the 'economic market' (ibid., pp. 192–8). On the one hand, because some members of the polity have 'external preferences' against other preferences, modern liberalism insists upon a 'scheme of civil rights whose effect will be to determine those political decisions that are antecedently likely to reflect strong external preferences and to remove those decisions from majoritarian political decisions altogether' (ibid., p. 197). On the other hand, given the 'anti-egalitarian consequences of free enterprise in practice' (ibid., p. 194), modern liberalism endorses 'a scheme of redistribution that leaves [the] pricing system intact but limits at least the inequalities in *welfare* that [the constitutive position] prohibits' (ibid., p. 196; emphasis mine). Finally, given the 'genuine consent' imperative, 'respecting people's capacity to choose their ends mean[s] providing them with the material prerequisites of human dignity, such as food and shelter, education and employment' (Sandel, 1996, p. 201).

It is clear, then, that modern liberalism embraces a consequence based, procedurally-detached political economy. In contrast to Madison's view that 'justice is the end of government' (Carey and McClellan, 2001, p. 271), and that 'that alone is a *just* government which *impartially* secures to every man whatever is his own' (Madison [1792b] 1999, p. 515; emphasis in original; see Chapter 2), the modern liberal insists that, given agents' rights against the state, economic growth, and distributive and 'social' justice are the state's ultimate desiderata. In this account, preference and need satisfaction, and a 'fairer' distribution of income and wealth are instrumentally important to the perfection of the free agency ideal. While it is true that these ideas gesture toward the constitutional jurisprudence of the New Court (see Chapter 4), it is also clear that they underwrite the relentless advance, in disregard of federalism and the separation of powers, of the 'activist state' (see Chapter 1 in this volume).

Finally, I acknowledge that Ronald Dworkin insists that utilitarianism is not constitutive of modern liberalism (1985, pp. 201–2). In fact, it *is* a defining characteristic of its constitutive and derivative political positions. As we shall see, the idea of rights as non-absolute trumps against external preferences is an attempt to perfect both majoritarian democracy and utilitarianism (R. Dworkin, 1978, p. 277). For its part, modern liberalism's impulse to 'perfect' the economic market to compensate for the 'anti-egalitarian consequences of free enterprise in practice' implicates the economist's utilitarian theory of the state, social welfare theory. Utilitarianism is, therefore, both an integral part of modern liberalism's constitutive political position, and instrumental to the achievement of the 'good ends' defined by that position. Consequence based and procedurally-detached, social welfare theory is both institutionless and intendedly value-free. While it is clear that it shares nothing in common with the Founders' political economy (see Chapter 2), the point of immediate interest is that, in modern liberals' hands, social welfare theory can be used to rationalize all manner of 'market interventions' and redistributive schemes. Given the logical, empirical and ontological problems that attend 'scientific' social welfare theory, *all* such interventions must be regarded as ad hoc. Add to this the problems associated with modern liberalism's rights construal and it is possible to question the legitimacy of a significant body of federal on-, off- and off-off-budget activity.

With all of this in mind, the balance of Chapter 5 focuses on a critical appraisal of utilitarian social welfare theory, and of the moral and political philosophy to which it is conjoined, modern liberalism.

5.2   UTILITARIANISM: A PRIMER

Given its pervasive role in modern liberalism's political and moral philosophy, it is appropriate that attention be paid to utilitarianism. I emphasize, first, that utilitarianism is a theory of the good; that utilitarians of every type argue that 'the good [is] equivalent to the desired' (Goodin, 1993, p. 243), and that the good ought always to be promoted (Pettit, 1993, p. 231). Equally important, 'there is nothing in [utilitarian] theory that says that people should have [particular] sorts of preferences'. Rather, utilitarianism 'is just a theory of what follows, *morally*, if people happen to [possess them]. It is good – *good for them* – to have their preferences satisfied, *whatever these preferences might be*' (Goodin, 1993, p. 243; emphasis mine). On some accounts, utilitarianism is associated with equal consideration, or impartiality. Indeed, in Ronald Dworkin's view, 'The utilitarian argument, that a policy is justified if it satisfies more preferences overall, seems . . . to be an egalitarian argument. It seems to observe impartiality' (1978, p. 234). For John Rawls, however, 'The fault of the utilitarian doctrine is that it mistakes impersonality for impartiality' (1971, p. 190). In any case, we know that, for modern liberalism, all preferences are not equal:

> Preference utilitarianism asks [government] officials to attempt to satisfy people's preferences so far as this is possible. But the preferences of an individual for the consequences of a particular policy may be seen to reflect . . . either a *personal* preference for his own enjoyment of some goods and opportunities, or an *external* preference for the assignment of goods and opportunities to others, or both. (R. Dworkin, 1978, p. 234; emphasis in original)

While there is an extensive literature on 'external preferences' or 'goods externalities', that is not my immediate concern. Rather, the essential point is that, for modern liberalism, the 'right of each person to respect and concern as an individual' requires that 'external' or political, altruistic or moralistic preferences be 'bracketed'; that they be excluded from majoritarian deliberation. The claim, in short, is that 'the domination of one set of external preferences, . . . preferences people have about what others shall do or have . . . invades rather than enforces the right of citizens to be treated as equals' (R. Dworkin, 1985, p. 196).[6]

While it is clear that 'bracketing' external preferences would trench upon the states' police powers (see Chapters 3 and 4), the point of immediate interest is that utilitarianism, like the Founders' contractariansim, grounds morality on a particular understanding of self-governance. That said, unlike the Founders, utilitarianism does not seek to promote just, in the sense of impartial, institutions. Rather, for utilitarians, 'the right action is that which maximizes utility (however construed) summed impersonally across all those affected by the action. That is the standard that we are to use, individually, in choosing our own actions'. Moreover, 'That is . . . the standard that public policy-makers are to use when making collective choices impinging on the community as a whole' (Goodin, 1993, p. 245).[7]

It is this form of preference utilitarianism that finds expression in the economist's theory of the state, and in modern liberalism's constitutive and derivative political positions. That said, immediate interest centers on the incompatibility of utilitarianism and the Founders' republican self-government project (see Chapter 2 in this volume).

As I have emphasized, the United States' Founders embraced a prior ethical commitment to the moral equivalence of persons. The associated impartiality imperative, an idea drawn from moral philosophy, has an analogue in political philosophy. The principle of equal political participation 'requires that all citizens have an equal right to take part in, and to determine the outcome of, the constitutional process that establishes the laws with which they are to comply'. So it is that:

> Justice as [impartiality] begins with the idea that where common principles are necessary and to everyone's advantage, they are to be worked out from the viewpoint of a suitably defined initial situation of equality in which each person is fairly represented. The principle of [equal political] participation transfers this notion from the [Kantian] original position to the constitution as the highest-order system of social rules for making rules. (Rawls, 1971, pp. 221–2)

While the 'original position' to which Rawls refers is discussed elsewhere (Chapter 2, Sections 2.3 and 2.4), the essential point is that the principle of equal political participation implies a constitutional imperative. Among other things, 'firm constitutional protections' must be provided 'for certain liberties, particularly freedom of speech and assembly, and liberty to form political associations' (Rawls, 1971, pp. 222–3). If this calls to mind Americans' English inheritance and the Founders' constitutional project, the essential point is that the principle of equal political participation implies 'some form of constitutional democracy' (Rawls [1989] 1999, p. 526).[8] Moreover, the principle of equal political participation requires that the Constitution 'be framed so that of all the feasible just arrangements, it is the one more likely than any other to result in a *just and effective system of legislation*' (Rawls, 1971, p. 221; emphasis mine). In short, the moral equivalence of persons demands that the constitutional rules of the game are consonant with the passage of just, in the sense of impartial, statutory law. This, I suggest, is the essence of the Founders' constitutional project.

In contrast, because it is outcomes based and procedurally-detached, utilitarianism is *incapable* of addressing the institutional imperatives that animated the Founders' constitutional enterprise. While it is true that rule-utilitarianism endorses rules that can be justified on utilitarian grounds, utilitarian arguments can always trump the rules. Whereas rule-utilitarianism '*limits* the application of the standard of utility to rules or social institutions and *requires compliance* with rules . . . having the requisite utilitarian justification' (Lyons, 1982, p. 128; emphasis in original), the rule-utilitarian must confront a logical conundrum: 'If a utilitarian believes that certain rules are justified on utilitarian grounds, [he does not] *contradict* himself by supposing that direct utilitarian arguments for deviating from the rules may be entertained'. Importantly, the utilitarian 'cannot regard the morally defensible rights under *utilitarian* institutions as having moral force' (ibid., p. 129; emphasis in original).[9]

On utilitarian logic, then, there can be no duty either to respect rights or to promote just, in the sense of impartial, institutions. Rather, there is only a duty to promote good outcomes. Moreover, whereas the Founders' prior ethical commitment to the moral equivalence of persons finds institutional expression in 'some form of constitutional democracy', the utilitarian justification of democratic institutions is necessarily contingent: '[T]he intellectual foundations of democratic institutions in [the utilitarian] perspective are weaker by an order of magnitude than those in the contractarian perspective'. This follows from the fact that 'Democratic institutions stand or fall [from the utilitarian perspective] on their alleged superiority in generating the attainment of an independently existing "public good". The whole defense is necessarily based on [economic] efficiency' (Brennan and Buchanan [1985a] 2000, p. 49).

It follows from all of this that, on utilitarian logic, both constitutional and post-constitutional politics are outcomes based and procedurally-detached. If this means that the only dimension of moral appraisal of political decisions is a comparative assessment of their consequences (Davis, 1993, p. 205), it also means that, rather than seeking to promote just institutions, the utilitarian imperative is to promote good outcomes. Utilitarians must, therefore, regard democratic institutions as merely instrumentally important rather than intrinsically valuable.

It should be clear, then, that nothing in the utilitarian enterprise could find expression in the Founders' procedurally based, consequence-detached republican self-government project. The problem is that utilitarianism is instrumentally important both to the economist's theory of the state, and to the public philosophy to which it is conjoined, modern liberalism.

5.3   ENDS OVER MEANS

Modern liberalism, like utilitarianism, is defined in opposition to the Founders' republican self-government project. The Founders insisted that the rights of morally equivalent persons are the result of path-dependent historical processes – the 'English inheritance' – and of majoritarian deliberation. For modern liberals, rights are antecedent to civil society. The Founders insisted that rights protection depends upon institutional constraints; upon federalism, the separation of powers and the other constitutional 'auxiliary precautions'. For modern liberals, rights protection requires that moralistic, altruistic and other 'external' preferences be 'remove[d] from majoritarian political institutions altogether' (R. Dworkin, 1985, p. 197). Given their prior ethical commitment to the moral equivalence of persons, the Founders embraced and promoted a *procedural* theory of justice as impartiality. For the Founders justice as impartiality implies a procedural imperative: both the Constitution and post-constitutional statutory law must be impartial, and the greatest possible equal political participation must be promoted. For Dworkin's part, '[T]he [modern] liberal . . . finds the [economic] market defective principally because it allows *morally irrelevant* differences, like differences in talent to affect [income and wealth] distribution, and, therefore considers that those who have less talent, as the market judges talent, have a *right* to some form of redistribution in the name of justice' (ibid., p. 199, emphasis mine).

While I shall return to these themes below, the point of immediate interest is that the modern liberal paradigm informs both federal policy (see Chapter 1) and modern constitutional jurisprudence (see Chapter 4):

> What seems increasingly clear in recent decades is that the [constitutional] revisionists . . . have given primacy to *ends* over *means*; that is, their commitment to majority rule is secondary to their commitment to democratic ends which, to a great extent, come down to *egalitarianism* mixed with *virtually unbridled liberty*. (Carey, 1995, p. 4; emphasis mine)

The passage is clearly evocative of Madison's concern with 'legislative encroachments' (see Chapter 2). That said, it is modern liberalism's peculiar understanding of the transcendental autonomous self that animates the 'revisionists':

> The *autonomous individual* . . . is viewed apart from the complex organic whole of society. His duties and responsibilities to others . . . are almost nonexistent. Beyond this, the individual becomes a moral universe to himself . . . . Thus, the individual is not subordinate to any higher or transcendental order not of his own making or derived from his own private stock of reason. (Carey, 1995, pp. 187–8; emphasis mine)[10]

If, as I suggest, it is this understanding of the autonomous individual that accounts for modern liberalism's generalized institutional skepticism, it also accounts for the failure to respect the Constitution's restraints on majoritarian democracy in general, and the states' police powers in particular. Yet, it is the transcendental autonomous self that animates the United States' public philosophy, 'the political theory implicit in our practices, the assumptions about citizenship and freedom that inform [American] public life' (Sandel, 1996, p. 4).

While it is clear that modern liberalism's autonomous individual offers a 'liberating vision' and makes a case for 'equal respect' (ibid., p. 12) it is also clear that the 'liberating vision' cannot be reconciled with the Founders' view of man as 'formed by society' and constrained by the 'justice of harmony and obedience' (see Chapter 2). For its part, modern liberalism's equal respect construal constitutes a distortion of the Founders' impartiality imperative (see Chapter 2). Whereas the Founders insisted that respect for the *duty* to treat others as ends rather than means must be cultivated, modern liberalism's disproportionate individualism is irreconcilable with the 'moral community' that is a *sine qua non* for republican self-government: 'A moral community exists among a set of persons to the extent that individual members of the group identify with a collective unit, a community, rather than conceive of themselves to be independent, isolated individuals' (Buchanan [1981] 2001, p. 188).

If a moral community, a 'national character', is what Washington and the Founders had in mind (Washington [1796b] 1997, p. 952), they would also associate themselves with Jefferson's view that 'Self-love . . . is no part of morality' ([1814b] 1984, p. 1336). Given their prior ethical commitment to the moral equivalence of persons, they would surely be concerned that, 'For several decades . . . [the United States'] moral order has been in the process of erosion. Larger and larger numbers of persons seem to become moral anarchists; they seem to be losing a sense of mutual respect one for another along with any feeling of obligation to abide by generalizable rules and codes of conduct' (Buchanan [1981] 2001, p. 197).

Whatever else is said, Buchanan's observation calls to mind Madison's remarks before the Virginia Ratifying Convention: 'Is there no virtue among us? If there be not . . . No theoretical checks – no form of government can render us secure. To suppose that any form of government will secure liberty and happiness without any virtue in the people, is a chimerical idea' ([1788b] 1999, p. 398).

The erosion of the United States' moral order is, I suggest, a reflection of the institutional skepticism that is characteristic of modern liberalism. I emphasize, first, that the transcendental, autonomous individual cannot, logically, be influenced by what Friedrich Hayek has called 'the process of cultural transmission' (Hayek [1970] 1997, p. 323). Equally important, agency requires immersion in contingent circumstance. In effect, the pretense of transcendental autonomy ignores a fundamental logical conundrum: if I am truly both autonomous and freed from any social bonds I have no motive to act (Scruton, 2002, p. 189). Most important, the transcendental autonomous person of the modern liberalism's imagination must regard inherited 'rules of conduct', whether formal or informal, as intrusive; as what Mill called 'the despotism of custom' ([1859] 2000, p. 7). This, despite the fact that the 'wisdom of our ancestors' is conducive to 'a condition in which individuals are able . . . to form expectations concerning the conduct of others' (Hayek [1970] 1997, p. 323).

In sum, modern liberalism promotes an understanding of the human agent and, it should be said, of 'citizenship' with which the United States' Founders cannot be associated. Moreover, in their relentless pursuit of 'autonomy' and of 'moral and political space' modern liberals do not simply define liberty in opposition to republican self-government. In their insistence that rights are antecedent to, rather than the result of, self-government, they deny Americans' 'English inheritance' and undermine both federalism and the separation of powers. Finally, modern liberalism denies the role and importance of the received 'social knowledge' that both identifies man as a social creature and informs his moralistic, altruistic and political 'external' preferences. If this denies a fundamental feature of observable reality, it is also corrosive of the states' police powers.

5.4   THE NEW POLITICAL MORALITY

I emphasize, first, that the ideas that animate *modern* liberalism, equality, natural rights and the transcendental autonomous self, find expression neither in *classical* liberalism nor in the Founders' moral and political philosophy.[11] For classical liberals, the imperatives are to respect the individual agent's autonomy, the institutionalization of a strong system of property rights, the voluntary exchange of comestibles and productive inputs and prohibitions against fraud and abuse. For the Founders, the moral equivalence of persons demands that the greatest possible equal political participation be promoted, and that the Constitution and statutory law both respect and promote the moral law (see Chapter 2). *Nothing* in the Founders' project contemplated the exclusion from democratic, majoritarian deliberation of moralistic, altruistic or political 'external' preferences. In contrast, modern liberalism's rights construal is inexorably bound up with its peculiar understanding of 'equal treatment':

> [Majoritarian] democracy is justified because it enforces the right of each person to respect and concern as an individual; but in practice the decisions of a democratic majority may often violate that right, according to the liberal theory of

what the right requires. Suppose a legislature elected by a majority decides to make criminal some act (like speaking in favor of an unpopular political position, or participating in eccentric sexual practices) . . . because the majority disapproves of those views or that sexual morality. The political decision, in other words, reflects not just some accommodation of *personal* preferences of everyone . . . but the domination of one set of *external* preferences, that is, preferences people have about what others shall do or have. The decision invades rather than enforces the right of citizens to be treated as equals. (R. Dworkin, 1985, p. 196; emphasis in original)

If, as I suggest, this understanding of 'equal treatment' and of rights against 'external' preferences is corrosive of the states' police powers, it also underwrites the expansion of the federal enterprise. What is in any case clear is that modern liberalism's contingent defense of majoritarian democracy is derivative of the idea that individuals possess rights, *antecedent* to civil society, against 'preferences people have about what others shall do or have'. Given their view that law should both reflect and promote virtue, and that the maximum possible *equal political participation* must be promoted, modern liberalism's understanding of rights would be unacceptable to the Founders. The same is true of modern liberalism's equal treatment imperative.

Whereas the Founders' prior ethical commitment to the moral equivalence of persons implies a *procedural* imperative, modern liberalism takes the equal treatment imperative to mean that government must 'be neutral on what might be called the question of the good life' (R. Dworkin, 1985, p. 191). It follows that modern liberalism's equal treatment construal, a concept of the right, requires that only *strictly personal* 'wants and needs' be satisfied, a concept of the good.[12] If, as I shall argue, this means that it deploys an internally inconsistent hybrid moral theory, the point of immediate interest is that modern liberalism is not reconcilable with the Founders' insistence upon the reciprocal relationship between law and morality (see Chapter 2).

It is against this background that modern liberalism rules out 'the state's use of coercion to make people morally better' (G. Dworkin, 1995, p. 363). So it is that modern liberalism insists that the state's authority and legitimacy depend upon an 'endorsement constraint':

> [Ronald Dworkin] develops an argument against state paternalism which . . . relies on the idea that the good life for persons is necessarily one that they create for themselves, that is lived from the inside as opposed to led from the outside. He argues for what Kymlicka has called the 'endorsement constraint'. (Ibid.)

For modern liberalism, neither constitutional nor statutory law 'can make a person's life better against his opinion that it does not' (R. Dworkin,

1991, p. 50). On this logic, and in clear opposition to the Founders' view, constitutional and statutory laws that reflect and promote preferences 'about what others shall do or have' are both violative of autonomy and corrosive of the state's authority and legitimacy.[13]

The differences between the Founders' moral and political philosophy and that of modern liberalism are revealed in R. Dworkin's answer to the rhetorical question: 'What does it mean for the government to treat its citizens as equals? . . . as free, or as independent, or with equal dignity'. Dworkin suggests that the question may be answered in 'two fundamentally different ways': 'The first supposes that government must be neutral on what might be called the question of the good life. The second supposes that government cannot be neutral on that question, because it cannot treat its citizens as equal human beings without a theory of what human beings ought to be' (R. Dworkin, 1985, p. 191).

Whereas Dworkin avers that modern liberalism 'takes as its constitutive political morality the first conception of morality' (ibid., p. 192), it is the second that captures the Founders' view (see Chapter 2). As it happens, Dworkin provides a thought experiment that brings the differences into stark relief.

Suppose that a liberal is asked to found a new state; that he is required to 'dictate [the new state's] constitution and fundamental institutions'. In particular, 'He must propose a general theory of political distribution, that is, *a theory of how whatever the community has to assign, by way of goods or resources or opportunities, should be assigned*' (ibid.; emphasis mine). If the Founders would be appalled at the prospect of a 'general theory of *political distribution*', a theory about 'how whatever the community has to *assign . . . should be assigned*', they would surely reject modern liberalism's 'principle of rough equality'. In Dworkin's view, the liberal founder of a new state 'will arrive initially at something like this principle of rough equality: resources and opportunities should be distributed, so far as possible, equally' (ibid.; emphasis mine). If, as I insist, nothing in the Founders' procedurally based, consequence-detached republican self-government project contemplates a commitment to state-sponsored 'resources and opportunities' redistribution schemes, it is equally clear that the Founders would not countenance the 'bracketing' of individuals' 'external' moralistic, altruistic and political preferences. In contrast, Dworkin insists that, because 'citizens have different theories of the good and hence different preferences':

> The liberal, as lawgiver . . . needs mechanisms to satisfy the principle of equal treatment in spite of these disagreements. He will decide that there are no better mechanisms available, as general political institutions, than the two main

institutions of our own political economy: the economic market, for decisions about what goods shall be produced and how they shall be distributed, and representative democracy, for collective decisions about what conduct shall be prohibited or regulated. (Ibid., pp. 193–4)

It is clear, then, that the 'economic market' and representative democracy are modern liberalism's key 'derivative political positions'; positions 'that are valued as strategies, as means of achieving the constitutive political positions' (ibid., pp. 183–4). However, given the 'anti-egalitarian consequences of free enterprise in practice' (ibid., p. 194), and given that individuals possess 'external preferences . . . about what others shall do or have' (ibid., p. 196), the 'liberal lawgiver' will seek to perfect both the market economy and majoritarian democracy.

Implicit in all of this is the presumption that a 'mixed economic system' can, through appropriate government-directed redistributive policies, eliminate the 'forbidden inequalities'. Yet Dworkin emphasizes that the 'liberal lawgiver . . . faces a difficult task':

His conception of equality requires an economic system that produces certain inequalities (those that reflect the true differential costs of goods and opportunities) but not others (those that follow from differences in ability, inheritance, and so on). The market produces both the required and the *forbidden inequalities*, and there is no alternative system that can be relied upon to produce the former without the latter. (Ibid., pp. 195–6; emphasis mine)

I emphasize, first, that the idea of 'forbidden inequalities' would be alien to the Founders' imagination. Thomas Jefferson's view is heuristic:

To take from one, because it is thought that his own industry and that of his fathers has acquired too much, in order to spare to others, who, or whose fathers have not exercised equal industry and skill, is to violate arbitrarily the first principle of association, 'the *guarantee* to every one of a free exercise of his industry, and the fruits acquired by it'. ([1816a] 1987, p. 573; emphasis in original)

It is significant that, immediately after his invocation of the 'first principle of association', Jefferson adds this: 'If the overgrown wealth of an individual be deemed dangerous to the State, *the best corrective is the law of equal inheritance to all in equal degree*' (ibid.; emphasis mine). While this is evocative of the generality or impartiality constraint discussed in Chapter 2, the point of immediate interest is that, in his adumbration of the perfectibility of the 'economic market', Dworkin invokes utilitarian social welfare theory, the economist's theory of the state (Brennan, 1995, p. 142).

Central to social welfare theory are its two 'fundamental welfare theorems'. The first theorem asserts that a perfectly competitive system will automatically move to a first-best Pareto-optimal or 'efficient' outcome. The second theorem indicates that, no matter to which point on the efficiency or welfare frontier a perfectly competitive system is impelled, a 'socially desired' distribution can be achieved by appeal to a system of 'lump sum' taxes and subsidies. While a critical appraisal of the theory is momentarily deferred, I emphasize that lump-sum taxes and subsidies are those that do not affect relative product and input prices. In light of this, it is significant that, because the 'economic market' produces both 'the required and the forbidden inequalities', 'The [modern] liberal must be tempted . . . to a reform of the market through *a scheme of redistribution that leaves its pricing system relatively intact* but sharply limits, at least, the inequalities in *welfare* that his [equal treatment] principle prohibits' (R. Dworkin, 1985, p. 196; emphasis mine).

Whatever else is said, Dworkin's invocation of 'efficiency', of 'welfare' and, implicitly, of lump-sum taxes and subsidies means that utilitarian social welfare theory is instrumentally important to the achievement of modern liberalism's constitutive equal treatment position. If this outcomes based 'utilitarian connection' means that it is irreconcilable with the Founders' procedurally based, consequence-detached republican self-government project, it also means that modern liberalism must confront fundamental logical, empirical and ontological problems (see Sections 5.5 through 5.8 below).

It is significant, then, that Dworkin's 'general theory of rights,' modern liberalism's second derivative political position, is an attempt to perfect *both* majoritarian democracy and utilitarianism:

> The concept of an individual political right . . . is a response to the philosophical defects of a utilitarianism that counts external preferences and the practical impossibility of a utilitarianism that does not. It allows us to enjoy the institutions of political democracy, which enforce overall or unrefined utilitarianism, and yet protect the fundamental right of citizens to equal concern and respect by prohibiting decisions that seem, antecedently, likely to have been reached by virtue of the external components of the preferences democracy reveals. (R. Dworkin, 1978, p. 277)[14]

Thus, whereas modern liberalism insists that moralistic and other 'external' preferences must *not* inform political decisions, its political morality requires that the autonomous individual's strictly personal preferences be satisfied; that these preferences represent the good to be promoted by public policy (R. Dworkin, 1985, p. 197).

If, as I have suggested, the Founders would insist that moralistic, altruistic and other 'external' preferences *must* enjoy a reciprocal relationship with constitutional and statutory law, they would also reject the idea that 'rights' depend upon a myopic appreciation of contingent circumstance. They would not countenance the idea that 'The scheme of rights necessary [to remove external preferences from majoritarian institutions] will depend on general facts about the prejudices and other external preferences of the majority at any given time' (ibid.). This, however, does not exhaust the difficulties associated with modern liberalism's 'utilitarian connection'. The fundamental logical problem is that modern liberalism is a hybrid moral theory.[15] On the one hand, because it assigns an instrumental role to rights, it incorporates elements of right-based moral theories. On the other hand, because it incorporates utilitarian social welfare theory it is a goal-based moral theory. It is sufficient for the moment to emphasize that insufficient attention has been paid to the irreconcilability of right- and goal-based moral theories and, therefore, to the logical opposition between utilitarianism and modern liberalism. While these ideas are more fully developed below, I turn next to the economist's utilitarian theory of the state.

5.5   ENTER THE ECONOMISTS

The economist's approach to government finds expression in the normative use of utilitarian social welfare theory. Economists identify 'welfare' or the 'public good' with utility (Warke, 2000, p. 374), and whereas the father of utilitarianism, Jeremy Bentham, contemplated constitutional reforms intended to ensure that 'utilitarian processes would prevail in the public arena' (ibid., p. 379), social welfare theory is institutionless. Finally, while utilitarianism is understood to be a part of the corpus of moral philosophy, social welfare theory is *intendedly* value-free.

It should be clear that there are no elements of correspondence between consequence based, procedurally-detached social welfare theory and the Founders' republican self-government project.[16] This conclusion is reinforced when account is taken of the distinction between economic and political efficiency, and between distributional 'equity' and justice as impartiality. On the one hand, the Founders sought to promote *political* efficiency, the minimization, through formal and informal institutional restraints, of the corrosive effects of narrowly self-interested 'factious' behavior.[17] On the other hand, social welfare theory's practitioners, both economists and politicians, understand *economic* efficiency to consist in first-best, Pareto-optimal *outcomes*. Moreover, whereas the Founders' project was animated by a Smithian/Kantian, procedurally based justice as impartiality imperative, social welfare theory's adherents understand the promotion of distributional 'equity' to consist in the reconciliation of outcomes based 'competitive' and 'ethical' equilibria. Because social welfare theory's normative use depends upon two theoretical constructs I shall consider them in turn.

The efficiency or welfare frontier embodies the technological and other constraints on the perfectly competitive economic system. The frontier is determinate, given the behavioral and technological assumptions that define the theory's frictionless decision environment. Central to all of this is *Homo economicus* or economic man. Autonomous, atomistic, narrowly self-interested and classically rational, economic man is assumed to be a constrained utility maximizer. Whereas the Founders regarded preference and value structures as mutable, and therefore endogenously determined, social welfare theory assumes that economic man's consistently ordered preferences are both exogenously determined and stable, and defined on goods and services whose technical, aesthetic and property rights characteristics are known with certainty. For their part, producers are assumed to employ the only output-maximizing technical alternatives available. Finally, classical or impersonal and instantaneous contracting proceeds on the assumption that instrumentally important property and exchange rights are unattenuated.[18] The duties correlative to property and exchange rights are therefore implicitly assumed to be respected. Given this assumption, both ex ante and ex post transaction costs are zero.

Given these analytically convenient, but patently unrealistic simplifying assumptions, the achievement of first-best Paretian optima or points on the efficiency frontier requires the satisfaction of three marginal equivalences or 'Paretian conditions'. As it happens, a defining characteristic of the long-run perfectly competitive equilibrium is that it is Pareto optimal. So it is that, given a resource endowment, the fixity of product and input prices ensures the satisfaction of the three Paretian conditions and, therefore, the attainment of a unique 'competitive equilibrium'.

It is on this logic that the theory's first fundamental welfare theorem asserts that a perfectly competitive system will *automatically* move to a first-best Pareto-optimal or 'efficient' competitive equilibrium. It is in this sense that outcomes based *economic* efficiency becomes an instrument of policy appraisal. For economists and their politician-clients – represented in the theory as 'the benevolent despot' and 'the omniscient economist' – violation of one or more of the Paretian conditions constitutes 'market failure'. This, in turn, is taken to be justificatory of outcomes based public policy intervention.

As has been emphasized (in Section 5.4), the second fundamental welfare theorem indicates that, no matter which competitive equilibrium is achieved, a 'socially desired' or 'ethical equilibrium' can be attained by appeal to a system of 'lump-sum' taxes and subsidies. The essential idea is that 'movements along the [efficiency] frontier . . . are secured by redistributions . . . which do not destroy the [three] marginal equivalences' (Graaff, 1967, p. 63). While the 'practicability of lump-sum redistributions' is itself a profound question – in fact, they are *not* 'practicable' – the key point is that the achievement of 'competitive' and 'ethical' equilibria is dependent upon the *existence* of a single-valued efficiency frontier and a single-valued, consistently ordered social welfare function. As we shall see, once account is taken of fundamental features of observable reality, neither condition can be met. It follows that, while the economist's 'scientific' approach to public policy appraisal can be used to rationalize any desired market intervention or redistribution scheme, *any* social welfare theory-animated government intervention must be regarded as ad hoc.

5.6   SOME MORAL AND POLITICAL PROBLEMS

As we have seen (in Section 5.4), utilitarianism cannot respect the moral force of rights.[19] The problem for utilitarian social welfare theory and, therefore, for modern liberalism, is that right- and goal-based theories are irreconcilable:

> Utilitarian arguments for institutional design (the arguments that utilitarians might use in favor of establishing or maintaining certain legal rights) do not logically or morally exclude direct utilitarian arguments concerning the exercise of, or interference with, such rights. As a consequence, evaluation of conduct from a utilitarian standpoint is dominated by direct utilitarian arguments and therefore ignores the moral force of justified legal rights. (Lyons, 1982, p. 113)

Reduced to its essentials, the problem is that, in a utilitarian framework, utility trumps rights. As Almond has observed, '[Rights] appear to be unacceptable to utilitarians since they impede the unfettered pursuit of the *social good*' (1993, p. 266; emphasis mine).[20] The problem for politicians and their economist-advisers is that this fundamental, logical conundrum calls into question both the existence of, and the path to, the notional efficiency frontier. This, in turn, calls into question *economic* efficiency, the only standard of normative appraisal to which social welfare theory gives rise.

Paradoxically, while it cannot, logically, respect the moral force of rights, *respect* for rights poses a different problem for utilitarian social welfare theory. If, as we know they do, individuals possess 'meddlesome' or 'nosy' preferences, and minimal privacy rights *are* respected, the 'impossibility of the Paretian liberal' militates against the use of a social welfare function as an interest-aggregation decision mechanism (Sen, 1995. p. 13).[21] When considered in concert with Arrow's Possibility Result (1951, pp. 24–31) and Buchanan's 'ontological objection' (1954, p. 116), it is clear that neither the notional idea of 'social preference' nor the 'ethical equilibrium' has an operational counterpart.

In the face of these logical conundrums, either modern liberals and social welfare theorists must argue that the rights that they regard as important are morally exigent in themselves and reject the economic efficiency standard, or they must embrace the economic efficiency standard and deny the moral force of rights.[22]

Rights, of course, are not the only dimension of moral appraisal. Given modern liberalism's commitment to the equal treatment imperative, and given social welfare theory's instrumental role in modern liberalism's political morality, the question is, can social welfare theory accommodate any plausible theory of justice?

Given the irreconcilability of utilitarianism and respect for rights, we know that neither the economists who deploy social welfare theory nor their politician-clients can, in the manner of libertarians, regard justice as respect for rights (Nozick, 1974, pp. 150–53). That said, I emphasize that social welfare theory does not deploy an explicit definition of justice. The theory addresses neither the procedural nor the distributive justice of 'competitive equilibria'. The same is true of the initial resource endowments that, along with relative prices, determine the unique, first-best Paretian allocation.

Setting aside the indeterminacy of the efficiency frontier and of the social welfare function, the question becomes, what is the moral content of the 'ethical' equilibrium? I emphasize, first, that preference satisfaction may not provide an adequate conception of individual or 'social' welfare. Preferences may be based upon malign, contestable, false, or idiosyncratic beliefs. Moreover, there may be circumstances in which preferences may have to be 'laundered' before they may be accorded moral weight (Hausman and McPherson, 1993, pp. 690–91). Given this understanding of observable reality, the moral weight of the ethical equilibrium may be called into question. Second, it is clear that distributive and 'social' justice are outcomes based or consequentialist. It follows that utilitarian social welfare theory is not reconcilable with the two theories of procedural justice that have been characterized as the 'leading contenders' (Barry, 1989, p. XIII). The first characterizes justice as mutual advantage (Roth, 2007, pp. 65–7), while the second, embraced by the Founders, regards justice as impartiality. Suffice it to say that, because it is consequence based and procedurally-detached, social welfare theory can accommodate neither of the contending contractarian theories of justice. While it is clear that nothing in the mutual advantage approach suggests that particular outcomes ought to be promoted, it is equally clear that the Founders' justice as impartiality construal is relentlessly non-consequentialist and anti-utilitarian (see Chapter 2).

While social welfare theory can accommodate neither the libertarian nor a procedural theory of justice, it *can* accommodate an end-state or time-slice theory of justice: 'Welfare economics is the theory of current time-slice principles of justice. The subject is conceived as operating on matrices representing only current information about distribution' (Nozick, 1974, p. 154). The essential point is that end-state or time-slice theories of justice are unhistoric. This, it is clear, is a defining characteristic of social welfare theory. The theory addresses neither the morality of the initial resource endowment nor the property and exchange rights that, along with relative product and input prices, determine a 'competitive equilibrium'. Moreover, the implicit assumption that structurally identical income or 'welfare' distributions are equally just is a logical corollary of social welfare theory's utilitarian ontology. On utilitarian logic, 'Two distributions are structurally identical if they present the same profile, but perhaps have different persons occupying the . . . slots. My having ten and you having five, and my having five and you having ten are structurally identical distributions' (ibid.). If, as Rawls suggests, this indifference is reflective of utilitarians' propensity to mistake impersonality for impartiality (1971, p. 190), the essential point is that the theory cannot *justify* this view. Finally, as Nozick has suggested, a time-slice theory of justice cannot tell the whole story about distributive shares.

In sum, utilitarian social welfare theory can accommodate neither the moral force of rights nor any plausible theory of justice. Equally important, the only standard of moral appraisal to which the theory gives rise, outcomes based and procedurally-detached economic efficiency, is itself indeterminate (see Section 5.8 below). If it is therefore clear that the theory cannot be instrumental to the achievement of modern liberalism's constitutive political position, it is equally clear that it is antithetical to the Founders' republican self-government project. All of this notwithstanding, the theory's 'scientific' pretensions (see again, Section 5.8) enable economists and their politician-clients to rationalize all manner of federal on-, off- and off-off budget policies.

The paucity of the theory's empirical content is revealed once account is taken of social welfare theory's peculiar, truncated understanding of 'government': a 'benevolent despot', informed by an 'omniscient being – the observing economist – who possesses whatever information we may require about tastes, [production] techniques, the future, and anything else' (Graaff, 1967, p. 13), engages in the single-minded pursuit of the supraindividual, socially desired 'ethical optimum' (p. 70). While it is clear that the 'omniscient being – observing economist' construal is intended to serve as a simplifying 'expository device' (p. 13), it is apparent that a patently unrealistic assumption has, in some hands, become a presumptive description of reality. While the 'benevolent despot' formulation has, appropriately, been characterized as a romanticized view of politics, the benevolent despot is best understood as a bifurcated man. Whereas the theory assumes that he is narrowly self-interested in his private activity, the implicit assumption is that he 'suppresses these motives and brings out the more "noble" ones in his political activity' (Buchanan [1962b] 1999, pp. 68–9). It is perhaps sufficient to note that the '"benevolent despot" model of government . . . is hopelessly at odds with assumptions made elsewhere in economics about human motives and social motivations' (Brennan, 1995, p. 147). If social welfare theory's romanticized view of politics ignores the narrow self-interest that animates rent seeking, it is also fundamentally at odds with the Founders' understanding of post-constitutional politics, and with their appreciation of the need for both formal and informal institutional constraints on discriminatory, factious behavior.

The differences between the Founders' political economy and the economist's theory of the state are both profound and revealing. At the most rudimentary level, economic man's exogenously determined, intertemporally stable, and narrowly self-interested preference structure can accommodate neither the intervention of social norms nor the cultivation of respect for the moral law. Moreover, because they embrace utilitarian impersonality, social welfare theorists cannot logically accommodate the Founders' Smithian/Kantian/Rawlsian impartiality imperative. Equally important, if utilitarian social welfare theorists can neither accommodate, nor assess the political efficiency of, the Founders' constitutional 'auxiliary precautions', they must confront a logical conundrum: on the one hand, in their utilitarian framework, outcomes based economic efficiency is the only dimension of moral appraisal available. On the other hand, nothing in the utilitarian framework justifies respect for rights or for other institutional restraints on utility maximizing behavior. If this means that federalism and the separation of powers can always be trumped by utilitarian considerations, it also means that the imperative to promote just, in the sense of impartial institutions is alien to the social welfare theorist's project. Finally, as utilitarians, social welfare theorists, like modern liberals, can provide only a contingent defense of majoritarian democracy. This would surely give the Founders pause.

5.7   MORE ON RIGHTS AND 'SOCIAL JUSTICE'

I have emphasized that Ronald Dworkin's explanation of the values that undergird modern liberalism's natural rights construal relies upon the individual's fundamental right to equal treatment. And central to this paradigm is the idea that individuals possess natural rights, antecedent to civil society, as non-absolute trumps against welfarist calculations informed by external preferences (Waldron, 1995b, p. 582).

Consider, first, that however they are construed, modern liberalism's transcendental, autonomous self has no motive to respect institutions generally and rights in particular (see Section 5.3 above). If, as I suggest, this means that modern liberalism is internally inconsistent, its 'utilitarian connection' compounds the problem. While it is clear that utilitarians cannot respect the moral force of rights, account should be taken of Jeremy Bentham's ontological objection to rights generally, and to natural rights in particular. In Bentham's utilitarian account, 'The language of natural rights . . . "is from beginning to end so much flat assertion: it lays down as a fundamental and inviolable principle whatever is in dispute"' (ibid., p. 581).[23]

Bentham's *utilitarian* objection to natural rights notwithstanding, 'the claim to "natural rights" has never been quite defeated' (MacDonald [1947–8] 1995, p. 21). As is well known, the claim that rights are antecedent to civil society is associated with John Locke. In his account, '"natural" rights attach, by virtue of his reason, to every man much as do his arms and legs. He carries them about with him from one society to another' (ibid., p. 27). Yet, while it is true that the natural rights claim 'has never quite been defeated', it is recognized that the natural rights doctrine 'has seemed particularly vulnerable to ethical skepticism'. As Jeremy Waldron has emphasized, 'The idea of *natural* rights is seen as a particularly glaring example of the "Naturalistic Fallacy", purporting to derive certain norms or evaluations from descriptive premises about human nature'. Given these epistemological difficulties, 'it becomes important, in the area of rights as elsewhere, for philosophers to identify clearly the deep assumptions on which their theories depend' (1995a, p. 3; emphasis in original). Unfortunately for modern liberalism, the 'deep assumptions' upon which its rights as trumps theory is based reduce to a truncated image of Kantian autonomy. That image, in turn, is logically incompatible with rights protection, *however* rights are construed. The question, then, is not whether the rights that modern liberalism asserts are 'natural' rights. The fundamental question is, can modern liberals protect the rights that they regard as instrumentally important or intrinsically valuable? Clearly, the answer is no.

But what of the Founders? Clearly, they did not regard rights as antecedent to civil society (see Chapter 2). At least on one account, an account with which the Founders would agree, 'Assertions about natural rights . . . are assertions of what *ought to be* as the result of human choice' (MacDonald [1947–8] 1995, p. 34; emphasis mine). Granting this, 'Standards are determined by human choice, not set by nature independently of men' (ibid., p. 31).[24] On this logic, '"natural rights" are the conditions of a good society. But what those conditions are is not given by nature mystically bound up with the essence of man . . . but is determined by human decisions' (ibid., p. 34). This, it is clear, is consistent with H.L.A. Hart's insistence that 'if there are any moral rights at all, it follows that there is at least one natural right, the equal right of all men to be free' ([1955] 1995, p. 77). If, as I suggest, the Founders would accept this idea, their embrace of the Smithan/Kantian two-person point of view, and their invocation of Americans' 'English inheritance' (see Chapter 2) suggest that they would agree that 'natural rights' are *political* claims.[25] These claims, in turn, assert that 'In any society and under every form of government men ought to be able to think and express their thoughts freely; to live their lives without arbitrary molestation with their persons and goods. They ought to be treated as equal in value, though not necessarily of equal capacity or merit' (MacDonald [1947–8] 1995, p. 33).

On this logic, the rights that determine the distribution of freedom are political claims that are themselves the result of a path-dependent process. So it is that the Constitution and the Bill of Rights are reflections of antecedent norms and laws. Moreover, as 'fundamental law', they are both progenitors of, and absent constitutional amendment, constraints upon, future norms and statutory law. If this means that 'liberty depends on sharing in self-government' (Sandel, 1996, p. 5), it also suggests that the character and content of rights and of rights attenuations cannot be the province of the transcendental, autonomous self's 'pure practical reason' (MacDonald [1947–8] 1995, p. 29).

It is clear that this was the Founders' view. It was this understanding that informed their appreciation of the nexus between self-government and rights, between self-government and virtue, and of the need to cultivate virtue. Nothing in the Founders' republican self-government project contemplated a natural right, antecedent to civil society, to a job, to a home, to health care, or to an education. While such 'rights' have found expression in modern liberalism's political morality, the Founders would insist that such political claims be the subject of public deliberation:

> Central to republican theory is the idea that liberty depends on sharing in self-government. This idea is not by itself inconsistent with liberal freedom.

Participating in politics can be one among the ways in which people choose to pursue their ends. According to republican political theory, however, sharing in self-rule involves something more. It means deliberating with fellow citizens about the common good and helping to shape the destiny of the political community. *But to deliberate well about the common good requires more than the capacity to choose one's ends and to respect others' rights to do the same. It requires a knowledge of public affairs and also a sense of belonging, a concern for the whole, a moral bond with the community whose fate is at stake. To share in self-rule therefore requires that citizens possess, or come to acquire, certain qualities of character or civic virtues.* (Sandel, 1996, pp. 5–6; emphasis mine)

If this is evocative of John Rawl's 'duty of justice' (1971, p. 115), and of Montesquieu's view that 'morals, customs, [and] received examples may give rise to [political liberty]' ([1750] 1977, p. 216), it is also consistent with James Buchanan's conception of moral community (see Section 5.3 above).[26] If it is clear that a self-governing 'moral community' is what the Founders envisioned, it is equally clear that they would reject modern liberalism's peculiar natural rights conception. The same is true of modern liberalism's 'social justice' construal; an idea that finds expression in a particular conception of 'economic rights for hard times':

During the long period of liberal ascendancy, from the New Deal through the 1960's, liberals felt confident that the immediate reduction of poverty was in every way good for the larger community. *Social justice* would, in Lyndon Johnson's phrase, make the society great. Liberals thus avoided the question of what liberalism requires when prosperity is threatened rather than advanced by justice. They offered no coherent and feasible account of what might be called *economic rights for hard times: the floor beneath which people cannot be allowed to drop for the greater good.* (R. Dworkin, 1985, p. 212, emphasis mine)

Drawing upon modern liberalism's constitutive and derivative political moralities and, it should be said, upon the Progressive movement's 'necessitous men' construal (see Section.5.1 above), Ronald Dworkin avers that '[Liberals] need not accept . . . that our future will be jeopardized if we try to provide everyone with the means to lead a life with choice and value' (1985, p. 212). It is on this logic that, 'respecting people's capacity to choose their ends mean[s] providing them with the material prerequisites of human dignity, such as food and shelter, education and employment' (Sandel, 1996, p. 201) (Section 5.1).

I emphasize, first, that this idea is difficult to reconcile with modern liberalism's transcendental autonomous self construal: whom among these individuals, freed of the burden of custom, tradition, societal norms and of contingent circumstance, will have *any* motive to act? More to the point, on what logic would transcendental autonomous individuals be sympathetic to the plight of 'necessitous men'? If this conundrum undermines the *logic* of modern liberalism's 'social justice' – 'economic rights for hard times' construal, it is nevertheless true that:

> The appeal to 'social justice' has . . . by now become the most widely used and most effective argument in political discussion. *Almost every claim for government action on behalf of particular groups is advanced in its name, and if it can be made to appear that a certain measure is demanded by 'social justice', opposition to it will rapidly weaken.* (Hayek [1973] 1997, p. 325; emphasis mine)

Moreover, whereas 'until recently one would have vainly sought . . . for an intelligible definition of [social justice]', it is nevertheless true that 'scarcely anyone doubts that the expression has a definite meaning, describes a high ideal, and points to grave defects of the existing social order which urgently call for correction' (ibid., p. 327).

While modern liberalism does not provide a *definition* of social justice, we know that the associated 'economic rights for hard times' are consequence based and procedurally-detached. This conception stands in sharp contrast to the Founders' procedurally-based, consequence-detached understanding of justice as impartiality. Whereas 'social justice' reflects the imperatives of the egalitarian reformer (Scruton, 2002, p. 79), justice as impartiality is a procedural notion contemplating relations among individuals. The Nobel laureate Friedrich Hayek's argument is heuristic:

> It might . . . be said that the main difference between the order of society at which classical liberalism aimed and the sort of society into which it is now being transformed is that the former was governed by principles of just individual conduct while the new society is to satisfy the demands for 'social justice' – or, in other words, that the former demanded just action by the individuals while the latter more and more places the duty of justice on authorities with power to command people what to do. ([1973] 1997, p. 326; emphasis mine)

The essential point is this: given their prior ethical commitment to the moral equivalence of persons, the Founders sought to promote both respect for the moral law, and just, in the sense of impartial, *institutions*. In contrast, modern liberalism seeks to promote egalitarian outcomes. Given this imperative, the 'liberal lawgiver' is presumed to be able to secure 'social justice' by appeal to social welfare theory's second fundamental welfare theorem (see Sections 5.3 and 5.4 above). Given the logical, empirical and ontological problems that attend social welfare theory (Sections 5.5 and 5.6), social justice-animated income redistribution schemes are necessarily ad hoc and, from the Founders' perspective, morally objectionable.

If this should give the 'liberal lawmaker' pause, the same is true of his propensity to associate differences in ability and inheritance with the production of 'forbidden inequalities' (R. Dworkin, 1985, pp. 195–6). If, as I have suggested, this idea would be alien to Thomas Jefferson's imagination, it is also clear that 'The natural distribution [of talents] is neither just nor unjust; nor is it unjust that persons are born into society at some particular position. These are simply natural facts' (Rawls, 1971, p. 103). It follows, then, that 'In order to employ this concept of "justice" in political debate . . . the advocate of "social justice" creates a peculiar unconscious fiction: the fiction that really all wealth, and perhaps all advantage, belongs to a single owner (society), which (in some inexplicable way) has the duty to ensure its "distribution"' (Scruton, 2002, p. 80).

The Founders did not, could not, embrace this 'fiction'. Their procedurally based, consequence-detached moral and political philosophy was conjoined to a political economy that did not contemplate the intendedly value-free maximization of 'social welfare'. Their republican self-government project was animated neither by the desire to promote 'social justice' or other 'good ends', nor by the imperative to 'perfect' the market system. Rather, given their non-teleological conception of the state, they sought to promote respect for the moral law, to maximize equal political participation and, through Madison's constitutional 'auxiliary precautions', to mitigate the effects of discriminatory factious behavior. In light of all of this, they would surely associate themselves with Nobel laureate James Buchanan's admonition that:

> confusion between the constitutional stage of choice . . . and collective actions taken within 'the [constitutional] law' will almost necessarily arise as long as the objectives of the state are seen as those of promoting 'social good'. To the extent that the institutions of law and government, along with the prevailing public attitudes toward these institutions, reflect this teleological conception of the state, constitutional order is necessarily undermined . . . a constitution is a set of rules which constrain the activities of persons and agents in the pursuit of their own ends and objectives. To argue directly or by inference that the constitution in itself embodies or should embody a 'social purpose' is to negate its very meaning. ([1977] 2001, p. 178)

5.8   MORE ON 'SCIENTIFIC' ECONOMICS

As we have seen, social welfare theory is instrumentally important to modern liberals. On the one hand, the first fundamental welfare theorem is deployed to rationalize 'market failure'-animated government interventions. For its part, the second fundamental welfare theorem is deployed to correct market-generated 'forbidden inequalities'. Simply stated, modern liberalism regards social welfare theory as an instrument of normative appraisal. And central to this project are the 'competitive' and 'ethical' equilibria against which observable market outcomes are to be evaluated.

Unfortunately, neither the efficiency frontier nor the social welfare function, the constructs upon which the determination of the two equilibria depends, has an operational counterpart. It follows that *a comparison of observed market outcomes with hypothetical and unrealizable benchmarks is unavailing*:

> The view that now pervades much public policy economics implicitly presents the relevant choice as between an ideal norm and an existing 'imperfect' institutional arrangement. This *nirvana approach* differs considerably from a *comparative institution* approach in which the relevant choice is between alternative real institutional arrangements. In practice, those who adopt the nirvana viewpoint seek to discover discrepancies between the ideal and the real and, if discrepancies are found, they deduce that the real is inefficient. Users of the comparative institution approach attempt to assess which alternative real institutional arrangement seems best able to cope with the economic problem. (Demsetz, 1969, p. 1; emphasis in original)

The passage just quoted is important, both because it emphasizes what has come to be called the *nirvana fallacy*, and because it draws a distinction between first-best Pareto optimality or 'economic' efficiency and institutional or political efficiency. As has been emphasized, consequence based, procedurally-detached 'economic' efficiency found no expression in the Founders' republican self-government project. For the Founders and, it should be said, for constitutional political economists, the explicitly normative process of institutional appraisal centers on *political efficiency*; on 'the efficacy of differing institutions in reducing or eliminating incentives for participants to invest in resources in rent seeking aimed to secure discriminatory advantage through majoritarian exploitation' (Buchanan and Congleton, 1998, p. 40).

If the United States' Founders would be shocked that the economist's theory of the state is both institutionless and intendedly value-free, they would be dismayed that, as an instrument of public policy appraisal, it never reaches the question of institutional appraisal and design; that, instead, it focuses on 'efficient' outcomes, and that the 'nirvana approach' is its defining characteristic. What follows is a brief adumbration of the problems that attend the nirvana approach 'in action'. The essential problem is that, once account is taken of basic features of observable reality, neither of the theory's fundamental theoretical constructs, the efficiency frontier and the social welfare function, has an operational counterpart. It follows that a comparison of observable outcomes with realizable ideals is not only unavailing, it invites all manner of casuistries.

We begin with the theoretical foundations of the efficiency frontier. The logic of the frontier requires that the underlying utility and production functions exhibit orthodox, neoclassical properties, and that the decision environment be 'frictionless'; that, in other words, property and exchange rights be respected, and that transaction costs be zero.

Central to the neoclassical paradigm is *Homo economicus*. As we have seen, 'economic man' is autonomous, atomistic, narrowly self-interested and, importantly, classically rational. In this account, *preference* structures are assumed to be consistently ordered, exogenously determined, and stable. The objects of choice are purchasable economic goods whose physical, technical and aesthetic properties are known with certainty, and whose associated property rights are both known and unattenuated. Significantly, because individuals are fully informed, information asymmetries and their concomitant, opportunistic behavior, are non-existent. Granting all of this, economic man's objectively defined and subjectively perceived decision environments are congruent. Finally, exchange is characterized by classical, rather than relational contracting (Furubotn and Richter, 2005, p. 549). It follows that, because fully informed agents engage in instantaneous, impersonal exchange, transaction costs are zero (ibid., p. 52).

I note first that the assumption that preference structures are both exogenously determined and stable is incompatible with the Founders appreciation of the self. If, for present purposes this is all-but-decisive, we also know that preference (and value) structures are endogenously determined. They are, in fact, path-dependent (Buchanan, 1994b, pp. 76–7).[27] It is beyond dispute that evolutionary and other path-dependencies including learning, the development of social norms and the emergence of new products influence preference and value structures.[28] Moreover, it is understood that higher order preferences, or 'preferences for preferences' (North, 1994) tend, in a manner evocative of the Founders' effort to promote private and public virtue, to animate efforts to alter others' preferences and values (Buchanan, 1994b, pp. 74–7). It follows that, as the Founders understood, economics must take account of the relationship between preferences and values, and of the setting within which preferences and values are formed (Buchanan, 1991, p. 186).

If path-dependencies may account for the 'anomalous behavior' that has been judged to be inconsistent with classical rationality (Tversky and Thaler, 1990), they also gesture toward another problem with implications for social welfare theory. It has long been recognized that, if interpersonal utility comparisons are ruled out, there is no possible method of aggregating individual rankings of social alternatives that meets five innocuous criteria (Arrow, 1951, pp. 24–31). What seems generally not to be recognized is that, in the presence of path-dependencies, 'essentially different individuals are in existence at different points in time'. It follows that, *with respect to any one individual*, 'Preferences are simply not comparable from one [time] period to the next' (Furubotn and Richter, 2005, p. 545).[29]

If it is clear that preference and, it should be said, value structures are neither exogenously determined nor intertemporally stable, it is also true that agents are neither autonomous nor relentlessly narrowly self-interested. At issue is the presumption, roughly congruent with modern liberalism's transcendental, autonomous self construal, that economic man has no 'social identity'. Empirical findings in evolutionary and other branches of psychology suggest that 'One or more of [a] collection of distinct [cognitive] processing units weighs or tries to weigh economic goods according to the logical laws of transitivity, but other processors register utility in at least five other ways' (Aaron, 1994, p. 15). While it is clear that utility derives from consumption, it also derives from self-reference, from helping others, from setting goals and achieving them, from interpersonal relationships and from caring about others as ends.[30] If, as the Founders insisted, this suggests that man has an innate moral sense,[31] it also suggests that ethical and behavioral norms enter as arguments of individuals' utility functions and as behavioral constraints (Buchanan, 1994a, pp. 128 and 135).[32] Equally important, account should be taken of what the Nobel laureate Amartya Sen has called 'a sense of identity with others':

> both in *reflective* choice and in *evolutionary* selection, ideas of identity can be important. . . The time has certainly come to displace the presumption of 'identity disregard' from the exalted position it has . . . occup[ied] in a substantial part of economic theory woven around the concept of 'the economic man', and also in political, legal and social theory (used in imitative admiration – a sincere form of flattery – of so-called rational-choice economics). (2006, p. 23)[33]

The essential point is this: given that social welfare theory is, to paraphrase Sen, 'woven around the concept of "the economic man"', it can accommodate neither the endogeneity of preferences and values, nor the interpersonal effects and multiple preference domains that influence individuals' behavior. If the single-equation, strictly personal, endogenously determined and intertemporally stable utility function of social welfare theorists' imagination cannot accommodate these phenomena, neither does it take account of cognitive limitations. Reduced to its essentials, there is a discrepancy 'between the perfect human rationality that is assumed in classical and neoclassical economic theory and the reality of human behavior'. Whereas it is not true 'that people are consciously and deliberately irrational . . . neither their knowledge nor their powers of calculation allow them to achieve the high level of optimal adaptation of means to ends that is posited in economics' (Simon, 1992, p. 3).

Whereas for economic man and, therefore, for social welfare theory, 'there is no gap between competence and the difficulty of the decision problem to be solved' (Heiner, 1983, p. 562), cognitive limitations are the defining characteristic of the boundedly rational agent (Conlisk, 1996).[34] While there is no generally accepted definition of bounded rationality (Furubotn and Richter, 2005, p. 47), it is generally agreed that the optimization of utility, profit or any other desideratum is 'a special case occurring when the competence-difficulty gap approaches zero' (Wilde et al., 1985, p. 403).[35] Given bounded rationality, behavioral patterns reflect '"rule-governed" behavior, such as instinct, habits, routines, rules of thumb, administrative procedures, customs, norms, and so forth' (Heiner, 1983, p. 567).[36] Thus, in contrast to 'what Hayek has called constructivist rationality (or "constructivism")' (Smith, 2003, p. 466), 'models of bounded rationality consist of simple step-by-step rules that function well under the constraints of limited search, knowledge and time'. Importantly, while 'the mechanism is not yet well-understood', the boundedly rational decision-maker's 'adaptive toolbox' takes account of 'conflicting motivations and goals' (Gigerenzer and Selten, 2002, pp. 8–9).[37] If it is clear that the boundedly rational agent's 'adaptive tool box' is irreconcilable with economic man's classical rationality, it also emphasizes the role of 'unconscious, autonomic, neuropsychological systems' and of path-dependencies; in particular, of subjective, 'autobiographic, experiential memory' (Smith, 2003, pp. 468–9).

Finally, I emphasize that 'welfare economics, and the entire ability of economists to make normative statements, is premised on the idea that giving people what they want makes people better off' (Camerer et al., 2005, p. 37). The problem for social welfare theorists, and for the theory's normative application, is that 'there is considerable evidence from neuroscience and other areas of psychology that the motivation to take an action is not always closely tied to hedonic consequences' (ibid.). The point of immediate interest is that 'it is possible to be motivated to take actions that bring no pleasure' and, conversely, to 'feel quite unmotivated to engage in activities that, at a purely cognitive level, you are quite sure you would find deeply pleasurable' (ibid.).[38] In this account, 'decision making involves the interaction of two separate, though overlapping systems, one responsible for pleasure and pain (the "liking system"), and the other for motivation (the "wanting system")'. Whatever else is said, the distinction between 'likes' and 'wants' has profound implications for utilitarianism generally, for utilitarian social welfare theory, for normative policy appraisal, and for 'optimal' public policy:

> Economics proceeds on the assumption that satisfying people's wants is a good thing. The assumption depends on knowing that people like what they want. If likes and wants diverge, this would pose a fundamental challenge to standard welfare economics. *Presumably, welfare should be based on 'liking'. But if we*

cannot infer what people like from what they want and choose, then an alternative method for measuring liking is needed. (Ibid.; emphasis mine)

Were nothing else to be said, the distinction between 'likes' and 'wants' calls into question both the empirical content of the 'economic man' convention and the ontological existence both of the efficiency frontier *and* of the social welfare function. It follows that the normative benchmarks against which market outcomes are to be appraised – 'competitive' and 'ethical' equilibria – are themselves unrealizable.

If the problems that attend the economic man construal militate against the normative use of social welfare theory's first and second fundamental welfare theorems, the same is true of the theory's production theoretic foundations. The root cause of the problem is that the representative producer is presumed to employ the only 'efficient' or output maximizing technical alternative available. On the one hand, the single-equation production function cannot accommodate a fundamental feature of observable reality: because human and non-human capital input types appear in differentiated forms the producer of any product confronts a 'choice of technique' problem. On the other hand, the efficiency assumption requires that production proceed under conditions of 'perfect adaptability'. While little attention has been paid to this implicit assumption, the logic of the 'efficiency' assumption requires that, as movement along the efficiency frontier proceeds, 'fixed' inputs must, instantaneously and costlessly, 'adapt' to changing rates of use of the 'variable' inputs.[39] What seems not be acknowledged is that, as 'adaptation' proceeds, the technical properties of the underlying production functions change. In effect, as 'perfect adaptation' proceeds, movement *along* the efficiency frontier is a *logical* impossibility. Setting aside the question of the ontological existence of the efficiency frontier (and, it should be said, of the 'practicability' of lump sum taxes and subsidies), it follows that appeal to the second fundamental welfare theorem is unavailing.

If the perfect adaptability assumption militates against the reconciliation of 'competitive' and 'ethical' equilibria, the 'choice of [production] technique' problem compromises the logic of the efficiency frontier. The problem is straightforward. Once account is taken of elementary technological considerations, the set of available technical options cannot be represented by a single-equation, 'output maximizing' production function. The existence at a point in time of differentiated forms of capital input types means that the firm's production function is properly understood to be a multi-equation construct. Each production subfunction, while capable of producing the desired product, has as its technical parameters the particular differentiates of the capital input types employed (Roth,

1979). Given this empirically observable understanding of its technical options, the firm confronts a 'choice of technique' problem. Given the firm's objective(s) it must choose among the available, competing technical options or production subfunctions.

In the situation envisioned, the boundedly rational producer does not possess exhaustive knowledge of the technical array. Moreover, confronted by positive transaction (decision) costs, he must decide *how* to decide among the available techniques. Yet any chosen decision rule is itself the outcome of a prior decision process, and so on. Given uncertain benefits and positive decision costs, the question becomes, 'how is the individual to resolve the infinite regress of whether it is worthwhile to obtain information concerning whether it is worthwhile to obtain information?' (Stiglitz, 1985, p. 23).[40] If, as has been suggested, 'the rational thing to do is to be irrational', and 'to choose a choice method without reason' (Pingle, 1992, p. 11), the essential point is this: given bounded rationality and positive decision costs, 'it is no longer possible to assume that each individual knows everything about existing technological alternatives'. Under the circumstances envisioned, 'The older formalism of the neoclassical case does not apply when individual knowledge endowments are limited, differ widely from person to person, and are subject to continuing change, and when the very process of decision making is costly and based on decision rules other than rational choice' (Furubotn, 1999, p. 183). On this logic, there can be no presumption that either incumbent firms or de novo industry entrants will employ the same production functions or 'techniques'. Moreover, if this is true *within* an industry it must be true *across* industries.

A corollary of all of this is that, when account is taken of bounded rationality, of positive decision costs, and of elementary technological considerations, the individual producer's production function is subjectively determined. This, in turn, compromises the logic of the efficiency frontier; a construct that is predicated on the assumption that producers within an industry employ identical, output maximizing production functions, and that firms across industries employ the same inputs!

In sum, whether interest centers on individuals' preference and value structures, or upon producers' technical options, the economist's theory of the state, social welfare theory, fails to take account of real and unavoidable constraints. The irremediable fact is that fundamental features of observable reality militate against the *derivation* of the efficiency frontier. Stated differently, these considerations call into question the ontological existence of the efficiency frontier (Furubotn, 1994; Frank, 1996, p. 119). Yet, even if the existence of the frontier were granted, fundamental logical problems remain. I emphasize, in particular, that the path to the frontier, to first-best Paretian optima or 'competitive equilibria', is not assured.

As has been emphasized, utilitarian social welfare theory is a hybrid moral theory. Consequence based and procedurally-detached, the theory nevertheless assigns an instrumental role to unattenuated property and exchange rights. Indeed, respect for rights is a necessary condition for the attainment of 'competitive equilibria'; of points on the efficiency frontier. Yet, as we have seen, in the utilitarian framework, utilitarian considerations trump rights (Lyons, 1982, p. 113). It follows that utilitarian considerations militate *against* the achievement of competitive equilibria.

If an analytically convenient assumption, unattenuated property and exchange rates, undermines social welfare theory's internal logic, the same is true of the zero transaction cost assumption. Whereas the theory regards zero ex ante and ex post transaction costs as a necessary condition for the attainment of competitive equilibria, in fact the assumption leads to a logical conundrum: a decision environment characterized by costless transactions is congenial to the formation of coalitions that, effectively, rule out the satisfaction of the marginal equivalences needed to attain first-best Paretian optima or competitive equilibria (Furubotn, 1991).

If it is clear that the efficiency frontier is indeterminate, the same is true of the social welfare function. I begin by noting that the complexity of individuals' preference and value structures militates against the specification of both the efficiency frontier and the social welfare function. The fundamental problem is that an emerging literature suggests that individual *preference and value systems involve a number of utility domains*. Each utility domain is defined by a utility subfunction defined for the same individual. While the arguments of some of these subfunctions include purchasable economic goods, others contemplate arguments that are reflective, among other things, of society's view of acceptable behavior. In effect, individuals' complex utility domains incorporate both preferences and values or moral tastes (Buchanan, 1994a, p. 128). In James Buchanan's account, the 'ecumenical utility-function approach' ([1983a] 2000, p. 122) recognizes that 'There are several "non-economic" men that live with *Homo economicus*, and it is folly to ignore their existence and their tempering influence because they are difficult to quantify' (p. 121).

The essential point is that an explicit accounting of utility domains, of the 'several "non-economic" men" that live with *Homo economicus*' cannot, in the manner of social welfare theory, be accomplished by appeal to a single-equation utility function. What is required is a multi-equation utility function. Yet it is immediately clear that this compromises the derivation of both the efficiency frontier and the social welfare function. Among other things, the juxtaposition of bounded rationality, information asymmetries and path dependencies ensures that individuals possess disparate preference and utility domains. Moreover, there is no assurance that any individual's utility domains will be intertemporally stable. Add to this the lack of congruence between 'wants' and 'likes', and the arguments of individuals' utility subfunctions will differ, both at a point in time, and over time. It follows that, because the spaces in which individuals' utility domains are incommensurable, *neither the efficiency frontier nor the social welfare function can be defined.*

Even if this problem were to be set aside, the impossibility of the Paretian liberal (see Section 5.6) militates against the specification of a social welfare function. The upshot is that, Amartya Sen's efforts to expand the informational base of social welfare theory notwithstanding (Roth, 1999, pp. 59–63), Arrow's Possibility Result (Section 5.6) and the impossibility of the Paretian liberal mean that the notional social welfare function has no operation counterpart.

Finally, the question of the ontological existence of the social welfare function finds expression in James Buchanan's observation that the *idea* of 'social preference' imputes 'rationality or irrationality as an attribute of a social group'. This, in turn, 'implies the imputation to that group of an organic existence apart from that of its individual components' (Buchanan, 1954, p. 116). From the public policy perspective it is significant that Amartya Sen finds this objection 'quite persuasive' when 'social preference' connotes 'the operation of social decision mechanisms such as voting procedures' (1995, p. 5).

Social welfare theory, the economist's theory of the state, is a theory of 'optimal' public policy. Its signature consequence based, procedurally-detached desideratum, economic efficiency, has motivated countless government market interventions. It is revealing that, writing more than four decades ago, James Buchanan observed that 'economists tend to be so enmeshed with efficiency notions that it seems extremely difficult for them to resist the ever-present temptation to propose yet more complex gimmicks and gadgets for producing greater "efficiency"' ([1962b] 1999, p. 62).

It is safe to say that nothing has changed since Buchanan's words were written. Remarkably, economists have taken little account of the theory's debilitating limitations. If economists have ignored the question of the ontological existence of the efficiency frontier, they seem implicitly to embrace the theory's 'romanticized view of politics'. As has been emphasized, the theory assumes that public policy is implemented by a benevolent despot advised by an 'omniscient being – the observing economist'. If it is clear that the benevolent despot has no empirical counterpart and would, in any case, be alien to the Founders' imagination, it is also clear that, 'Since no one other than an omniscient "observing economist" can have the information that would permit a system to reach full efficiency at the hypothetical [efficiency] frontier, *there is no chance for normal market participants to bring about the ideal results discussed in traditional welfare theory*' (Furubotn and Richter, 2005, p. 528, footnote 12; emphasis mine). If economists' continuing embrace of the nirvana fallacy is inexplicable, so too is the fact that economists have for more than 50 years systematically ignored Lipsey and Lancaster's 'General Theory of Second Best' (1956).

Recall first that the attainment of a point on the efficiency frontier requires that three marginal equivalences or 'Paretian conditions' be satisfied. Consider now that:

> The general theorem of the second best optimum states that if there is introduced into a general equilibrium system a constraint which prevents the attainment of one of the Paretian conditions, the other Paretian conditions, though still attainable, are, in general, no longer desirable. In other words, *given that one of the Paretian optimum conditions cannot be fulfilled, then an optimum situation can be achieved only by departing from all of the Paretian conditions.* (Lipsey and Lancaster, 1956, p. 1; emphasis mine)

It is revealing that the 'negative corollary' of the general theorem is that 'it is not true that a situation in which more, but not all, of the [three] optimum conditions are fulfilled is necessarily, or is even likely to be, superior to a situation in which fewer are fulfilled' (ibid., p. 12). It is clear, for example, that a regulated, fixed price, accompanied by a mandate to engage in marginal cost pricing – a familiar construction in price-regulated 'natural monopoly' industries – is not 'likely to be [Pareto] superior to a situation in which fewer [of the Pareto conditions] are fulfilled'. It is on this logic that Lipsey and Lancaster emphasize that 'It should be obvious . . . that the principles of the general theory of second best show the futility of "piecemeal welfare economics"' (ibid., p. 17).

Lipsey and Lancaster's point is straightforward: if the economist and his politician-clients are intent upon using social welfare theory to shape public policy, account must be taken of a general equilibrium system; of a system in which, quite literally, everything is related to everything else. It is on this logic that Lipsey and Lancaster emphasize that 'To apply to only a small part of an economy welfare rules which would lead to a Paretian optimum if they were applied everywhere, may move the economy away from, not toward, a second best optimum position' (ibid.).

I emphasize, first, that the General Theory of Second Best engages social welfare theory on its own terms. Stated differently, no account is taken of the indeterminacy of the efficiency frontier or of the social welfare function. That said, the general theorem of the second best shows the 'futility of piecemeal [or *partial equilibrium*] welfare economics'. Yet, it is clear that, whether claimed 'market failures' are characterized as generalized externalities, public goods, or 'monopoly elements', public policy interventions are, necessarily, 'piecemeal'. The essential point is that, while applications of the first and second fundamental welfare theorems must occur in the context of a general equilibrium system, explicit account cannot be taken of all of the interrelationships that characterize an economy (Salanié, 2000, p. 138).[41]

Let us be clear: whereas the 'omniscient' economist of social welfare theorists' imagination must understand all of the objective (and inter-related) features of a 'world where many imperfections exist and only a few can be removed at any one time' (Lipsey and Lancaster, 1956, p. 13), this is precisely the world contemplated by the General Theory of Second Best. Despite this logical conundrum it is remarkable that the view persists that 'Ideally, the purpose of antitrust and regulation policies is to foster improvements judged in efficiency terms. . . The object is to increase the efficiency with which the economy operates, recognizing that we may fall short of . . . replicating a perfectly competitive market, but nevertheless we can achieve substantial improvements over what would prevail in the absence of such government intervention' (Viscusi et al., 2005, p. 9).

The hubris of its practitioners notwithstanding, the point is that social welfare theory cannot, legitimately, be used to justify either 'market imperfection'-animated government interventions or income redistribution schemes. The normative use of the theory is compromised by its indeterminacy, by its romanticized view of politics, by its inability to accommodate a procedural theory of justice, and by its reliance upon logically irreconcilable right- and goal-based moral theories. If it is clear that utilitarian social welfare theory has nothing in common with the Founders' procedurally based, consequence-detached political economy, it is equally clear that it cannot legitimately serve as a theory of the state.

I note finally that, like social welfare theory, *macroeconomics* is both institutionless and relentlessly utilitarian. Characteristically, macroeconomists insist that 'The goal of [macroeconomic] policy is economic welfare. . . Economic welfare can be thought of simply as happiness, the things that individual members of society want – stable prices, full employment, and a high standard of living' (Gordon, 2000, p. 455). Indeed, it is precisely these consequence based, procedurally-detached ideas that animate the federal government's statutory macroeconomic policy 'goals'. As we saw in Section 1.3 in Chapter 1, the Employment Act of 1946 declares that it is the 'continuing policy and responsibility of the Federal Government to use all practicable means' to promote 'the general welfare', 'useful employment opportunities', full employment, increased real income, 'balanced growth', a balanced federal budget, 'adequate productivity growth', an improved trade balance 'through increased exports and improvement in the international competitiveness of agriculture, business, and industry', and 'reasonable price stability'. And all of this is to be accomplished while according 'proper attention to national priorities' (US Congress Joint Economic Committee, 2002, p. 3).

It is immediately clear that the statutory language takes no account of the Founders' understanding of the Constitution's General Welfare, Necessary and Proper, Commerce and Legislative Powers Clauses (see Chapter 4). I emphasize, in particular, that the phrase 'practicable means' ignores both the Founders' view of *permissible* means (see also Chapter 2), and of the Necessary and Proper Clause's original meaning. As we have seen, the Clause 'authorizes Congress to enact laws that are "appropriate" and plainly adapted for carrying into execution Congress's *enumerated powers*' (Chapter 4). For its part, the invocation of the phrase 'general welfare' invites all manner of casuistries. We know, for example, that Madison, Jefferson and Wilson insisted that the General Welfare Clause did *not* confer upon Congress the right to do whatever *it* thinks to be in the national interest. Whereas federal taxation and spending must be in the *national* interest (and consistent with the federal government's enumerated powers), it was left to the *states* to attend to their residents' welfare. Moreover, we know that Jefferson, Madison and the early Congresses rejected as unconstitutional and immoral 'bounties, premiums and other artificial encouragements' (see Chapters 1 and 2). And we know that, the holdings of the New Court notwithstanding, the Supreme Court long held that if activities were either not interstate commerce, or 'bore no sufficient nexus to interstate commerce', they were not encompassed by the Commerce Clause. Finally, we know that the Founders' understanding of the separation of powers did not contemplate the delegation of Congress's legislative or 'policy-making' powers (Chapter 4).

The Founders' views notwithstanding, the pot-pourri of macroeconomic policies and 'responsibilities' codified in the Employment Act of 1946 reflects the reciprocal relationship between what the Founders would style 'legislative encroachments' and the New Court's expansive reading of the Constitution. Were nothing else to be said, the nebulous statutory imperative to promote 'useful employment opportunities', 'balanced growth', 'adequate productivity growth', 'the international competitiveness of agriculture, business and industry' and 'reasonable price stability' – while, at the same time, affording 'proper attention to national priorities' – has enabled both the Congress, and the entities to which it delegates rulemaking powers, to do whatever they think to be in the national interest. It is in this sense that the Employment Act of 1946 is a metaphor for the combination of congressional overreach and judicial deference that has both eroded federalism and the separation of powers and underwritten the relentless expansion of the federal enterprise (see Chapter 1).

Ultimately, however, the goals and 'responsibilities' that find expression in federal on-, off- and off-off budget policies are reflective of a public philosophy and a political economy that emphasize the wants, needs and prerogatives of the transcendental, autonomous, and narrowly self-interested individual. For modern liberalism, the imperative to 'perfect' both majoritarian democracy and the 'market economy' has as its corollaries that rights, antecedent to civil society, do not depend upon federalism and the separation of powers; that the ultimate desideratum is the maximization of strictly personal preferences, and that 'forbidden [income] inequalities' must be redressed. For its part, the economist's relentlessly outcomes based, institutionless and *intendedly* value-free theory of the state regards 'wants and needs' satisfaction as equivalent to the public good. Moreover, because economists embrace a romanticized model of politics and *assume* that rights will be respected, federalism and the separation of powers fade as a concern. Finally, his pretension that the first and second fundamental welfare theorems are 'scientific' enables the economist to rationalize all manner of 'efficiency enhancing' market interventions and income redistribution schemes.

It seems clear that economists and politicians would do well to remember Madison's admonition that, if republican self-government is to survive:

> *Ambition must be made to counteract ambition. . .* It may be a reflection of human nature, that such devices should be necessary to control the abuses of government. But what is government itself, but the greatest of all reflections on human nature? If men were angels, no government would be necessary. . . In framing a government which is to be administered by men over men, the great difficulty lies in this: you must first enable the government to control the governed; and in the next place oblige it to control itself. A dependence on the people is, no doubt, the primary control on the government, but *experience has taught mankind the necessity of auxiliary precautions.* (Carey and McClellan, 2001, pp. 268–9; emphasis mine)

NOTES

1. See also Section 3.5 in Chapter 3 of this volume.
2. For more on this, see Rawls (1971, p. 102).
3. See, for example, Jefferson ([1787e] 1984, pp. 290–91) and ([1787c] 1993, p. 213).
4. See, for example, Jefferson ([1787a] 1984, p. 918) and ([1804] 1984, p. 1144).
5. It should be emphasized that my quarrel is with modern, as opposed to classical liberalism. For more on this, see Section 5.4 below.
6. See also R. Dworkin (1978, p. 235).
7. These ideas have a long history. For example, Jeremy Bentham believed that only

utilitarian arguments could justify political decisions (R. Dworkin, 1978, p. 233). The same could be said, today, about preference and welfare utilitarians. Whereas the former, a group that includes most economists, asserts a public policy imperative to promote preference satisfaction, the latter argues for the suppression of 'short-sighted preference satisfaction in favour of protecting people's long-term welfare interests' (Goodin, 1993, p. 244). Because they sometimes assume that it is possible to determine what people 'need', rather than what they 'want', welfare utilitarians may argue that public policy should promote 'welfare' or 'need' satisfaction (Hausman and McPherson, 1993, p. 706).

8. See also Rawls (1996, pp. XVIII and XX).
9. For more on the logical problems associated with rule-utilitarianism, see Scruton (1994, pp. 282–3).
10. Justice Kennedy's Opinion in *Lawrence* v. *Texas* (545 US (2003)) refers explicitly to the transcendental autonomous self: 'Freedom extends beyond spatial bounds. Liberty presumes an autonomy of self that includes freedom of thought, belief, expression, and certain intimate conduct. The instant case involves liberty of the person both in its spatial and more transcendental dimensions' (p. 1). While Justice Kennedy's language is evocative of modern liberalism's understanding of the self, Justice Thomas's Dissent reflects a different view: 'just like Justice Stewart, I "can find [neither in the Bill of Rights nor any other part of the Constitution] a general right of privacy" . . . or as the Court terms it today, the "liberty of the person both in its spatial and more transcendental dimensions"' (p. 1).
11. For more on the differences between modern and classical liberalism, see Roth (2007, pp. 72–3). For more comprehensive discussions of classical liberalism, see Buchanan (2005) and Epstein (2003).
12. The economics literature does recognize that it is doubtful that 'racist, sadistic and other antisocial preferences should count as contributing to individual well-being'. Hausman and McPherson have suggested that one approach to this problem is to 'launder' preferences (1993, pp. 690–91).
13. The 'endorsement constraint' is, I suggest, the primary source of modern liberalism's institutional skepticism. Indeed, Jeremy Waldron has noted that 'Liberals demand that the social order should in principle be capable of explaining itself at the tribunal of each person's understanding' (1987, p. 149).
14. See also R. Dworkin (1985, p. 198).
15. The same is true of social welfare theory, the economist's theory of the state. See, especially Section 5.6 in Chapter 5 in this volume.
16. See, especially, Section 2.2 in Chapter 2 of this volume.
17. See, especially, Sections 2.3 and 2.4 in Chapter 2.
18. For more on the distinction between classical and relational contracting, see Furubotn and Richter (2005).
19. This is true, whether utilitarianism is expressed in hedonistic, preference or welfare form.
20. The Nobel laureate Amartya Sen agrees that 'no direct and basic importance is attached in the utilitarian framework to rights and liberties in the evaluation of states of affairs' (1995, p. 13). That said, he insists that 'The need to guarantee some "minimal liberties" on a priority basis can be incorporated in social choice formulations' (ibid.). Sen's project is animated by his insistence that rights cannot be consequence-detached. He argues that utilitarian analysis can be employed in 'inverse form' to determine which rights to protect. While Sen's idea is to embed rights in 'states of affairs' as consequences, the problem is that rights and their correlative duties 'have a normative life of their own, with implications that are neither reducible to, nor traceable by, direct considerations of utility' (Lyons, 1982, p. 133). It follows that, whether the rights one seeks to protect are regarded as instrumentally important or intrinsically valuable, they cannot be derived from desired states of affairs or consequences. This objection applies, moreover, to rule-utilitarianism. For more on the relationships between rights and utility, see R. Dworkin (1978, p. 94–6).

21. For more on 'Politics and Meddlesome Preferences', see Buchanan ([1986b] 2000, pp. 410–18).
22. For more on this, see Lyons (1982, pp. 124–8).
23. As is well known, Bentham 'dismissed absolute natural rights as "nonsense upon stilts"' (Almond, 1993, p. 266).
24. MacDonald's argument is based on the 'Naturalistic Fallacy' to which Jeremy Waldron refers. See MacDonald (1947–8, pp. 30–31).
25. In her paean to 'The Majesty of the Law', former Supreme Court Justice Sandra Day O'Connor highlights Americans' 'English inheritance' (2004, pp. 34–5). For his part, Alan Dershowitz's 'rights from wrongs' construction emphasizes path-dependencies and the role of majoritarian self-government: 'rights are those fundamental preferences that *experience and history* . . . have taught are so essential that the citizenry should be *persuaded* to entrench them and not make them subject to easy change by shifting majorities' (2004, p. 81; emphasis mine).
26. As we have seen, the United States' Founders shared Montesquieu's view that republican self-government and liberty depend upon civic virtue. They also shared his view that 'political liberty is formed by a certain distribution of the three powers; by the separation of powers among the 'Judiciary Power', the 'Legislative Power', and the 'Executive Power'. See Montesquieu ([1750] 1977, p. 216 and Book XI, Chapters 1–7). See also Chapter 2 this volume.
27. See also Furubotn and Richter (2005, pp. 542–6).
28. For experimental evidence on the effect of group attachment and social learning on economic behavior, see Harbough and Krause (2000). For a survey of game-theoretic and empirical results that suggest that cooperative behavior may be attributable to the development of social norms, see Ostrom (2000) and Fehr and Gächter (2000). For an adumbration of a sociological view of the endogeneity of preference structures, see Baron and Hannan (1994, p. 1117). Henrich (2000) presents evidence that 'economic decisions and economic reasoning may be heavily influenced by cultural differences – that is, by socially transmitted rules about how to behave in certain circumstances (economic or otherwise) that may vary from group to group as a consequence of different cultural trajectories'. Given this 'social learning', Henrich argues that 'the assumption that humans share the same economic decision-making process must be reconsidered' (ibid., p. 973). Finally, experimental results involving equity, reciprocity and competition have been rationalized by appeal to evolutionary biology. See, for example, Bolton and Ockenfels (2000) and Robson (2001). For a discussion of the empirical problems that attend efforts to distinguish among endogeneity interactions, 'contextual interactions' and 'correlated effects', see Manski (2000, pp. 128–30).
29. The United States' Founders would likely agree with this assessment. We know that they assumed that preference and value structures are mutable. Moreover, we know that they insisted that there is a reciprocal and path-dependent relationship between value structures and society's formal and informal institutions (see Chapter 2).
30. See also Hausman and McPherson (1993, p. 688).
31. Michael S. Gazzainga, a Professor of Cognitive Neuroscience, 'support[s] the idea that there could be a universal set of biological responses to moral dilemmas, a sort of ethics, built into our brains' (2005, p. XIX). Building on the work of Adam Smith, Brennan and Pettit develop a model of the demand for and supply of approbation or, in their language, 'esteem'. In their account, 'The forces of esteem are distinctively associated, not with the market, and not with the state, but with what is nowadays often described as civil society'. They argue, in particular, that 'One of the most interesting projects in institutional design is to investigate the conditions under which the intangible hand [the demand for approbation] can be expected to work well and, in particular, to work for the production of . . . the common good' (2004, p. 5).
32. See Dowell et al. (1998) for a model that incorporates moral concerns in utility functions and constraints.
33. In Sen's account, 'a person's behavior may be swayed by . . . her adherence to some

norms of acceptable conduct . . . or by her sense of duty . . . toward others with whom one does not identify in any obvious sense'. Recognizing this, Sen, adds that 'a sense of identity with others can be a very important . . . influence on one's behavior which can easily go against narrowly self-interested conduct' (2006, p. 23). See also Goette et al. for a discussion of the relationship between membership in a social group and the internalization of roles, norms and values that affect behavior (2006). Finally, Bernhard et al. find that 'in-group favoritism is a strong force in altruistic norm enforcement and sharing decisions' (2006, p. 221).

34. To paraphrase Richard Thaler (2000), *Homo economicus* will, in the future, begin losing IQ, and will become more emotional. He predicts, in short, that, 'over the next couple of decades', '*Homo economicus* will evolve into *Homo sapiens*' (p. 140), and that economists will study human cognition (p. 137).

35. See also Heiner (1983, p. 568).

36. The Nobel laureate Douglass North suggests that 'Ronald Heiner (1983), in a path-breaking article, not only made the connection between the mental capacities of humans and the external environment, but suggested the implications for arresting economic progress' (1994, p. 363, footnote 7). For evidence in support of Heiner's theory of rule-governed behavior, see Kaen and Rosenman (1986) and Wilde et al. (1985). For critiques of his approach, see Bookstaber and Langsam (1985) and Garrison (1985). For Heiner's reply, see (1985b). For 'Further Modeling and Applications of the Theory', see Heiner (1985a).

37. For a discussion of what Vernon Smith has styled 'ecological rationality', see Smith (2003, pp. 469–71).

38. Camerer et al. proffer the following example: 'Berridge believes that the later stages of many drug addictions present prototypical examples of situations of what he terms "wanting" without "liking"; drug addicts often report an absence of pleasure from taking the drugs they are addicted to, coupled with an irresistible motivation to do so' (2005, p. 37).

39. See Furubotn (1964, p. 22). See also Furubotn (1965), Roth (1974) and Stigler (1987, pp. 136–8).

40. See also Winter (1964) and Conlisk (1988).

41. A recent book, *The Welfare Economics of Public Policy*, is subtitled *A Practical Approach to Project and Policy Evaluation*. Given their avowed purpose, it is significant that the authors concede that 'the simplistic partial equilibrium models of Pigou and Marshall . . . may not account for significant interactions', while 'the full general equilibrium models of Arrow and Debreu . . . are typically not estimable (except under crude assumptions regarding, for example, substitution or applicability of a representative consumer model)' (Just et al., 2004, p. 641).

6. What would the Founders do?

6.1 A REPRISE

America's Founders embraced a prior ethical commitment to the moral equivalence of persons. This idea informed their moral and political philosophy, their political economy, their understanding of the Constitution, and their vision of post-constitutional republican self-government.

Given their conception of the right, the moral equivalence of persons, the Founders were not, indeed they could not be, utilitarians. If, as I have argued, the Founders would not countenance a moral and political philosophy committed to distributive justice and to the promotion of 'want' and 'need' satisfaction, they *were* concerned with the specification of *permissible* ends, and with the promotion of just, in the sense of impartial, constitutional and post-constitutional statutory law. Indeed, the Constitution's Madisonian 'auxiliary precautions' were animated by the idea that the Constitution must both reflect and promote respect for the moral law; by the idea that restraints on the federal government are a *sine qua non* for equal political participation and, therefore, for liberty, and by the idea that, if the effects of narrowly self-interested discriminatory 'factious' behavior are to be mitigated, ambition must be set against ambition. It is in this sense that, for the Founders, federalism, the separation of powers and the other 'auxiliary precautions' were both instrumentally important, and intrinsically valuable.

The Founders' procedurally based, consequence-detached moral and political philosophy was conjoined to a political economy whose desideratum is decidedly not the maximization of preference based 'social welfare' or the promotion of outcomes based 'social justice'. Whereas the economist's utilitarian theory of the state, social welfare theory, is deployed to rationalize 'efficiency-enhancing' market interventions and income and wealth redistribution schemes, the Founders' political economy focuses on *political efficiency*; on the minimization of narrowly self-interested and discriminatory rent seeking and majoritarian cycling.

In contrast, contemporary federal on-, off- and off-off budget policy is informed by the public philosophy of modern America, modern liberalism and by the political economy to which it is conjoined, social welfare theory. Given the moral, logical, empirical and ontological problems that attend both modern liberalism and social welfare theory, this is remarkable. Setting this aside, the essential point is this: on the one hand, modern liberalism's peculiar rights as trump cards construal means that liberty does not depend upon federalism and the separation of powers. On the other hand, modern liberalism's commitment to *economic* efficiency, to the maximization of strictly personal preferences and to the correction of the 'anti-egalitarian consequences of free enterprise in practice' means that utilitarian social welfare theory's first and second fundamental welfare theorems are instrumentally important to the 'perfection' of the 'economic market'. Yet, as we have seen, the relentless pursuit of economic efficiency and of 'socially desired' income allocations proceeds at the expense of federalism and the separation of powers. If, as I argue, institutionless, intendedly value-free and utilitarian social welfare theory can be used to rationalize all manner of ad hoc 'market interventions' and redistribution schemes, its 'romanticized view' of politics militates against consideration of the procedural questions that animated the Founders' republican self-government project.

Let us be clear: the Founders would reject a moral and political philosophy that insists both that individuals be given 'moral and political space', and that federal policy be dedicated to the satisfaction of 'wants' and 'needs' and the pursuit of distributive or 'social' justice. Moreover, given their understanding of rights as the result of self-government, the Founders would abhor the mestastization of 'rights', among other things, to education, employment, health care and housing – all claimed to be antecedent to civil society. And, given their concern with the 'rage of legislation', Jefferson, Wilson and others of the Founding generation would be dismayed that the urge to 'perfect the economic market' has been the catalyst both to a burgeoning body of tax, regulatory, environmental, labor and other law, and to its concomitant, the explosive growth of agency rule-making. Finally, the Founders would understand that the expansion of the federal enterprise has been facilitated by the Supreme Court's expansive readings of the Constitution's General Welfare, Necessary and Proper, Interstate Commerce and Legislative Powers Clauses. Just as Madison feared, the relentless advance of the 'responsive state' has been underwritten by 'the high sanction given to a latitude in expounding the Constitution which seems to break down the landmarks intended by a specification of the Powers of Congress' (Madison [1819] 1999, p. 734).

From the Founders' perspective, we have failed to take account of one of their fundamental insights; namely, that constitutional restraints on majoritarian democracy are a necessary condition for the survival of a self-governing republic. Moreover, we take little or no cognizance of the fact that, if the moral equivalence of persons requires that the greatest possible equal political participation be promoted, the worth or fair value of equal political participation requires that the Constitution 'underwrite a fair opportunity to take part in and to influence the political process' (Rawls, 1971, p. 224). If this means, as the Founders clearly intended, that federalism and the separation of powers must be respected, it also means that 'procedures guaranteeing adequate time for discussion, debate, and votes – known as "regular order" – in committee, on the floor, and in conference, which are essential if congress is to play its critical role [*must not be*] routinely ignored to advance the majority agenda' (Mann and Ornstein, 2006, p. 7).

6.2   A THOUGHT EXPERIMENT

The Founders' perspective is the focus of this, the final chapter. At issue are the federal on-, off- and off-off-budget activities discussed in Chapter 1. Informed by the Founders thinking (Chapter 2), by a critical assessment of the Supreme Court's constitutional jurisprudence (Chapters 3 and 4), and by an equally critical appraisal of the 'public philosophy of modern America' and the political economy to which it is conjoined (Chapter 5), I engage in a thought experiment: suppose that the Founders were asked to assess extant and prospective federal activities. Given their moral and political philosophy, their political economy and their textualist approach to constitutional jurisprudence, the question is, which federal on-, off-, and off-off-budget activities would be judged to be immoral, unconstitutional, or both? In brief but heuristic outline, I deploy the following evaluative standards:

- Respect for the moral law and its corollaries, the promotion of the maximum possible equal political participation, and the passage of just, in the sense of impartial, laws.
- Respect for Hamilton's Smithian/Kantian maxim that 'as no man can be sure that he may not be tomorrow the victim of a spirit of injustice, by which he may be a gainer to-day . . . every man must now feel, that the inevitable tendency of such a spirit is to sap the foundations of public and private confidence, and to introduce in its stead universal distrust and distress' (Carey and McClellan, 2001, pp. 406–7).
- Respect for Jefferson's, Madison's and the early Congresses' objection to federal provision of 'bounties, premiums and other aids' (Hamilton [1791] 2001, p. 671) to manufacturers and the private sector generally.

- Respect for Hamilton's view of the Constitution as 'the standard to which we are to cling . . . rejecting all changes but through the channel itself provides for amendments' ([1802] 2001, p. 989).
- Respect for Madison's admonition that, in interpreting the Constitution, 'It is but too common to read the expressions of a remote period thro' the modern meaning of them, & to omit guards agst. misconstruction not anticipated' (Madison [1833] 1999, p. 865), and for Jefferson's concern that 'The judiciary of the United States is the subtle corps of sappers and miners constantly working under ground to undermine the foundations of our confederated fabric. They are construing our constitution from a co-ordination of a general and special government to a general and supreme one alone' ([1820] 1984, p. 1446).
- Respect for Jefferson's insistence that 'I believe the States can best govern our home concerns, and the General Government our foreign ones. I wish, therefore, to see maintained that wholesome distribution of powers established by the constitution for the limitation of both; and never to see all offices transferred to Washington, where, further withdrawn from the eyes of the people, they may more secretly be bought and sold as at market' ([1823] 1984, pp. 1476).
- Respect for Madison's warning that 'what is of most importance is the high sanction given to a latitude in expounding the Constitution which seems to break down the landmarks intended by a specification of the Powers of Congress, and to substitute for a definite connection between means and ends, a Legislative discretion as to the former to which no practical limit can be assigned' ([1819] 1999, p. 734).

Finally, my evaluation of federal activity is informed by Madison's *The Federalist* No. 45, and by James Wilson's careful, systematic codification of the federal government's enumerated powers. I note first that:

> Wilson was one of only six persons to sign both the Declaration of Independence and the Constitution; only Gouverneur Morris spoke more frequently in the Philadelphia Convention of 1787; and scholars rank Wilson as the second most influential member of that convention, behind only James Madison. (Hall and Hall, 'Introduction', 2007, p. XIII)

Wilson's celebrated Lecturers on Law, 'Delivered in the College of Philadelphia, in the Years One Thousand Seven Hundred and Ninety and One Thousand Seven Hundred and Ninety One', include discussions of the Constitutions of the United States and of Pennsylvania, and of the 'Legislative Department'. Of immediate interest is Wilson's characterization of the 'powers vested in congress by the constitution of the United States':

> On this subject, we discover a striking difference between the constitution of the United States and of Pennsylvania. By the latter, each house of the general assembly is vested with every power necessary for a branch of the legislature of a free state. In the former, no clause of such an extensive and unqualified import is to be found. The reason is plain. The latter institutes a legislature with general, the former with enumerated powers. (Hall and Hall, 2007, p. 870)

With this as background, Wilson lists the enumerated powers of the 'national government':

> One great end of the national government is to 'provide for the common defense'. . .
>
> Another great end of the national government is, 'to ensure domestick tranquility'. That it may be enabled to accomplish this end, congress may call for the militia to suppress insurrections.
>
> Again, the national government is instituted to 'establish justice'. For this purpose, congress is authorized to erect tribunals inferiour to the supreme court. . .
>
> It is an object of the national government to 'form a more perfect union'. On this principle, congress is empowered to regulate commerce among the several states, to establish post offices, to fix the standard of weights and measures, to coin and regulate the value of money, and to establish, throughout the United States, a uniform rule of naturalization.
>
> Once more, at this time: the national government was intended to *promote the general welfare*'. For this reason, congress have power to regulate commerce with the Indians and with foreign nations, and to promote the progress of science and of useful arts, by securing, for a time, to authors and inventors, an exclusive right to their compositions and discoveries.
>
> An exclusive property in places fit for forts, magazines, arsenals, dockyards and other useful buildings . . . will be of great publick utility, perhaps, of evident publick necessity. They are, therefore, vested in congress, by the constitution of the United States.
>
> For the exercise of the foregoing powers, and for the accomplishment of the foregoing purposes, a revenue is unquestionably indispensable. That congress may be enabled to exercise and accomplish them, it has power to lay and collect taxes, duties, imposts, and excises. (Wilson, pp. 870–72; emphasis mine)

To this list of the national government's enumerated powers, Wilson adds that:

The powers of Congress are, indeed, enumerated; but it was intended that those powers, thus enumerated, should be effectual, and not nugatory. In conformity to this, . . . congress has power to make all laws, which shall be *necessary and proper* for carrying into execution every power vested by the constitution in the government of the United States. (Ibid., p. 872; emphasis mine)

It is appropriate that James Wilson's understanding of the federal government's enumerated powers be invoked as an evaluative standard. As we know, Wilson has been recognized as one of the Constitution's chief architects (Hall and Hall, 'Introduction', Volume I, 2007, p. XX). Equally important, as Kermit Hall has emphasized, 'Wilson . . . advocated for federalism and the related concept of dual sovereignty':

Since the people were the foundation of all government, they could construct as many levels of authority as they wished. Thus, the people could not only establish a *national government of enumerated powers but simultaneously lend their support to state governments vested with the traditional police powers of health, safety, morals and welfare.* (Ibid., pp. XIX–XX; emphasis mine)

Wilson, in short, provides both informed and clear guidance as to the powers and responsibilities of the national and state governments:

In [a federal] republik, *the rights of internal legislation may be reserved to all the states, of which it is composed*; while the adjustment of their several claims, the power of peace and war, the regulation of commerce, the right of entering into treaties, the authority of taxation, and the direction and government of the common force of the confederacy may be vested in the national government. (Hall and Hall, Volume I, 2007, p. 666; emphasis mine)

Finally, as its author, Wilson stressed the nexus between the Necessary and Proper Clause and the federal government's *enumerated* powers. As was emphasized in Chapter 2, Wilson insisted that 'the clause at the end of the eighth section [of Article 1 of the Constitution] . . . gives no more or other powers . . . beyond the particular enumeration . . . those words are limited and defined by the following, "for carrying into execution the foregoing [enumerated] powers"' (Kurland and Lerner, 1987c, p. 241).[1] Significantly, Wilson *rejected* the 'general objection to this system, that "the powers of Congress are unlimited and undefined, and that [the Congress] will be the judges, in all cases, of what is necessary and proper for them to do"' (ibid.).

With these evaluative standards in mind I consider, in turn, the federal on-, off- and off-off-budget activities discussed in Sections 1.1, 1.3 and 1.4 in Chapter 1. I proceed on the assumption that the programmatic and other details adumbrated in Chapter 1 need not be reprised, and that the argument developed in Chapters 1 through 5 can be deployed without further explanatory or justificatory effort.

6.3   BAILOUTS, STIMULUS AND ALL THAT: THE FOUNDERS' VIEW

Divisions A, B and C of the three-part bill that became law on 3 October 2008 would, on various dimensions of appraisal, be unacceptable to the Founders. Division A includes the Troubled Asset Relief Program (TARP).

It is first of all clear that the underlying bill is a metaphor for what James Wilson called the 'rage of legislation', and Jefferson styled the 'instability of our laws'. Hurriedly cobbled together without appeal to 'regular order', the bill institutionalizes, extends or modifies tax provisions benefiting 'targeted', well-defined beneficiaries (Divisions B and C). On the one hand, therefore, the bill adds to the body of discriminatory 'tax expenditures' that the Founders would find morally reprehensible. On the other hand, the *process* that gave rise to the bill violates the principle of maximum possible equal political participation. Moreover, as it has been implemented, Division A (TARP) is itself a metaphor for blatant disregard of the constitutional separation of powers. Whereas Division A contemplates the purchase of 'troubled assets' from 'financial institutions', the Treasury Department has institutionalized 12 programs that do not involve the purchase of troubled assets. Rather, the programs are designed to benefit such disparate beneficiaries as automobile manufacturers and part suppliers, home buyers, small businesses and investors buying securities backed by consumer loans, student loans, credit card debt and legacy mortgage-backed securities.

While it is possible to question whether TARP is consistent with the federal government's enumerated powers, this much is clear: the Supreme Court's expansive reading of the Constitution's Legislative Powers Clause notwithstanding (see Section 4.5, Chapter 4), TARP, as implemented, represents a usurpation of Congress's legislative powers. Add to this the bailouts and preferential tax provisions that are their defining characteristics, and it is clear that the Founders would have opposed the passage of the Emergency Economic Stabilization Act of 2008 (Division A), the Energy Improvement and Extension Act of 2008 (Division B), and the Tax Extenders and Alternative Minimum Tax Relief Act of 2008 (Division C). Granting this, the Secretary of the Treasury would *not* now have 'the authority to purchase and hold up to roughly $699 billion in assets at one time'. Moreover, the 'Total Projected Funding at Risk', a total 'including

TARP funds, loans and guarantees from other agencies, and private money' that 'could reach nearly $3 trillion' would *not* be at risk.[2]

The Founders' view of the American Recovery and Reinvestment Act of 2009, the Stimulus Bill, would, in its essentials, be congruent with their assessment of TARP and its related legislation. They would oppose the passage of a 781-page, $787 billion bill replete with discriminatory tax provisions and targeted grants and subsidies. And they would insist that a 14.5-hour Stimulus Bill 'debate' represents both an affront to republican self-government and a threat to liberty.

If, as I argue, the Founders would reject the Stimulus Bill (and, thereby, reduce federal spending by $787 billion), they would, I am confident, have opposed the passage of the Omnibus Appropriations Act, 2009. At issue is the Congress's 'now-routine' appeal to omnibus bills and the concomitant, systematic disregard of congressional budget process law.

The eminent historian of the United States' Founding, Forrest McDonald, has emphasized that 'The Constitution is primarily a structural and procedural document, specifying who is to exercise what powers and how. It is a body of law, designed to govern, not the people, but government itself' (2004, p. 185). If the Founders *hoped* that the Constitution's procedural restraints would disperse power and defend liberty, they *insisted* that post-constitutional statutory law must reflect the maximum possible equal political participation.

The passage of the $410 billion Omnibus Appropriations Act of 2009 is symptomatic of Congress's disregard, not only of the body of budget process law, but of the imperative to produce legislation that is the product of a slow, systematic and transparent deliberative process. As has now become commonplace, having failed to pass nine of 12 appropriations bills, the Congress resorted first to a Continuing Resolution and, then, to an ad hoc Omnibus Bill. If it is clear, as Mann and Ornstein have suggested, that omnibus appropriations bills result 'in stealth legislation that has not really passed majority muster' (2006, p. 173), it is equally clear that the Founders would both reject omnibus bills and insist upon 'Procedures guaranteeing adequate time for discussion, debate, and votes . . . in committee, on the floor, and in conference'. They would insist, in short, that all legislative deliberation reflect the procedural constraints known as 'regular order' (ibid., p. 7). The Founders would understand that departures from regular order do not simply disenfranchise members of the polity and their elected representatives; they are corrosive of trust in, and the legitimacy of, government. And, above all, they threaten liberty and erode the foundations of our self-governing republic.

It should be clear that these remarks apply, perforce, to an 'earmarking process' that is inherently discriminatory, that lacks transparency and that underwrites congressional incumbency. The same is true of deliberate efforts to truncate the budget process so as to facilitate the passage of controversial legislation. Simply stated, the Founders would regard appeals to earmarks and to the budget reconciliation process as incompatible with the moral equivalence of persons, and with the associated procedural imperative to promote the greatest possible equal political participation.

6.4   FEDERAL ON- AND OFF-BUDGET ACTIVITY: THE FOUNDERS' VIEW

We saw in Chapter 1, Section 1.1 and Section 6.3 above that 'regular order' has been 'routinely ignored to advance the majority agenda' (Mann and Ornstein, 2006, p. 7). Indeed, it may fairly be said that the 'demise of regular order' has been accompanied by the 'death of budget process law'. The result has been that Congress has routinely substituted continuing resolutions and omnibus bills for budgets. Whereas a 'budget for any fiscal year' *should be* the product of a systematic, 11-month *deliberative* process (Section 1.1), '[The House] Rules Committee . . . has facilitate[d] the now-routine process of folding many significant issues into huge omnibus bills and bringing them to the House floor for *up-or-down votes without any notice or time for members to read or absorb them*' (Mann and Ornstein, 2006, p. 173; emphasis mine) (Section 1.1 and Section 6.3 above).

There can be no doubt that the Founders would find this to be morally abhorrent! This is true, moreover, irrespective of the character and content of omnibus bills. As has been repeatedly emphasized, the Founders' prior ethical commitment to the moral equivalence of persons has as a corollary the moral imperative to promote the greatest possible equal political participation. Were nothing else to be said, this consideration would be decisive: *from the Founders' perspective, Congress's neglect of the equal political participation imperative calls into question the entire corpus of federal on- and off-budget acitivity.*[3]

While the Founders would also object to the character and content of federal on- and off-budget activity, I focus for the moment on a different, defining characteristic of the 'Unified Budget'. Recall, first, that the Unified Budget combines on- and off-budget programs. Recall also that the Unified Budget has been in deficit in all but 12 of the post-World War II fiscal years (see Chapter 1, Sections 1.2 and 1.3). While the corollary of this has been an accelerating rate of increase in the statutory 'debt limit', a limit currently in excess of $12 trillion, the essential point is this: from the Founders' perspective, the moral equivalence of persons demands that future generations – those who cannot agree to bear the future costs of debt-financed programs – be treated impartially. On this logic, and given that statutory balanced budget constraints are unavailing,[4] the Founders would insist upon a constitutional balanced budget constraint.

If, as I argue, the Founders would promote a constitutional balanced budget amendment, they would also object to the *composition* of federal on- and off-budget spending. In particular, they would object to the secular displacement of national defense spending by 'non-defense discretionary' and 'mandatory human resource programs' (see Tables 1.1 and 1.2 in Chapter 1).

My assessment of the Founders' response to the relative decline of national defense spending – both as a percentage of the Unified Budget and as a percentage of real Gross Domestic Product – is informed by the following considerations: first, we have it on the authority of James Madison and James Wilson that national defense is first among the federal government's *enumerated* powers (see Chapter 2, Section 2.3 and Section 6.2 above). Second, the Founders would quickly learn that it is the federal government's commitment to, and pursuit of, goals and policies other than national defense that accounts for the changing composition of federal on- and off-budget spending. They would note, in particular, that the Employment Act of 1946 'declares that it is the continuing policy and responsibility of the Federal Government' to promote an array of consequence based, procedurally-detached policy goals (see Chapter 1, Section 1.3). They would be aware that standing House and Senate Committees hold periodic 'Humphrey-Hawkins' Hearings to assess the federal government's progress toward the achievement of these goals.[5] The Founders would be aware that the federal government's policy goals bear little correspondence either to their procedurally based, consequence-detached republican self-government project (Chapter 2), or to the federal government's enumerated powers (Chapter 2, Section 2.3 and Section 6.2 above). They would understand that many of the 'goals' are inherently ambiguous – (promotion of) 'the general welfare', 'useful employment opportunities', 'full employment and production', 'balanced growth', 'adequate productivity growth', 'proper attention to national priorities' and 'reasonable price stability' are examples – and are, therefore, conducive to all manner of interpretations and policy 'imperatives'. They would be aware that the spirit and scope of the federal government's outcomes-based statement of federal 'policy and responsibility' was both affirmed and expanded in the Fiscal Year 2010 federal Budget. The Founders would understand that federal policy is informed by a public philosophy that: (1) insists that rights are antecedent to civil society (so that federalism and the separation of powers fade as a rights-protection concern), and (2) regards the economist's utilitarian social welfare theory as instrumentally important to the maximization of strictly personal utility, to the 'perfection' of the market system, and to the correction of 'forbidden' income and wealth inequalities (see Chapter 5). Finally, the Founders would understand that the Supreme Court has underwritten the relentless expansion of the federal government's outcomes based, procedurally-detached enterprise (see Chapter 4). The Court's 'generous' readings of the General Welfare, Necessary and Proper, Commerce and Legislative Powers Clauses would call to mind Madison's observation that 'the [Supreme] Court . . . has manifested a propensity to enlarge the general authority in derogation of the local' ([1823] 1999, p. 802), and Jefferson's view that 'The judiciary of the United States . . . [is] construing our constitution from a co-ordination of a general and special government to a general and supreme one alone' ([1820] 1984, p. 1446).

It would be clear to the Founders that the Supreme Court's deferential constitutional jurisprudence (Chapter 4) has both facilitated the federal government's usurpation of the states' police powers (see also Chapter 2, Section 2.3, and this chapter, Sections 6.2 and 6.5) and systematically eroded the separation of powers. I suggest, first, that the Founders would recall both Madison's concern with untrammeled 'Legislative discretion' as to means judged by Congress to be necessary ([1819] 1999, p. 734) to the achievement of constitutionally sanctioned powers, and Jefferson's fear that Congress might 'take everything under their management which *they* should deem for the *public welfare*, & which is susceptible of the application of money' ([1792a] 1984, p. 677; emphasis in original).

It is against this background that the Founders would assess Means Tested Entitlements, Medicare and Social Security, the spending categories that constitute the principal components of the federal government's 'mandatory human resource programs'; programs for which Fiscal Year 2010 inflation-adjusted outlays are estimated to total $1.629 trillion (Table 1.2, Chapter 1, this volume).

Consider first Means Tested Entitlements, a collection of programs that has increased from 4.1 percent of federal outlays in fiscal year (FY) 1962 to an estimated 15.6 percent in FY 2010 (Office of Management and Budget, 2009c, p. 138). Importantly, 'Means Tested Entitlements' include 'Medicaid, SNAP (formerly food stamps), family support assistance (AFDC), temporary assistance to needy families, [the] welfare contingency fund, child care entitlement to States, child nutrition programs, foster care and adoption assistance, State children's health insurance, supplemental security income (SSI), veterans pension, and [the] refundable portions of various tax credits that are subject to an income phase out' (ibid., p. 139). Setting aside the payment of veterans' pensions, a category that clearly falls under the rubric of national defense, the Founders would recognize that means testing is inherently discriminatory. It follows that, given their prior ethical commitment to the moral equivalence of persons, and given their understanding that justice in the sense of impartiality is the 'end of government' (see Sections 2.2 and 2.3, Chapter 2), they would reject all means tested programs. Equally important, they would recognize that transfer programs, whether means tested or not, are not among the federal government's enumerated powers (Chapter 2, Section 2.3 and Section 6.2 above). They would recall Madison's admonition that 'The very existence of . . . local sovereignties is a controul on the pleas for a constructive amplification of the powers of the General Govt.', and that 'Within a single State possessing the entire sovereignty, the powers given to the Govt. by the people are understood to extend to all the Acts whether as means or ends required for the welfare of the Community and falling within the range of just government' ([1819] 1999, p. 736). And they would embrace Jefferson's understanding that 'The capital and leading object of the constitution was to leave with the States all authorities which respected their own citizens only, and to transfer to the United States those which respected citizens of foreign or other States: to make us several as to ourselves, but one as to all others' ([1823] 1984, p. 1475). In short, the Founders would insist that, given the states' police powers, *the institutionalization of transfer programs is a prerogative of the several states, not of the federal government*. A corollary of this is that the Founders' view of the unfolding federal health-care reform debate would be informed by two ideas. First, their citizens' health, like other aspects of their citizens' 'general welfare', is counted among the *states'* police powers: 'States have an inherent "police power" to promote public safety, health, morals, public convenience, and general prosperity' (Congressional Research Service, 2004, p. 1681).[6] Second, even if the health-care reform debate does not reach the question of the states' police powers (see Section 6.5 below), the Founders would object to the use of 'budget reconciliation' to facilitate passage of a health-care reform bill (Chapter1, Section 1.1). From their perspective, because departures from 'regular order' violate the principle of maximum possible equal political participation they are both immoral and a threat to liberty.

Whether or not the United States Senate employs budget reconciliation to secure passage of a health-care reform bill, the essential point is this: *Helvering* was decided in 1937 (see Chapter 4, Sections 4.2 and 4.3). In the period since 1937:

not once has the [Supreme] Court invalidated an act of Congress because it violated the General Welfare Clause. Yet the federal government has immersed itself in matters ranging from public schools to hurricane relief, drug enforcement, welfare, retirement systems, medical care, family planning, housing, and the arts – *not a single one of which can be found among Congress's enumerated powers.* (Levy and Mellor, 2008. p. 29; emphasis mine)[7]

There can be no doubt that this would, from the Founders' perspective, be decisive. Means Tested Entitlements – accounting, as we have seen, for an estimated 15.6 percent of FY 2010 federal outlays – are unconstitutional. This is true, moreover, whether or not the programs are means tested. That said, I emphasize again that transfer programs are the prerogative of the states. The Founders would surely recall Madison's admonition that 'the powers not delegated to the United States, by the Constitution, nor prohibited by [the Constitution] to the states, are reserved to the states respectively, or to the people' ([1800] 1999, p. 610).

These remarks apply with equal force to Medicare and Social Security; programs that are estimated to account for 34 percent of FY 2010 federal outlays (Office of Management and Budget, 2009c, pp. 23 and 236). While it is clear that neither program is contemplated by the federal government's enumerated powers, their institutionalization, like that of Means Tested Entitlements, may be traced to the interaction of two powerful forces. On the one hand, the programs are a metaphor for what Madison called 'legislative encroachments' ([1819], 1999, p. 734). On the other hand, the congressional impulse to expand its powers beyond those granted by the Constitution has been underwritten by the Supreme Court's 'great deference to Congress's decision that a spending program advances the general welfare'. Indeed, as we have seen (in Chapter 4, Section 4.3), the Court 'has even questioned whether [a restriction on the spending power] is judicially enforceable' (Congressional Research Service, 2004, pp. 163–4). While the argument developed in Chapter 4, Sections 4.2 and 4.3 will not be reprised, the essential point is that the New Court's General Welfare and Necessary and Proper Clause jurisprudence has facilitated the relentless expansion of federal on- and off-budget activity.

As we saw in Sections 4.2 and 4.3, the central problem is this: the Supreme Court takes little or no cognizance of the fact that the General Welfare Clause limits Congress's *taxing* power. I emphasize in particular that, whereas Article I, Section 8, Clause I, the General Welfare Clause, authorizes tax levies for debt payment, for the common defense, and for the *general* welfare, it does *not* authorize the special exclusions, exemptions, deductions or other 'targeted' tax provisions that are today characterized as 'tax expenditures' (see Chapter 1, Section 1.4 and Section 6.5 below). For its part, Article I, Section 8, Clause 18, the Necessary and Proper Clause, authorizes Congress to 'make all Laws which shall be *necessary and proper for carrying into Execution the foregoing powers*'; that is, for carrying into execution the federal government's *enumerated* powers.

This, as we have seen, is the view articulated by James Wilson, the *author* of the Necessary and Proper Clause (see Chapter 4, Section 4.3). It follows that, while it is an instrumentally important 'means' by which the federal government's *enumerated powers* can be exercised, federal spending must be 'necessary and proper' for the 'Execution' of those powers.

Finally, the constitutional constraints on federal spending and taxes would, along with their commitment to the impartiality imperative, inform the Founders' appraisal of federal tax policy. The Tax Code of the United States is replete with blatantly discriminatory preferential tax provisions or 'tax expenditures' (see Chapter 1, Section 1.4 this volume). Because they fall under the rubric of off-off-budget activity, discussion of the Founders' view of these provisions is deferred to Section 6.5 below. For the moment, interest centers on tax rate 'progressivity', another defining characteristic of the Tax Code.

I suggest, first, that the Founders would agree with Buchanan and Congleton that tax rate progressivity is a predictable consequence of the functioning of majoritarian democracy. Reduced to its essentials, 'members of the exploiting majority have more to gain from tax discrimination against the rich than against middle- or low-income groups' (Buchanan and Congleton, 1998, p. 91; Chapter 1, Section 1.3). Equally important, the Founders would recognize that tax rate progressivity is a reflection of modern liberalism's insistence that 'those who have less talent, as the market judges talent, have a right to some form of redistribution in the name of [social] justice' (R. Dworkin, 1985, p. 199; see Chapter 5, Sections 5.3, 5.4 and 5.7). If the Founders would reject modern liberalism's 'general theory of political distribution', a theory about 'how whatever the community has to assign . . . should be assigned' (R. Dworkin, 1985, p. 192), they would surely reject modern liberalism's claim that 'resources and opportunities should be distributed, so far as possible, equally' (ibid.; Section 5.4). *Nothing* in the Founders' moral and political philosophy (Chapter 2, Section 2.2), their political economy (Section 2.4) or their understanding of the Constitution as a restraint on discriminatory factious behavior (Section 2.3) can be construed to mean that they would endorse tax rate progressivity. Finally, given their interest in economics (Sections 2.2 and 2.4), the Founders would surely know that modern liberalism's relentless effort to 'perfect the economic market' and to 'correct forbidden [income and wealth] inequalities' has been underwritten by the economist's utilitarian theory of the state; a theory that, despite its indeterminacy (see Section 5.8), can and has been used to rationalize both 'market imperfection'-animated credit, insurance and regulatory activity (see Section 6.5 below), and income and wealth redistribution policies (Chapter 5, Sections 5.5 and 5.8).

In short, the Founders would reject the moral and political philosophy that promotes, and the political economy that has been used to rationalize, income redistribution. Add to this Madison's admonition that 'that alone is a just government which impartially secures to every man whatever is his own' ([1792b] 1999, p. 515) and it is clear that the Founders would reject both tax rate progressivity and the body of discriminatory tax expenditures (see next section). Given their prior ethical commitment to the moral equivalence of persons it seems plausible to suggest that they would seek both to abolish the Tax Code, and to institutionalize a proportional income or expenditure tax (Chapter 1, Section 1.3).

6.5   FEDERAL OFF-OFF-BUDGET ACTIVITY: THE FOUNDERS' VIEW

'Targeted' federal loan, loan guarantee and insurance programs are the products of the intersection of modern liberalism's commitment to 'perfect the economic market' and to 'reduce income inequality and increase access' (Chapter 1, Section 1.4, Chapter 5, Sections 5.3 and 5.4), and the normative use of the economist's theory of the state, social welfare theory (Section 5.5). On the one hand, social welfare theory's first fundamental welfare theorem is deployed to rationalize 'market failure'-animated government interventions. On the other hand, the second fundamental welfare theorem is deployed to correct market-generated 'forbidden inequalities' (Section 5.8). As we have seen, all of this proceeds despite the problems that attend both modern liberalism and social welfare theory (Sections 5.5, 5.6, 5.7 and 5.8).

While, as I have suggested, the Founders would reject both modern liberalism's moral and political philosophy (Sections 5.3 and 5.4) and the economist's consequence based procedurally-detached theory of the state (Sections 5.6, 5.7 and 5.8), the essential point is this: the Founders would be aware that, with the possible exception of deposit and terrorism insurance (Chapter 1, Section 1.4), the federal government's enumerated powers do not contemplate the institutionalization of loan, loan guarantee or insurance programs. Neither modern liberalism's insistence that 'resources and opportunities should be distributed, so far as possible, equally' (R. Dworkin, 1985, p. 192) nor the social welfare theorist's 'market imperfection' analysis can, legitimately, overcome this *constitutional* constraint. That said, while the Founders would acknowledge that the provision of credit and insurance programs is a prerogative of the *states*, they would counsel that the in-period and intergenerational discrimination that characterizes such programs renders them *morally* objectionable (Sections 1.4 and 5.7).

Given the nature of my thought experiment we may assume that the Founders would, today, be aware that the states' police powers have, over time, been attenuated. Indeed, the Founders would agree that, 'If a [state] police power regulation goes too far, it will be recognized as a taking of property for which compensation must be paid' (Congressional Research Service, 2004, p. 1681). This understanding is informed by the Fifth Amendment's Takings Clause: 'nor shall private property be taken for public use, without just compensation'. The phrase 'public use' is crucial. In its controversial ruling in *Kelo et al.* v. *City of New London* (2005), the Supreme Court held that, because the City of New London's economic development plan 'unquestionably serves a *public purpose*, the takings challenged here satisfy the *public use* requirement of the Fifth Amendment' (Opinion, p. 13; emphasis mine). It is sufficient for present purposes to emphasize that, in their *Kelo* Dissents, Justices O'Connor and Thomas gesture toward Madison's and Jefferson's arguments against 'misconstruction' or 'broad construction' of the Constitution (see Chapter 2, Section 2.3). Justice O'Connor's language is clear and unambiguous: 'the Court today . . . holds that the sovereign may take private property currently put to ordinary private use, and give it over for new, ordinary private use, so long as the new use is predicted to generate some secondary benefit for the public' (Dissent, p. 8). While, as Justice O'Connor suggests, 'The Founders cannot have intended [this] perverse result', the *Kelo* decision appears to relax the constraint on the 'sovereign's' eminent domain power.[8]

If the Founders would reject the Supreme Court's expansive reading of the Takings Clause, they would surely not endorse the Supreme Court's 'discovery' of a Commerce Clause-driven 'national' police or regulatory power. We know, for example, that in *United States* v. *Darby* (312 US (1941)), the Supreme Court asserted that Congress's Commerce Clause power is analogous to the states' police power. Just as Madison feared (see Section 2.3), the Court's acquiescence to Congress's 'legislative encroachments' has been animated by the growth of interstate commerce. In *New York* v. *United States* (1992), the Court held that 'As interstate commerce has become ubiquitous, activities once considered purely local have come to have effects on the national economy, and have accordingly come within the scope of the Congress' commerce power'. If the *New York* Court's 'effects on the national economy' construction gestures toward the Supreme Court's 'affecting commerce' standard (see Chapter 4, Sections 4.2 and 4.4), the essential point is this: the Supreme Court's Commerce Clause jurisprudence has resulted in 'the virtual disappearance of the distinction between interstate and intrastate commerce' (Congressional Research Service, 2004, p. 212). As I have emphasized, the result is that the Supreme Court has gradually 'turned the commerce power into the equivalent of a general regulatory power and undid the Framers' original structure of limited and delegated powers' (Forte, 2005, p. 204).

This would be obvious to the Founders. They would be aware that, even prior to the late 1930s constitutional revolution (see again, Sections 4.2 and 4.4), 'not all [federal] measures taken to promote objectives which had traditionally been regarded as the responsibilities of the States had been held invalid' (Congressional Research Service, 2004, p. 1615). Among other things, the Supreme Court 'sustained federal laws penalizing the interstate transportation of lottery tickets, of women for immoral purposes, of stolen automobiles, and of tick-infected cattle' (ibid.). That said, the Founders would be aware that the New Court's Commerce Clause jurisprudence has properly been characterized as 'one of the most confused areas of constitutional law', and that the New Court's Commerce Clause holdings have borne little relation either to Chief Justice Marshall's 1824 *Gibbons* v. *Ogden* holding, or to the Court's pre-1938 Commerce Clause jurisprudence. Just as Madison feared, the New Court has held that activities 'which are antecedent to or subsequent to a move across state lines are conceived to be part of an integrated commercial whole and therefore subject to the reach of [Congress's] commerce power' (see Chapter 2, Section 2.3, Chapter 4, Sections 4.2 and 4.4).

The Founders would surely recognize that the New Court's Commerce Clause jurisprudence has accompanied the emergence of *national* economic and social legislation, itself a reflection of the Progressive movement, and of modern liberalism's determination to 'perfect the economic market' and to correct 'the anti-egalitarian consequences of free enterprise in practice' (see Chapter 5, Sections 5.1, 5.3, 5.4 and 6.1 above). Equally important, the Founders would understand that the New Court has given its imprimatur to the federal government's embrace of economic and social 'responsibilities' not contemplated by its enumerated powers (Chapter 5, Sections 1.3, 4.4 and 6.4).

If, as I have suggested, the Founders would reject modern liberalism and the economic theory to which it is conjoined, social welfare theory (see Chapter 5, Sections 5.3, 5.4, 5.5, 5.6, 5.7 and 5.8), they would surely insist that the New Court's Commerce Clause jurisprudence is animated by 'principles of decision' that exhibit excessive deference to congressional regulatory action. I suggest, in particular, that the Founders would find the 'affecting commerce' and 'class-of-activities' standards (Section 4.4) to be inherently ambiguous, antithetical to the states' police powers, and congenial to essentially unconstrained federal regulatory activity.

Following Madison, the Founders would acknowledge that 'In the great system of Political Economy . . . everything is related immediately or remotely to every other thing', so that 'a Power over any one thing, if not limited by some obvious and precise affinity, may amount to a Power over every other'. Given the interdependencies that characterize an economy, the Founders would agree with Madison that the danger is that 'Ends & means may shift their character at the will & according to the ingenuity of the Legislative Body' ([1819] 1999, p. 734).[9]

Given the 'ingenuity of the Legislative Body', and given that 'everything is related immediately or remotely to every other thing' (Madison [1819] 1999, p. 734), the Founders would not be satisfied that the New Court's rational basis test is an effective restraint on the relentless expansion of federal regulatory activity. As we have seen (in Chapter 4, Section 4.4), the test asks only if Congress had a 'rational basis' for a finding that a regulated activity 'affects' interstate commerce, or if there is a 'reasonable connection between the regulatory means selected and the asserted ends'.

If the inherently subjective rational basis test is instrumentally important to the Supreme Court's equally ambiguous 'affecting commerce' standard, the same is true of the class-of-activities standard. At issue is Congress's ability to determine that an *intrastate* activity is 'within a class the activities of which affect commerce' (Congressional Research Service, 2004, p. 215). Because the 'test' reduces to the question of whether a local activity is 'merely an element of a much broader commercial market' (Chapter 4, Section 4.4), it is difficult to imagine a circumstance in which Congress's Commerce Clause power does *not* apply. Indeed, as I have emphasized, for 53 years following *Wickard* v. *Filburn* (1942), no federal law was held to be unconstitutional because it exceeded Congress's Commerce Clause power (see again, Chapter 4, Section 4.4). That said, while the Court's rulings in *United States* v. *Lopez* (1995), *United States* v. *Morrison* (2000) and *Gonzalez* v. *Oregon* (2005) *limited* Congress's Commerce Clause powers, its holding in the most recent Commerce Clause case, *Gonzalez* v. *Raich* (2005) does the opposite (Chapter 4, Section 4.4).

It is safe to say that the Founders would be impatient with the Court's ambiguous and accommodative 'rational basis' test and the associated, equally vacuous 'affecting commerce' and 'class-of-activities' standards. Above all, they would insist upon respect for the *states'* police powers. They would, in short, associate themselves with the Dissents in *Raich*, a case in which Justice Stevens, writing for the majority, avers that:

> In assessing the scope of Congress' authority under the Commerce Clause, we stress that the task before us is a modest one. We need not determine whether respondents' activities, taken in the aggregate, substantially affect interstate commerce in fact but only whether a 'rational basis' exists for so concluding. . . Given the enforcement difficulties that attend distinguishing between marijuana cultivated locally and marijuana grown elsewhere . . . and concerns about

diversion into illicit channels, we have no difficulty concluding that Congress had a rational basis for believing that failure to regulate the intrastate manu- facture and possession of marijuana would leave a gaping hole in the [federal Controlled Substances Act]. Thus, as in *Wickard*, when it enacted compre- hensive legislation to regulate the interstate market in a fungible commodity, Congress was acting well within its authority to 'make all Laws which shall be necessary and proper' to 'regulate Commerce . . . among the several States'. . . . *That the regulation ensnares some purely intrastate activity is of no moment.* (Opinion, p. 19; emphasis mine)

If Justice Steven's invocation of the rational basis test is unexception- able, his assertion that '[if the federal] regulation ensnares some purely intr- astate activity [it] is of no moment' would, from the Founders' perspective, be unacceptable. Equally important, while his allusion to the Necessary and Proper Clause is clearly appropriate (see Chapter 4, Section 4.3 and 6.2 above), the Founders would surely agree with Justice Thomas's Dissent:

One searches the Court's Opinion in vain for any hint of what aspect of American life is reserved to the States. Yet this Court knows that '[t]he Constitution created a Federal Government of limited powers'. . . . That is why today's decision will add no measure of stability to our Commerce Clause juris- prudence: This Court is willing neither to enforce limits on federal power, nor to declare the Tenth Amendment a dead letter. If stability is possible, it is only by discarding the stand-alone substantial effects test and revisiting our defini- tion of 'commerce among the several states'. *Congress may regulate interstate commerce – not things that affect it, even when summed together, unless truly 'necessary and proper' to regulating interstate commerce.* (Dissent, pp. 14–15; emphasis mine)

While Justice Thomas's allusion to the federal government's limited powers and to the Tenth Amendment would please the Founders (see Chapter 2, Section 2.3) so too would his explicit rejection of the affecting commerce and class-of-activities standards. The Founders would, moreo- ver, associate themselves with Justice O'Connor's implicit critique of the Court's rational basis test:

Today's decision allows Congress to regulate intrastate activity without checks, so long as there is some implication by legislative design that regulating intra- state activity is essential (and the Court appears to equate 'essential' with 'nec- essary') to the interstate regulatory scheme. (Dissent, p. 5)

The Founders would recognize that Justice O'Connor's construction is evocative of Jefferson's admonition that we 'not make [the Constitution] a blank paper by construction' ([1803] 1984, p. 1140), and of Hamilton's insistence that 'To avoid an arbitrary discretion in the courts, it is indis- pensible that they should be bound down by strict rules and precedents'

(Carey and McClellan, 2001, p. 407) (see Section 2.3).[10] The Founders would note, as well, Justice O'Connor's admonition that '[The Supreme Court] would do well to recall how James Madison, the father of the Constitution, described our system of joint sovereignty to the people of New York:. . . The powers reserved to the several States will extend to all the objects which, in the ordinary course of affairs, concern the lives, liberties, and properties of the people, and the internal order, improvement, and prosperity of the State' (Dissent, p. 16) (see Chapter 2, Section 2.3). The Founders would agree that:

> [The Supreme Court] enforce[s] the 'outer limits' of Congress' Commerce Clause authority not for their own sake, but to protect historic spheres of state sovereignty from excessive federal encroachment and thereby to maintain the distribution of power fundamental to our federalist system of government. . .
>
> This case exemplifies the role of States as laboratories. The States' core police powers have always included authority to define criminal law and to protect the health, safety and welfare of their citizens'. (Ibid., p. 1)

The Founders would agree that the Supreme Court's Commerce Clause jurisprudence undermines the 'limited constitution' of Hamilton's, Jefferson's and Madison's imagination, underwrites the 'legislative encroachments' that Madison feared, and '[manifests] a propensity to enlarge the general authority in derogation of the local, and to amplify [the Supreme Court's] jurisdiction' (Madison [1823] 1999, p. 802; see Chapter 2, Section 2.3). Justice Thomas's Dissent in *Raich* is consistent with this interpretation: 'This Court has carefully avoided stripping Congress of its ability to regulate *inter*state commerce, but it has casually allowed the Federal Government to strip States of their ability to regulate *intra*state commerce' (p. 14).

These considerations would, from the Founders' perspective, inform the health-care reform debate. On the one hand, their citizens' health, like other dimensions of their 'general welfare', is counted among the *states'* police powers (see Chapter 2, Section 6.4 above). Stated differently, medical care is not among the federal government's enumerated powers (Chapter 2, Section 6.2). That said, as we have seen (Chapter 4, Section 4.4), 'except for the due process and equal protection clauses of the Fourteenth Amendment, [the Commerce Clause] is the most important limitation . . . on the exercise of the state [police] power' (Congressional Research Service, 2004, p. 169). It is not surprising, therefore, that some have claimed that 'If the federal government has any right to reform, revise or remake the American health-care system, it must be found in the [Commerce Clause]' (Rivkin and Casey, 2009, p. A23).

Given the evident tension between the states' police power and the federal government's commerce power, the Founders would insist upon an answer to this question: does the power vested in Congress by Article I, Section 8 of the Constitution, '[t]o make all Laws which shall be necessary and proper for carrying into Execution' its authority to 'regulate Commerce with foreign Nations, and among the several States' include the power to 'reform' the US health-care system? Given its holding in *Raich*, and given the body of New Court Commerce Clause jurisprudence, it is likely that the Court would, again, defer to Congress's discretion. That said, the Founders would, I suggest, regard medical care as an *intra*state activity. Granting this, they would associate themselves with Justice O'Connor's *Raich* Dissent:

> Today's decision suggests that the federal regulation of local activity is immune to Commerce Clause challenge because Congress chose to act with an ambitious, all-encompassing statute, rather than piecemeal. In my view, allowing Congress to set the terms of the constitutional debate in this way, i.e., by packaging regulation of local activity in broader schemes, is tantamount to removing meaningful limits on the Commerce Clause. (p. 4)

If, as Justice O'Connor suggests, 'The hard work for courts . . . is to identify objective markers for confining the analysis in Commerce Clause cases' (p. 6), it is also true that 'Even if Congress may regulate purely intrastate activity when essential to exercising some enumerated power. . . Congress may not use its incidental authority to subvert basic principles of federalism and dual sovereignty' (Thomas, Dissent, p. 9). That said, Justice Thomas notes that:

> In *McCulloch v. Maryland* . . . this Court, speaking through Chief Justice Marshall, set forth a test for determining when an Act of Congress is permissible under the Necessary and Proper Clause:

> 'Let the end be legitimate, let it be within the scope of the constitution, and all means which are appropriate, which are plainly adapted to that end, which are not prohibited, but consist with the letter and the spirit of the constitution, are constitutional'. (pp. 3–4)

The Founders would, of course, accept that the commerce power is among the federal government's enumerated powers. But if, as I suggest, they would regard citizens' health to be among the states' 'traditional police powers' (p. 9), they would surely question whether federal health-care reform legislation is an 'end . . . within the scope of the constitution'. They would, therefore, oppose any *federal* 'health-care reform' bill – whether or not it is 'deficit-neutral'.

It would be apparent to the Founders that the explosive growth of the federal government's regulatory enterprise is only partially attributable to the New Court's accommodative Commerce Clause jurisprudence. It would be equally apparent that the Court's generous reading of the Legislative Powers Clause has played an important role (see Chapter 4, Section 4.5). At issue is the Congress's propensity to delegate rule-making authority to Executive 'department' administrative agencies.

Recall first that the Founders regarded the separation of powers (and the other auxiliary precautions) as both instrumentally important and intrinsically valuable; instrumentally important as a constraint on factious behavior and, therefore, as a defense of liberty, and intrinsically valuable as an institutional reflection of respect for the moral equivalence of persons (Chapter 2, Sections 2.2 and 2.3). It follows that they would view administrative agencies' exercise of legislative *and* judicial powers both as a threat to liberty and as inconsistent with the moral law.

A corollary of this is that, for the Founders, the 'constitutional principles' that inform the New Court's non-delegation jurisprudence (Chapter 2, Section 4.5) – the provision of 'standards' and due process – would be unavailing. The Court's authorization of administrative agency behavior, whether it be 'filling up the details', 'legislating contingently' or 'expressing policy judgment' (Chapter 2, Section 4.5) would, for the Founders, be deeply corrosive of the separation of powers. Moreover, the Founders would be aware that '[i]t seems reasonably clear that the Court does not really require much in the way of standards from congress', and that the 'justifications' for congressional delegation of rule-making authority are decidedly unpersuasive. On the one hand, the 'market failure' justification is reliant upon a consequence based procedurally-detached economic theory (Chapter 5, Section 5.5) that is defined in opposition to the Founders' procedurally based consequence-detached republican self-government project (Chapter 2, Sections 2.2, 2.3 and 2.4). Equally important, despite its obvious moral, logical, empirical and ontological problems (Chapter 2, Sections 5.6, 5.7 and 5.8), social welfare theory is conjoined to modern liberalism, a moral and political philosophy that focuses on 'wants and needs' satisfaction, promotes economic rather than political efficiency, and endorses what are, effectively, ad hoc market interventions and income and wealth redistribution schemes (Chapter 2, Sections 5.3, 5.4 and 5.8). All of this would be alien to the Founders' imagination. On the other hand, the 'complexity of society' justification for congressional delegation of rule-making authority would, from the Founders' perspective, be equally unpersuasive. As we have seen (in Chapter 4, Sections 4.2 and 4.5), the logic is that 'In a complex society, Congress cannot specify every detail of legislative policy' (Uhlmann, 2005, p. 230). Granting this,

'Room must be left for the exercise of [administrative agencies'] discretionary judgment . . . if Congress decides to regulate many subjects extensively' (ibid.). The presumption is therefore that, provided that Congress 'set[s] forth "intelligible principles" or "standards" to guide as well as limit the agency or official', administrative agencies may 'fill up the details' (Congressional Research Service, 2004, p. 81; see Chapter 4, Section 4.2).

Nothing in this construction would, from the Founders' perspective, be compelling. The Founders would be aware that, 'Since 1935, the Court . . . has approved, "without deviation, Congress' ability to delegate [legislative] power under broad standards"' (Congressional Research Service, 2004, pp. 75–6; see Chapter 4, Section 4.2). If this means that administrative agencies are neither guided nor limited 'in the performance of [their] assigned task[s]', the decisive considerations are these: first, given the problems that inhere in the political philosophy and the political economy that animate the regulatory impulse, the 'complexity of society' cannot justify the 'rage of [regulatory] legislation' and the concomitant metastasization of agency rule making. Second, given their prior ethical commitment to the moral equivalence of persons, the Founders would not countenance regulations (or statutory laws) that concentrate benefits and disperse costs. This is true, moreover, whether Congress or a rule-making administrative agency seeks to 'perfect the economic market' or to correct 'forbidden' income or wealth inequalities (Chapter 5, Sections 5.3 and 5.4). Third, the exigencies of contingent circumstance – the 'complexity of society' – do not have as their corollary that the federal government can 'do better' (Chapter 5, Section 5.8). Fourth, and above all, the pursuit of consequence based procedurally-detached regulatory goals would, from the Founders' perspective, represent a threat to liberty. Resort to agency rule-making, whether by means of 'filling up the details', contingent legislation, or the exercise of 'policy judgment' serves only to exacerbate that threat.

Granting all of this, the Founders would insist that the separation of powers be respected, that 'ambition must be made to counteract ambition' (Chapter 2, Section 2.2), and that, paraphrasing Justice Harlan (Chapter 4, Section 4.5), fundamental policy decisions be made, not by appointed officials, but by 'the body immediately responsible to the people'. If this means that the pace of regulatory and other legislation is slowed then, following Jefferson and Wilson, so much the better (Chapter 4, Section 2.3).

The remaining component of off-off-budget activity, tax expenditures (Chapter 1, Section 1.4), would receive the Founders' virtually unqualified disapprobation. While the Founders would likely be sympathetic to the provision of benefits and allowances to active Armed Forces and to military veterans (Office of Management and Budget, 2009b, pp. 307, 312 and

326), they would reject the discriminatory special exclusions, exemptions, deductions, tax credits, preferential tax rates and deferrals of tax liability provided under the rubrics of International Affairs, General Science, Space and Technology, Energy, Natural Resources and Environment, Agriculture, Commerce and Housing, Transportation, Community and Regional Development, Education, Training, Employment, and Social Services, Health, Income Security, Social Security, General Government and Interest (ibid., pp. 307–26).

The Founders' objections would be informed, in part, by constitutional questions. They would, among other things, question the delegation of rule-making authority to the Internal Revenue Service (Chapter 4, Section 4.5) and, more generally, the usurpation of the states' police powers (Chapter 4, Sections 4.3, 4.4, and 6.4 above). Equally important, they would reject both the moral and political philosophy and the political economy that animate preferential tax code provisions (Chapter 5, Sections 5.3, 5.4 and 5.5). That said, the Founders would insist that inherently discriminatory tax policies are inconsistent with the moral equivalence of persons (Chapter 2, Sections 2.2, 2.3 and 2.4), corrosive of trust and of the legitimacy of government and, ultimately, a threat to liberty. In short, they would, as I have suggested (in Chapter 1, Section 1.4), embrace Madison's admonition that:

> The apportionment of taxes, on the various descriptions of property, is an act which seems to require the most exact impartiality; yet there is, perhaps, no legislative act in which greater opportunity and temptation are given to a predominant party, to trample on the rules of justice. (Carey and McClellan, 2001, p. 45)

A corollary of all of this is that the Founders would reject both tax rate progressivity *and* the body of discriminatory tax expenditures. In short, they would seek both to abolish the Tax Code and to institutionalize a proportional income or expenditure tax (Chapter 1, Section 1.4). Moreover, given their prior ethical commitment to the moral equivalence of persons, their commitment to the greatest possible equal political participation, their insistence that post-constitutional law both reflect and promote respect for the moral law, and their political economy, the Founders would promote a set of *institutional* restraints or constitutional 'auxiliary precautions'. The 'precautions', in turn, would be informed by the realization that statutory restraints on representative democracy are unavailing; that no Congress can bind succeeding Congresses, and that Senate and House Rules Committees can promulgate procedural rules that ignore regular order generally, and budget process law in particular. With this in mind, the Founders would promote:

- A constitutional generality or impartiality constraint (see Chapter 1, Sections 1.3 and 2.4).
- A constitutional Balanced Budget amendment that includes a prohibition against federal off-off-budget credit and insurance programs.
- A constitutional amendment prohibiting the passage of omnibus appropriations bills and continuing resolutions, and requiring the passage of an Annual Budget. Passage of the Budget, in turn, must contemplate public committee hearings and 'mark-ups', with House, Senate and Conference debates and votes conducted in public.
- Following Jefferson and Wilson, a constitutional amendment requiring that all bills (other than the Annual Budget) be 'laid upon the table' for a period of six months; that, during the six-month period, all bills must be available to the public, and debated in public committee hearings and 'mark-ups'; and that, after the six-month period, floor debates and votes in both Chambers and in Conference, be conducted in public.
- A constitutional amendment, drafted by James Wilson, stipulating that the constitutionality of federal spending programs is determined by appeal to the federal government's enumerated powers, rather than by Congress's determination of what is in the national interest, or by the 'conditioning of funds'.
- A constitutional amendment stipulating that, so long as a state, in the exercise of its traditional police powers (see Chapter 4, Section 6.4 above) does not *restrict* or *impede* the flow of interstate commerce, its local activity is not subject to the federal interstate commerce power.
- A constitutional amendment prohibiting administrative agency rule-making.

Some may say that this 'menu' of proposed constitutional amendments is 'unrealistic'; that the probability of their adoption approaches zero. The response, it seems to me, is clear. On the one hand, as Buchanan and Tullock have shown, 'The self-interest of the individual participant at [the constitutional] level leads him to take a position as a "representative" or "randomly distributed" participant in the succession of collective choices anticipated' ([1962] 1999, p. 96). This conception, in turn, is evocative of Hamilton's observation that 'no man can be sure that he may not be tomorrow the victim of a spirit of injustice, by which he may be a gainer to-day' (Carey and McClellan, 2001, p. 405).[11] On the other hand, we know that, given the moral equivalence of persons, the Founders insisted that *all* members of the polity have a duty to promote just, in the sense of

impartial, institutions, and that the greatest possible equal political participation must be promoted (Chapter 2, Sections 2.2, 2.3 and 2.4). Finally,
we have it on Madison's authority that:

> If it be asked, what is the consequence, in case the congress shall misconstrue
> [the Necessary and Proper Clause], and exercise powers not warranted by its
> true meaning? I answer, the same as if they should misconstrue or enlarge any
> other power vested in them; as if the general power had been reduced to par-
> ticulars, and one of these were to be violated; the same in short, as if the state
> legislatures should violate their respective constitutional authorities. In the first
> instance, the success of the usurpation will depend on the executive and judici-
> ary departments, which are to expound and give effect to the legislative acts;
> *and in the last resort, a remedy must be obtained from the people*, who can, by the
> election of more faithful representatives, annul the acts of the usurpers. (Carey
> and McClellan, 2001, p. 235; emphasis mine)

If we, the people, can 'by the election of more faithful representatives,
annul the acts of the usurpers', President Washington's 19 September 1796
'Farewell Address' emphasizes that there is an additional remedy:

> It is important, likewise, that the habits of thinking in a free Country should
> inspire caution in those entrusted with its administration, to confine themselves
> within their respective Constitutional spheres; avoiding in the exercise of the
> Powers of one department to encroach upon another. The spirit of encroach-
> ment tends to consolidate the powers of all the departments in one, and thus
> to create whatever the form of government, a real despotism. A just estimate
> of that love of power, and proneness to abuse it . . . is sufficient to satisfy us of
> the truth of this proposition. The necessity of reciprocal checks in the exercise
> of political power; by dividing and distributing it into different depositories,
> and constituting each the Guardian of the Public Weal against invasions by the
> others, has been evinced by experiments ancient and modern; some of them in
> our country and under our own eyes. To preserve them must be as necessary
> as to institute them. *If in the opinion of the People, the distribution or modifica-*
> *tion of the Constitutional powers be in any particular wrong, let it be corrected*
> *by an amendment in the way which the Constitution designates.* ([1796a] 1997,
> pp. 970–71; emphasis mine)[12]

The Founders have been betrayed. Were they here today they would
recognize the existential threat to our self-governing republic. We have a
duty to do the same – and to act appropriately.

NOTES

1. See also Engdahl (2005, pp. 146–7).
2. See SIGTARP (2009c, pp. 3, 4 and 31).

3. Recall that off-budget activity subsumes 'transactions of the Federal Government that would be treated as budgetary had congress not designated them by statute as "off-budget". Currently transactions of the Social Security trust fund and the Postal Service fund are the only sets of transactions that are so designated' (Office of Management and Budget, 2009b, p. 414). The essential point is that the 'Unified Budget' combines on- and off-budget programs (ibid., p. 415). For more on this, see Section 1.2 in Chapter 1.

4. The reason for this is that 'no Congress can bind a succeeding Congress by a simple statute' (US Senate Committee on the Judiciary, 1981, p. 42).

5. The hearings are styled 'Humphrey-Hawkins' to reflect revisions to the Employment Act of 1946 made by Title I of the Full Employment and Balanced Growth Act of 1978, Public Law 95-523, the Humphrey-Hawkins Bill (US Congress, Joint Economic Committee, 2002, p. III).

6. See also Epstein (2006, p. 9).

7. Madison, Jefferson and James Wilson would surely agree. See Chapter 2, Section 2.3 and Chapter 6, Section 6.2.

8. For more on the Supreme Court's *Kelo* decision, see Roth (2007, pp. 159–61).

9. See also the discussion in Section 2.3, Chapter 2.

10. See also Hamilton's *The Federalist* Nos. 32 and 82 (Carey and McClellan, 2001).

11. See also Sections 2.3 and 2.4 in Chapter 2.

12. The text is similar to Alexander Hamilton's 30 July 1796 'A Draft of [President Washington's] Farewell Address'. See, especially ([1796] 2001, p. 862).

References

Aaron, H.J. (1994), 'Public policy, values, and consequences', *Journal of Economic Perspectives*, **8**(2), 3–21.

Adamy, Janet and Greg Hitt (2009), 'House panel pushes on $1 trillion health bill', *The Wall Street Journal*, 1–2 August.

Almond, B. (1993), 'Rights', in Peter Singer (ed.), *A Companion to Ethics*, Cambridge, MA: Blackwell Publishers, Ltd., pp. 259–69.

Armey, Dick (1996), 'How taxes corrupt', *The Wall Street Journal*, 19 June.

Arrow, K.J. (1951), *Social Choice and Individual Value*, New Haven: Yale University Press.

Baron, J.N. and M.T. Hannan (1994), 'The impact of economics on contemporary sociology', *Journal of Economic Literature*, **32**(3), 1111–46.

Barry, Brian (1989), *Theories of Justice*, Berkeley: University of California Press.

Bayh, Evan (2009), 'Deficits and fiscal credibility', *The Wall Street Journal*, 4 March.

Bendavid, Naftali (2009), 'House democrats unveil spending bill for rest of '09', *The Wall Street Journal*, 24 February.

Berger, Raoul (1997), *Government by Judiciary: The Transformation of the Fourteenth Amendment, Second Edition*, Indianapolis: Liberty Fund.

Bernhard, Helen, Ernst Fehr and Urs Fischbacher (2006), 'Group affiliation and altruistic norm enforcement', *American Economic Association Papers and Proceedings*, **96**(2), 217–21.

Black, Duncan (1958), *Theory of Committees and Elections*, Cambridge: Cambridge University Press.

Bolton, G.E. and A. Ockenfels (2000), 'ERC: A theory of equity, reciprocity, and competition', *American Economic Review*, **90**(1), 166–93.

Bookstaber, R. and J. Langsam (1985), 'Predictable behavior: Comment', *American Economic Review*, **75**(3), 571–5.

Brennan, Geoffrey (1995), 'The contribution of economics', in Robert E. Goodin and Philip Pettit (eds), *A Companion to Contemporary Political Philosophy*, Cambridge, MA: Blackwell Publishers, Ltd., pp. 123–56.

Brennan, Geoffrey and James M. Buchanan (1985a), 'The myth of benevolence', in Geoffrey Brennan, Hartmut Kliemt and Robert D. Tollison (eds) (2000), *The Collected Works of James M. Buchanan*, vol. 10, Indianapolis: Liberty Fund, pp. 38–52.

Brennan, Geoffrey and James M. Buchanan (1985b), 'Preface', in Geoffrey Brennan, Hartmut Kliemt and Robert D. Tollison (eds) (2000), *The Collected Works of James M. Buchanan*, vol. 10, Indianapolis: Liberty Fund, pp. XV–XXI.

Brennan, Geoffrey and James M. Buchanan (1985c), *The Reason of Rules: Constitutional Political Economy*, reprinted in Geoffrey Brennan, Hartmut Kliemt and Robert D. Tollison (eds) (2000), *The Collected Works of James M. Buchanan*, vol. 10, Indianapolis: Liberty Fund.

Brennan, Geoffrey and Philip Pettit (2004), *The Economy of Esteem: An Essay on Civil and Political Society*, Oxford: Oxford University Press.

Brutus (1788), 'Unlimited authority in tax revenues?', in Bernard Bailyn (ed.) (1993), *The Debate on the Constitution, Part One*, New York: Literary Classics of the United States, Inc., pp. 691–7.

Buchanan, James M. (1954), 'Social choice, democracy, and free markets', *Journal of Political Economy*, **62**(2), 114–23.

Buchanan, James M. (1962a), 'Easy budgets and tight money', in Geoffrey Brennan, Hartmut Kliemt and Robert D. Tollison (eds) (2000), *The Collected Works of James M. Buchanan*, vol. 13, Indianapolis: Liberty Fund, pp. 435–49.

Buchanan, James M. (1962b), 'Politics, policy and the Pigovian margins', in Geoffrey Brennan, Hartmut Kliemt and Robert D. Tollison (eds) (1999), *The Collected Works of James M. Buchanan*, vol.1, Indianapolis: Liberty Fund, pp. 60–74.

Buchanan, James M. (1967), *Public Finance in Democratic Process: Fiscal Institutions and Individual Choice*, reprinted in Geoffrey Brennan, Hartmut Kliemt and Robert D. Tollison (eds) (1999), *The Collected Works of James M. Buchanan*, vol. 4, Indianapolis: Liberty Fund.

Buchanan, James M. (1972), 'Rawls on justice as fairness', in Geoffrey Brennan, Hartmut Kliemt and Robert D. Tollison (eds) (2001), *The Collected Works of James M. Buchanan*, vol. 17, Indianapolis: Liberty Fund, pp. 353–9.

Buchanan, James M. (1975), *The Limits of Liberty: Between Anarchy and Leviathan*, reprinted in Geoffrey Brennan, Hartmut Kliemt and Robert D. Tollison (eds) (2001), *The Collected Works of James M. Buchanan*, vol. 7, Indianapolis: Liberty Fund.

Buchanan, James M. (1977), 'Criteria for a free society', in Geoffrey Brennan, Hartmut Kliemt and Robert D. Tollison (eds) (2001), *The Collected Works of James M. Buchanan*, vol. 18, Indianapolis: Liberty Fund, pp. 173–84.

Buchanan, James M. (1978), 'From private preferences to public philosophy', in Geoffrey Brennan, Hartmut Kliemt and Robert D. Tollison (eds) (2000), *The Collected Works of James M. Buchanan*, vol. 13, Indianapolis: Liberty Fund, pp. 39–56.

Buchanan, James M. (1981), 'Moral community, moral order, or moral anarchy', in Geoffrey Brennan, Hartmut Kliemt and Robert D. Tollison (eds) (2001), *The Collected Works of James M. Buchanan*, vol. 17, Indianapolis: Liberty Fund, pp. 187–201.

Buchanan, James M. (1983a), 'The achievement and the limits of public choice in diagnosing government failure and in offering bases for constructive reform', in Geoffrey Brennan, Hartmut Kliemt and Robert D. Tollison (eds) (2000), *The Collected Works of James M. Buchanan*, vol. 13, Indianapolis: Liberty Fund, pp. 112–26.

Buchanan, James M. (1983b), 'The public choice perspective', in Geoffrey Brennan, Hartmut Kliemt and Robert D. Tollison (eds) (2000), *The Collected Works of James M. Buchanan*, vol. 13, Indianapolis: Liberty Fund, pp. 15–24.

Buchanan, James M. (1985), 'The moral dimension of debt financing', in Geoffrey Brennan, Hartmut Kliemt and Robert D. Tollison (eds) (2000), *The Collected Works of James M. Buchanan*, vol. 14, Indianapolis: Liberty Fund, pp. 486–92.

Buchanan, James M. (1986a), 'Contractarianism and democracy', in Geoffrey Brennan, Hartmut Kliemt and Robert D. Tollison (eds) (2001), *The Collected Works of James M. Buchanan*, vol. 16, Indianapolis: Liberty Fund, pp. 215–24.

Buchanan, James M. (1986b), 'Politics and meddlesome preferences', in Geoffrey Brennan, Hartmut Kliemt and Robert D. Tollison (eds) (2000), *The Collected Works of James M. Buchanan*, vol. 1, Indianapolis: Liberty Fund, pp. 410–18.

Buchanan, James M. (1987a), 'Constitutional economics', in Geoffrey Brennan, Hartmut Kliemt and Robert D. Tollison (eds) (2001), *The Collected Works of James M. Buchanan*, vol. 16, Indianapolis: Liberty Fund, pp. 3–14.

Buchanan, James M. (1987b), 'The constitution of economic policy', *American Economic Review*, **77**(3), 243–50.

Buchanan, James M. (1989a), 'The ethics of constitutional order', in Geoffrey Brennan, Hartmut Kliemt and Robert D. Tollison (eds) (1999), *The Collected Works of James M. Buchanan*, vol. 1, Indianapolis: Liberty Fund, pp. 368–73.

Buchanan, James M. (1989b), 'On the structure of an economy', in Geoffrey Brennan, Hartmut Kliemt and Robert D. Tollison (eds) (2001), *The Collected Works of James M. Buchanan*, vol. 18, Indianapolis: Liberty Fund, pp. 263–75.

Buchanan, James M. (1990), 'The domain of constitutional economics', in Geoffrey Brennan, Hartmut Kliemt and Robert D. Tollison (eds) (1999), *The Collected Works of James M. Buchanan*, vol. 1, Indianapolis: Liberty Fund, pp. 377–95.

Buchanan, James M. (1991), *The Economics and the Ethics of Constitutional Order*, Ann Arbor: University of Michigan Press.

Buchanan, James M. (1994a), 'Choosing what to choose', *Journal of Institutional and Theoretical Economics*, **150**(1), 123–35.

Buchanan, James M. (1994b), *Ethics and Economic Progress*, Norman: University of Oklahoma Press.

Buchanan, James M. (1995), 'Federalism as an ideal political order and an objective for constitutional reform', in Geoffrey Brennan, Hartmut Kliemt and Robert D. Tollison (eds) (2001), *The Collected Works of James M. Buchanan*, vol. 18, Indianapolis: Liberty Fund, pp. 67–78.

Buchanan, James M. (1997a), 'Democracy within constitutional limits', in Geoffrey Brennan, Hartmut Kliemt and Robert D. Tollison (eds) (2001), *The Collected Works of James M. Buchanan*, vol. 16, Indianapolis: Liberty Fund, pp. 225–34.

Buchanan, James M. (1997b), 'Generality as a constitutional constraint', in Geoffrey Brennan, Hartmut Kliemt and Robert D. Tollison (eds) (1999), *The Collected Works of James M. Buchanan*, vol. 1, Indianapolis: Liberty Fund, pp. 419–28.

Buchanan, James M. (2005), *Why I, Too, Am Not a Conservative: The Normative Vision of Classical Liberalism*, Cheltenham, UK and Northampton, MA, USA: Edward Elgar.

Buchanan, James M. and Roger D. Congleton (1998), *Politics by Principle not Interest: Towards Nondiscriminatory Democracy*, Cambridge: Cambridge University Press.

Buchanan, James M. and Gordon Tullock (1962), *The Calculus of Consent: Logical Foundations of Constitutional Democracy*, reprinted in Geoffrey Brennan, Hartmut Kliemt and Robert D. Tollison (eds) (1999), *The Collected Works of James M. Buchanan*, vol. 3, Indianapolis: Liberty Fund.

Camerer, Colin, George Loewenstein and Drazen Prelec (2005), 'Neuroeconomics: How neuroscience can inform economics', *Journal of Economic Literature*, **63**(2), 9–64.

Carey, George W. (1995), *In Defense of the Constitution*, Indianapolis: Liberty Fund.

Carey, George W. and James McClellan (eds) (2001), *The Federalist*, Indianapolis: Liberty Fund.

Congressional Research Service (2004), *The Constitution of the United States: Analysis and Interpretation*, Washington, DC: US Government Printing Office.

Conlisk, J. (1988), 'Opitimization costs', *Journal of Economic Behavior and Organization*, **9**(3), 213–18.

Conlisk, J. (1996), 'Why bounded rationality?', *Journal of Economic Literature*, **34**(2), 669–700.

Covel, Simona and Kelly K. Spors (2009), 'US proposal aims to aid smaller companies', *The Wall Street Journal*, 17 March.

Davis, N.A. (1993), 'Contemporary deontology', in Peter Singer (ed.), *A Companion to Ethics*, Cambridge, MA: Blackwell Publishers Ltd, pp. 205–18.

Demsetz, H. (1969), 'Information and efficiency: Another viewpoint', *Journal of Law and Economics*, **12**(1), 1–22.

Dershowitz, Alan (2004), *Rights from Wrongs*, New York: Basic Books.

Dixit, Avinash (1996), *The Making of Economic Policy: A Transaction Cost Politics Perspective*, Cambridge: Cambridge University Press.

Dowell, R.S., R.S. Goldfarb and W.B. Griffith (1998), 'Economic man as a moral individual', *Economic Inquiry*, **36**(4), 645–53.

Dworkin, Gerald (1995), 'Autonomy', in Robert E. Goodin and Philip Pettit (eds), *A Companion to Contemporary Political Philosophy*, Cambridge, MA: Blackwell Publishers Ltd., pp. 359–65.

Dworkin, Ronald (1978), *Taking Rights Seriously*, Cambridge, MA: Harvard University Press.

Dworkin, Ronald (1985), *A Matter of Principle*, Cambridge, MA: Harvard University Press.

Dworkin, Ronald (1991), 'Foundations of liberal equality', in *Tanner Lectures on Human Values,* Salt Lake City: University of Utah Press.

Eastman, John C. (2005), 'Spending clause', in David F. Forte and Matthew Spalding (eds), *The Heritage Guide to the Constitution*, Washington, DC: The Heritage Foundation, pp. 93–6.

Editorial, 'Governors v. congress', *The Wall Street Journal*, 23 February 2009.

Editorial, 'Kent for rent', *The Wall Street Journal*, 29 April 2009.

Editorial, 'No help for the blue dogs', *The Wall Street Journal*, 28 July 2009.

Editorial, 'Health-care secrets', *The Wall Street Journal*, 29–30 August 2009.

Edwards, Jonathan, D.D. (1794), 'A Sermon Preached Before His Excellency Samuel Huntington, Esq. L.L.D. Governor, and the Honorable Assembly of the State of Connecticut, May 8, 1794', in Ellis Sandoz (ed.) (1998), *Political Sermons of the American Founding Era, 1730–1805, Volume 2*, Indianapolis: Liberty Fund, pp. 1187–216.

Ely, Richard T. (1914), *Property and Contract in their Relations to the Distribution of Wealth*, vol. 2, New York: Macmillan.

Engdahl, David (2005), 'Necessary and proper clause', in David F. Forte and Matthew Spalding (eds), *The Heritage Guide to the Constitution*, Washington, DC: The Heritage Foundation, pp. 146–50.

Epstein, Richard A. (2003), *Skepticism and Freedom*, Chicago: The University of Chicago Press.

Epstein, Richard A. (2006), *How Progressives Rewrote the Constitution*, Washington, DC: Cato Institute.

Epstein, Richard A. (2009), 'Is the bonus tax unconstitutional?', *The Wall Street Journal*, 26 March.

Fehr, E. and S. Gächter (2000), 'Fairness and retaliation: The economics of reciprocity', *Journal of Economic Perspectives*, **14**(3), 159–81.

Fleischacker, Samuel (2002), 'Adam Smith's reception among the American Founders', *Willliam and Mary Quarterly*, **59**(4), 897–924.

Forte, David, A. (2005), 'Commerce among the states', in David F. Forte and Matthew Spalding (eds), *The Heritage Guide to the Constitution*, Washington, DC: The Heritage Foundation, pp. 101–7.

Frank, R.H. (1996), 'The political economy of preference falsification: Timur Kuran's "Private truths, public lies"', *Journal of Economic Literature*, **34**(1), 115–23.

Fuller, Lon L. (1971), *The Morality of Law*, New Haven: Yale University Press.

Furubotn, E.G. (1964), 'Investment alternatives and the supply schedule of the firm', *Southern Economic Journal*, **31**(1), 21–37.

Furubotn, E.G. (1965), 'The orthodox production function and the adaptability of capital', *Western Economic Journal*, **3**(3), 288–300.

Furubotn, E.G. (1991), 'General equilibrium models, transaction costs, and the concept of efficient allocation in a capitalist economy', *Journal of Institutional and Theoretical Economics*, **147**(4), 662–86.

Furubotn, E.G. (1994), *Future Development of the New Institutional Economics: Extension of the Neoclassical Model or New Construct?*, Jena: Max-Planck Institute for Research into Economic Systems.

Furubotn, E.G. (1999), 'Economic efficiency in a world of frictions', *Journal of Law and Economics*, **8**(3), 179–97.

Furubotn, E.G. and R. Richter (2005), *Institutions and Economic Theory: The Contribution of the New Institutional Economics, Second Edition*, Ann Arbor: The University of Michigan Press.

Garrison, R.W. (1985), 'Predictable behavior: Comment', *American Economic Review*, **75**(3), 576–8.

Gazzainga, Michael S. (2005), *The Ethical Brain*, Washington, DC: Dana Press.

Gigerenzer, G. and R. Selton (eds) (2002), *Bounded Rationality: The Adaptive Toolbox*, Cambridge, MA: The MIT Press.

Goette, Lorenz, David Huffman and Stephan Meier (2006), 'The impact of group membership on cooperation and norm enforcement: Evidence using random assignment to real social groups', *American Economic Association Papers and Proceedings*, **96**(2), 212–16.

Goodin, R.E. (1993), 'Utility and the good', in Peter Singer (ed.), *A Companion to Ethics*, Cambridge, MA: Blackwell Publishers, Ltd., pp. 241–8.

Gordon, Robert J. (2000), *Macroeconomics, Eighth Edition*, Reading, MA: Addison-Wesley.

Graaff, J. de V. (1967), *Theoretical Welfare Economics*, Cambridge: Cambridge University Press.

Hall, Kermit L. and Mark David Hall (eds) (2007), *Collected Works of James Wilson*, Indianapolis: Liberty Fund.

Hamilton, Alexander (1775), 'Letter to John Jay', in Joanne B. Freeman (ed.) (2001), *Alexander Hamilton: Writings*, New York: Literary Classics of the United States, Inc., pp. 43–6.

Hamilton, Alexander (1788a), 'Speech in the New York Ratifying Convention on the Distribution of Powers', in Joanne B. Freeman (ed.) (2001), *Alexander Hamilton: Writings*, New York: Literary Classics of the United States, Inc., pp. 502–11.

Hamilton, Alexander (1788b), 'Speech in the New York Ratifying Convention on Interests and Corruption', in Joanne B. Freeman (ed.) (2001), *Alexander Hamilton: Writings*, New York: Literary Classics of the United States, Inc., pp. 496–501.

Hamilton, Alexander (1791), 'Report on the Subject of Manufactures', in Joanne B. Freeman (ed.) (2001), *Alexander Hamilton: Writings*, New York: Literary Classics of the United States, Inc., pp. 647–734.

Hamilton, Alexander (1792), 'To George Washington', in Joanne B. Freeman (ed.) (2001), *Alexander Hamilton: Writings*, New York: Literary Classics of the United States, Inc., pp. 760–88.

Hamilton, Alexander (1796), 'A Draft of the Farewell Address', in Joanne B. Freeman (ed.) (2001), *Alexander Hamilton: Writings*, New York: Literary Classics of the United States, Inc., pp. 851–68.

Hamilton, Alexander (1802), 'Letter to James A. Bayard', in Joanne B. Freeman (ed.) (2001), *Alexander Hamilton: Writings*, New York: Literary Classics of the United States, Inc., pp. 987–90.

Hampton, Jean (1995), 'Contract and consent', in Robert E. Goodin and Philip Pettit (eds), *A Companion to Contemporary Political Philosophy*, Cambridge, MA: Blackwell Publishers, Ltd., pp. 379–93.

Harbough, W.T. and K. Krause (2000), 'Children's altruism in public good and dictator experiments', *Economic Inquiry*, **38**(1), 95–109.

Hart, H.L.A. (1955), 'Are there any natural rights?', in Jeremy Waldron (ed.) (1995), *Theories of Rights*, New York: Oxford University Press, pp. 70–90.

Hausman, D.M. and M.S. McPherson (1993), 'Taking ethics seriously: Economics and contemporary moral philosophy', *Journal of Economic Literature*, **31**(2), 671–731.

Hayek, Friedrich A. von (1960), *The Constitution of Liberty*, Chicago: The University of Chicago Press.

Hayek, Friedrich A. von (1970), 'The errors of constructivism', in Jerry Z. Muller (ed.) (1997), *Conservatism*, Princeton: Princeton University Press, pp. 318–25.

Hayek, Friedrich A. von (1973), 'The mirage of social justice', in Jerry Z. Muller (ed.) (1997), *Conservatism*, Princeton: Princeton University Press, pp. 325–34.

Heiner, R.A. (1983), 'The origin of predictable behavior', *American Economic Review*, **73**(4), 560–95.

Heiner, R.A. (1985a), 'Origin of predictable behavior: Further modeling and applications', *American Economic Association Papers and Proceedings*, **75**(2), 391–6.

Heiner, R.A. (1985b), 'Predictable behavior: Reply', *American Economic Review*, **75**(3), 579–85.

Henrich, J. (2000), 'Does culture matter in economic behavior? Ultimatum game bargaining among the machiguenga of the Peruvian Amazon', *American Economic Review*, **90**(4), 973–9.

Himmelfarb, Gertrude (2004), *The Roads to Modernity: The British, French, and American Enlightenments*, New York: Alfred A. Knopf.

Hitt, Greg and Aaron Lucchetti (2009), 'House passes bonus tax bill', *The Wall Street Journal*, 20 March.

Hyneman, Charles S. and Donald S. Lutz (eds) (1983a), *American Political Writing during the Founding Era: 1760–1805, Volume I*, Indianapolis: Liberty Press.

Hyneman, Charles S. and Donald S. Lutz (eds) (1983b), *American Political Writing during the Founding Era: 1760–1805, Volume II*, Indianapolis: Liberty Press.

Jackson, Andrew (1832), 'Veto Message', in James D. Richardson (ed.) (1896), *Messages and Papers of the Presidents*, vol. 2, Washington, DC: US Government Printing Office, p. 590.

Jefferson, Thomas (1785), 'To Peter Carr', in Merrill D. Peterson (ed.) (1984), *Thomas Jefferson: Writings*, New York: Literary Classics of the United States, Inc., pp. 814–18.

Jefferson, Thomas (1786), 'To James Madison', in Merrill D. Peterson (ed.) (1984), *Thomas Jefferson: Writings*, New York: Literary Classics of the United States, Inc., pp. 848–52.

Jefferson, Thomas (1787a), 'Letter to James Madison', in Merrill D. Peterson (ed.) (1984), *Thomas Jefferson: Writings*, New York: Literary Classics of the United States, Inc., pp. 914–18.

Jefferson, Thomas (1787b), 'Letter to James Madison', in Bernard Bailyn (ed.) (1993), *The Debate on the Constitution, Part One*, New York: Literary Classics of the United States, Inc., pp. 209–13.

Jefferson, Thomas (1787c), 'Thomas Jefferson Replies to James Madison', in Bernard Bailyn (ed.) (1993), *The Debate on the Constitution, Part One*, New York: Literary Classics of the United States, Inc., pp. 209–13.

Jefferson, Thomas (1787d), 'Letter to Peter Carr', in Merrill D. Peterson (ed.) (1984), *Thomas Jefferson: Writings*, New York: Literary Classics of the United States, Inc., pp. 900–905.

Jefferson, Thomas (1787e), 'Notes on the State of Virginia', in Merrill D. Peterson (ed.) (1984), *Thomas Jefferson: Writings*, New York: Literary Classics of the United States, Inc., pp. 123–325.

Jefferson, Thomas (1792a), 'Conversations with the President', in Merrill D. Peterson (ed.) (1984), *Thomas Jefferson: Writings*, New York: Literary Classics of the United States, Inc., pp. 674–8.

Jefferson, Thomas (1792b), 'To the President of the United States', in Merrill D. Peterson (ed.) (1984), *Thomas Jefferson: Writings*, New York: Literary Classics of the United States, Inc., pp. 992–1001.

Jefferson, Thomas (1803), 'Letter to Wilson Cary Nicholas', in Merrill D. Peterson (ed.) (1984), *Thomas Jefferson: Writings*, New York: Literary Classics of the United States, Inc., pp. 1139–41.

Jefferson, Thomas (1804), 'Letter to Jean Baptiste Say', in Merrill D. Peterson (ed.) (1984), *Thomas Jefferson: Writings*, New York: Literary Classics of the United States, Inc., pp. 1143–4.

Jefferson, Thomas (1807), 'Letter to John Norvell', in Merrill D. Peterson (ed.) (1984), *Thomas Jefferson: Writings*, New York: Literary Classics of the United States, Inc., pp. 1176–9.

Jefferson, Thomas (1814a), 'Letter to Peter Carr', in Merrill D. Peterson (ed.) (1984), *Thomas Jefferson: Writings*, New York: Literary Classics of the United States, Inc., pp. 1346–52.

Jefferson, Thomas (1814b), 'Letter to Thomas Law', in Merrill D. Peterson (ed.) (1984), *Thomas Jefferson: Writings*, New York: Literary Classics of the United States, Inc., pp. 1335–9.

Jefferson, Thomas (1816a), 'Letter to Joseph Milligan', in Philip B. Kurland and Ralph Lerner (eds) (1987), *The Founders' Constitution, Volume One*, Chicago: The University of Chicago Press, p. 573.

Jefferson, Thomas (1816b), 'Letter to P.S. Dupont de Nemours', in Merrill D. Peterson (ed.) (1984), *Thomas Jefferson: Writings*, New York: Literary Classics of the United States, Inc., pp. 1384–8.

Jefferson, Thomas (1820), 'Letter to Thomas Ritchie', in Merrill D. Peterson (ed.) (1984), *Thomas Jefferson: Writings*, New York: Literary Classics of the United States, Inc., pp. 1445–7.

Jefferson, Thomas (1823), 'Letter to Justice William Johnson', in Merrill D. Peterson (ed.) (1984), *Thomas Jefferson: Writings*, New York: Literary Classics of the United States, Inc., pp. 1469–77.

Just, Richard E., Darrell L. Hueth and Andrew Schmitz (2004), *The Welfare Economics of Public Policy: A Practical Approach to Project and Policy Evaluation*, Cheltenham, UK and Northampton, MA, USA: Edward Elgar.

Kaen, F.R. and R.E. Rosenman (1986), 'Predictable behavior in financial markets: Some evidence in support of Heiner's hypothesis', *American Economic Review*, **76**(1), 212–20.

Kant, I. (1785), *Fundamental Principles of the Metaphysic of Morals*, translated by T.K. Abbot (1988), New York: Prometheus Books.

Kent, James (1794), 'An Introductory Lecture to a Course of Law Lectures', in Charles S. Hyneman and Donald S. Lutz (eds) (1983), *American Political Writing during the Founding Era: 1760–1805, Volume II*, Indianapolis: Liberty Press, pp. 936–49.

Ketcham, Ralph (ed.) (2003), *The Anti-Federalist Papers and The Constitutional Convention Debates*, New York: Signet.

Kurland, Philip B. and Ralph Lerner (eds) (1987a), *The Founders' Constitution, Volume One*, Chicago: University of Chicago Press.

Kurland, Philip B. and Ralph Lerner (eds) (1987b), *The Founders' Constitution, Volume Two*, Chicago: University of Chicago Press.

Kurland, Philip B. and Ralph Lerner (eds) (1987c), *The Founders' Constitution, Volume Three*, Chicago: University of Chicago Press.

Kymlicka, W. (1993), 'The social contract tradition', in Peter Singer (ed.), *A Companion to Ethics*, Cambridge, MA: Blackwell Publishers, Ltd., pp. 186–96.

Langdon, Samuel, D.D. (1788), 'A Sermon Preached At Concord, in the State of New-Hampshire; Before the Honourable Court at the Annual Election, June 5, 1788', in Ellis Sandoz (ed.) (1998), *Political Sermons of the American Founding Era, 1730–1805, Volume 1*, Indianapolis: Liberty Fund, pp. 943–67.

Lathrop, Joseph (1786), 'A Sermon Preached in the First Parish in West-Springfield, December 14, 1786, Being the Day appointed by Authority for Publick Thanksgiving', in Ellis Sandoz (ed.) (1998), *Political Sermons of the Founding Era: 1730–1805, Volume 1*, Indianapolis: Liberty Fund, pp. 867–81.

Levy, Leonard W. (2001), *Origin of the Bill of Rights*, New Haven and London: Yale Note Bene, Yale University Press.

Levy, Robert A. and William Mellor (2008), *The Dirty Dozen*, New York: Sentinel.

Lilly, Scott (2004), 'When congress acts in the dark of night, everyone loses', *Roll Call*, 6 December.

Lilly, Scott (2005), 'Is the politics of pork poisoning our democracy?', *Roll Call*, 15 August.

Lipsey, R. and K. Lancaster (1956), 'The general theory of second best', *Review of Economic Studies*, **24**(63), 11–32.

Lyons, David (1982), 'Utility and rights', in Jeremy Waldron (ed.) (1995), *Theories of Rights*, New York: Oxford University Press, pp. 110–36.

MacDonald, Margaret (1947–48), 'Natural rights', in Jeremy Waldron (ed.) (1995), *Theories of Rights*, New York: Oxford University Press, pp. 21–40.

Madison, Bishop James (1795), 'Manifestations of the Beneficence of Divine Providence Towards America', in Ellis Sandoz (ed.) (1998), *Political Sermons of the American Founding Era, 1730–1805, Volume 2*, Indianapolis: Liberty Fund, pp. 1305–20.

Madison, James (1787a), 'Vices of the Political System of the United States', in Jack N. Rakove (ed.) (1999), *James Madison: Writings*, New York: Literary Classics of the United States, Inc., pp. 69–80.

Madison, James (1787b), 'Letter to Thomas Jefferson', in Jack N. Rakove (ed.) (1999), *James Madison: Writings*, New York: Literary Classics of the United States, Inc., pp. 142–58.

Madison, James (1788a), 'Letter to Thomas Jefferson', in Jack N. Rakove (ed.) (1999), *James Madison: Writings*, New York: Literary Classics of the United States, Inc., pp. 418–23.

Madison, James (1788b), 'Speech in the Virginia Ratifying Convention on the Judicial Power', in Jack N. Rakove (ed.) (1999), *James Madison: Writings*, New York: Literary Classics of the United States, Inc., pp. 393–400.

Madison, James (1789a), 'Remarks in Congress on Proposed Constitutional Amendments', in Jack N. Rakove (ed.) (1999), *James Madison: Writings*, New York: Literary Classics of the United States, Inc., pp. 467–70.

Madison, James (1789b), 'Speech in Congress Proposing Constitutional Amendments', in Jack N. Rakove (ed.) (1999), *James Madison: Writings*, New York: Literary Classics of the United States, Inc., pp. 437–52.

Madison, James (1792a), 'Government of the United States', in Jack N. Rakove (ed.) (1999), *James Madison: Writings*, New York: Literary Classics of the United States, Inc., pp. 508–9.

Madison, James (1792b), 'Property', in Jack N. Rakove (ed.) (1999), *James Madison: Writings*, New York: Literary Classics of the United States, Inc., pp. 515–17.

Madison, James (1800), 'Report on the Alien and Sedition Acts', in Jack N. Rakove (ed.) (1999), *James Madison: Writings*, New York: Literary Classics of the United States, Inc., pp. 608–62.

Madison, James (1819), 'Letter to Spencer Roane', in Jack N. Rakove (ed.) (1999), *James Madison: Writings*, New York: Literary Classics of the United States, Inc., pp. 733–7.

Madison, James (1822), 'Letter to William T. Barry', in Jack N. Rakove (ed.) (1999), *James Madison: Writings*, New York: Literary Classics of the United States, Inc., pp. 790–94.

Madison, James (1823), 'Letter to Thomas Jefferson', in Jack N. Rakove (ed.) (1999), *James Madison: Writings*, New York: Literary Classics of the United States, Inc., pp. 798–802.

Madison, James (1833), 'Letter to William Cabell Rives', in Jack N. Rakove (ed.) (1999), *James Madison: Writings*, New York: Literary Classics of the United States, Inc., pp. 863–6.

Mann, Thomas E. and Norman J. Ornstein (2006), *The Broken Branch*, Oxford: Oxford University Press.

Manski, C.F. (2000), 'Economic analysis of social interactions', *Journal of Economic Perspectives*, **14**(3), 115–36.

McAdams, Richard H. and Eric B. Rasmusen (2004), 'Norms in law and economics', mimeo, pp. 1–49.

McClintock, Samuel (1784), 'A Sermon Preached Before the Honorable The Council, and the Honorable The Senate, and House of Representatives, of the State of New Hampshire, June 3, 1784. On Occasion of the Commencement of the New Constitution and Form of Government', in Ellis Sandoz (ed.) (1998), *Political Sermons of the American Founding Era, 1730–1805, Volume 1, Second Edition*, Indianapolis: Liberty Fund, pp. 791–813.

McDonald, Forrest (2004), *Recovering the Past: A Historian's Memoir*, Lawrence, Kansas: The University Press of Kansas.

Mill, John Stuart (1859), 'On Liberty', reprinted in Stefan Collini (ed.) (2000), *Cambridge Texts in the History of Political Thought*, Cambridge: Cambridge University Press.

Mixon, F.G., Jr and D.L. Hobson (2001), 'Intergovernmental grants and the positioning of presidential primaries and caucuses: empirical evidence from the 1992, 1996, and 2000 election cycles', *Contemporary Economic Policy*, **19**(1), 27–38.

Montesquieu, Charles (1750), *The Spirit of Laws, A Compendium of the First English Edition*, edited, with an Introduction, Notes, and Appendixes, by David Wallace Carrithers (1977), Berkeley and Los Angeles: University of California Press.

Moore, Zephaniah Swift (1802), 'An Oration on the Anniversary of the

Independence of the United States of America', in Charles S. Hyneman and Donald S. Lutz (eds) (1983), *American Political Writing during the Founding Era: 1760–1805, Volume II*, Indianapolis: Liberty Press, pp. 1206–19.

Muller, Jerry Z. (1993), *Adam Smith in His Time and Ours: Designing the Decent Society*, Princeton: Princeton University Press.

Napolitano, Andrew P. (2009), 'Health-care reform and the constitution', *The Wall Street Journal*, 15 September 2009.

North, D.C. (1994), 'Economic performance through time', *American Economic Review*, **84**(3), 359–68.

Nozick, Robert (1974), *Anarchy, State and Utopia*, New York: Basic Books.

O'Connor, Sandra Day (2004), *The Majesty of the Law*, New York: Random House.

Office of Information and Regulatory Affairs, OMB (2008), *2008 Report to Congress on the Benefits and Costs of Federal Regulations and Unfunded Mandates on State, Local, and Tribal Entities*, Washington, DC: US Government Printing Office.

Office of Management and Budget (2008), *Analytical Perspectives*, Budget of the United States Government, Fiscal Year 2009, Washington, DC: US Government Printing Office.

Office of Management and Budget (2009a), *A New Era of Fiscal Responsibility*, Washington, DC: US Government Printing Office.

Office of Management and Budget (2009b), *Analytical Perspectives*, Budget of the United States Government, Fiscal Year 2010, Washington, DC: US Government Printing Office.

Office of Management and Budget (2009c), *Historical Tables*, Budget of the United States Government, Fiscal Year 2010, Washington, DC: US Government Printing Office.

Omnigraphics, Inc. (2009), *Government Assistance Almanac*, Detroit, MI: Omnigraphics, Inc.

O'Neill, O. (1993), 'Kantian ethics', in Peter Singer (ed.), *A Companion to Ethics*, Cambridge, MA: Blackwell Publishers, Ltd., pp. 175–85.

Ornstein, Norman, J. (1981), 'The breakdown of the budget process', *The Wall Street Journal*, 24 November.

Ostrom, E. (2000), 'Collective action and the evolution of social norms', *Journal of Economic Perspectives*, **14**(3), 137–58.

Paton, H.J. (1964), *Immanuel Kant: Groundwork of the Metaphysics of Morals*, New York: Harper Torchbooks.

Peabody, Rev. Stephen (1797), 'A Sermon Delivered at Concord, Before the Honourable General Court of the State of New Hampshire, at the Annual Election, Holden on the First Wednesday in June, 1797', in Ellis

Sandoz (ed.) (1998), *Political Sermons of the American Founding Era, 1730–1805, Volume 2*, Indianapolis: Liberty Fund, pp. 1322–38.

Peterson, Merrill D. (ed.) (1984), *Thomas Jefferson: Writings*, New York: Literary Classics of the United States, Inc.

Pettit, P. (1993), 'Consequentialism', in Peter Singer (ed.), *A Companion to Ethics*, Cambridge, MA: Blackwell Publishers, Ltd., pp. 230–40.

Pingle, M. (1992), 'Costly optimization: An experiment', *Journal of Economic Behavior and Organization*, **17**(1), 3–30.

Posner, Richard A. (1997), 'Social norms and the law: An economic approach', *American Economic Review Papers and Proceedings*, **87**(2), 365–9.

Pound, Roscoe (1909), 'Liberty of contract', *Yale Law Journal*, **18**(454), 471–2.

Rakove, Jack N. (1997), *Original Meanings*, New York: Vintage Books.

Ramsay, David (1788), 'Oration at Charleston, South Carolina', in Bernard Bailyn (ed.) (1993), *The Debate on the Constitution, Part Two*, New York: Literary Classics of the United States, Inc., pp. 506–13.

Rawls, John (1971), *A Theory of Justice*, Cambridge, MA: The Belknap Press of Harvard University Press.

Rawls, John (1989), 'Themes in Kant's moral philosophy', in Samuel Freeman (ed.) (1999), *John Rawls: Collected Papers*, Cambridge, MA: Harvard University Press, pp. 497–528.

Rawls, John (1996), *Political Liberalism*, New York: Columbia University Press.

Regulatory Information Service Center (2008), *Unified Agenda*, **73**(227), Washington, DC: US General Services Administration.

Ring, Kevin A. (2004), *Scalia Dissents*, Washington, DC: Regnery Publishing, Inc.

Rivkin, David B., Jr. and Lee A. Casey (2009), 'Mandatory insurance is unconstitutional', *The Wall Street Journal*, 18 September, p. A. 23.

Robson, A.J. (2001), 'The biological basis of economic behavior', *Journal of Economic Literature*, **39**(1), 11–33.

Roth, T.P. (1974), 'The demand for a single variable productive service and the adaptability of capital', *Artha Vijnana*, **15**(4), 421–31.

Roth, T.P. (1979), 'Empirical cost curves and the production-theoretic short-run: A reconciliation', *Quarterly Review of Economics and Business*, **19**(3), 35–47.

Roth, T.P. (1999), *Ethics, Economics and Freedom: The Failure of Consequentialist Social Welfare Theory*, Aldershot, UK: Ashgate.

Roth, T.P. (2002), *The Ethics and the Economics of Minimalist Government*, Cheltenham, UK and Northampton, MA, USA: Edward Elgar.

Roth, T.P. (2007), *Morality, Political Economy and American*

Constitutionalism, Cheltenham, UK and Northampton, MA, USA: Edward Elgar.

Rush, Benjamin (1788a), 'Letter to David Ramsay', in Bernard Bailyn (ed.) (1993), *The Debate on the Constitution, Part Two*, New York: Literary Classics of the United States, Inc., pp. 417–19.

Rush, Benjamin (1788b), 'Letter to Jeremy Belknap', in Bernard Bailyn (ed.) (1993), *The Debate on the Constitution, Part Two*, New York: Literary Classics of the United States, Inc., pp. 256–7.

Salanié, Bernard (2000), *The Microeconomics of Market Failure*, Cambridge, MA and London: The MIT Press.

Sandel, Michael J. (1996), *Democracy's Discontent: America in Search of a Public Philosophy*, Cambridge, MA: The Belknap Press of Harvard University Press.

Schweikart, Larry and Michael Allen (2004), *A Patriot's History of the United States*, New York: Sentinel.

Scruton, Roger (1982), *Kant*, Oxford: Oxford University Press.

Scruton, Roger (1994), *Modern Philosophy: An Introduction and Survey*, New York: Penguin Books.

Scruton, Roger (2002), *The Meaning of Conservatism*, South Bend, IN: St. Augustine's Press.

Sen, Amartya (1995), 'Rationality and social choice', *American Economic Review*, **85**(1), 1–24.

Sen, Amartya (2006), *Identity and Violence: The Illusion of Destiny*, New York: W.W. Norton & Company.

Simon, Herbert A. (1992), 'Introductory comment', in Massimo Egide, Robin Marris and Ricardo Viale (eds), *Economics, Bounded Rationality and the Cognitive Revolution*, Aldershot, UK and Brookfield, VT USA: Edward Elgar, pp. 3–7.

Simon, Ruth (2009), 'Loan-modification plan revised to address second mortgages', *The Wall Street Journal*, 29 April.

Smith, Adam (1759), *The Theory of Moral Sentiments*, reprinted in D.D. Raphael and A.L. Macfie (eds) (1976), The Glasgow Edition of *The Works and Correspondence of Adam Smith*, Oxford: Oxford University Press.

Smith, Adam (1776), *An Inquiry into the Nature and Causes of the Wealth of Nations*, reprinted in W.B. Todd (ed.) (1976), The Glasgow Edition of *The Works and Correspondence of Adam Smith*, vol. II, Oxford: Oxford University Press.

Smith, Melancton (1787), 'Letter from the Federal Farmer', in Ralph Ketcham (ed.) (2003), *The Anti-Federalist Papers*, New York: Signet Classic Printing, pp. 264–9.

Smith, V. (2003), 'Constructivist and ecological rationality in economics', *American Economic Review*, **93**(3), 465–508.

Solomon, Deborah and Damian Paletta, (2009), 'US eyes banks pay over-haul', *The Wall Street Journal*, 13 May.

Special Inspector General for the Troubled Asset Relief Program (SIGTARP) (2009a), *Initial Report to Congress, February 6, 2009*, Washington, DC: Office of the Special Inspector General for the Troubled Asset Relief Program.

Special Inspector General for the Troubled Asset Relief Program (SIGTARP) (2009b), *Quarterly Report to Congress, April 21, 2009*, Washington, DC: Office of the Special Inspector General for the Troubled Asset Relief Program.

Special Inspector General for the Troubled Asset Relief Program (SIGTARP) (2009c), *Quarterly Report to Congress, July 21, 2009*, Washington, DC: Office of the Special Inspector General for the Troubled Asset Relief Program.

Stigler, George (1987), *The Theory of Price*, New York: Macmillan.

Stiglitz, Joseph (1985), 'Information and economic analysis: A perspective', *Economic Journal: Supplement*, **95**(380a), 21–41.

Stone, Timothy (1792), 'Election Sermon', in Charles S. Hyneman and Donald S. Lutz (eds) (1983b), *American Political Writing during the Founding Era: 1760–1805, Volume II*, Indianapolis: Liberty Fund, pp. 839–57.

Sununu, John E. (2009), 'National health care with 51 votes', *The Wall Street Journal*, 27 April.

Supreme Court of the United States, *The Brig Aurora*, 11 US (1813).

Supreme Court of the United States, *McCulloch* v. *Maryland*, 17 US (1819).

Supreme Court of the United States, *Gibbons* v. *Ogden*, 22 US (1824).

Supreme Court of the United States, *Wayman* v. *Southard*, 23 US (1825).

Supreme Court of the United States, *United States* v. *E.C. Knight Co.*, 156 US (1895).

Supreme Court of the United States, *United States* v. *Joint Traffic Association*, 171 US (1898).

Supreme Court of the United States, *Lochner* v. *New York*, 198 US (1905).

Supreme Court of the United States, *Adair* v. *United States*, 208 US (1908).

Supreme Court of the United States, *Coppage* v. *Kansas*, 236 US (1915).

Supreme Court of the United States, *United States* v. *Shreveport Grain and Elevator Co.*, 287 US (1932).

Supreme Court of the United States, *A.L.A. Schechter Poultry Corp.* v. *United States*, 295 US (1935).

Supreme Court of the United States, *Panama Refining Co.* v. *Ryan*, 293 US (1935).

Supreme Court of the United States, *United States* v. *Butler*, 297 US (1936).

Supreme Court of the United States, *Helvering* v. *Davis*, 301 US (1937).

Supreme Court of the United States, *NLRB* v. *Jones & Laughlin Steel Corp.*, 301 US (1937).

Supreme Court of the United States, *NLRB* v. *Fainblatt*, 306 US (1939).

Supreme Court of the United States, *Sunshine Anthracite Coal Co.* v. *Adkins*, 310 US (1940).

Supreme Court of the United States, *United States* v. *Darby*, 312 US (1941).

Supreme Court of the United States, *United States* v. *Wrightwood Dairy Co.*, 315 US (1942).

Supreme Court of the United States, *Wickard* v. *Filburn*, 317 US (1942).

Supreme Court of the United States, *Arizona* v. *California*, 373 US (1963).

Supreme Court of the United States, *NLRB* v. *Reliance Fuel Oil Co.*, 371 US (1963).

Supreme Court of the United States, *American Trucking Associations* v. *Atchison, Topeka & Santa Fe Railroad*, 387 US (1967).

Supreme Court of the United States, *Permian Basin Area Rate Cases*, 390 US (1968).

Supreme Court of the United States, *Hodel* v. *Virginia Surface Mining & Reclamation Association*, 452 US (1981).

Supreme Court of the United States, *Chevron, USA., Inc.* v. *Natural Resources Defense Council, Inc.*, 467 US (1984).

Supreme Court of the United States, *Russell* v. *United States*, 471 US (1985).

Supreme Court of the United States, *South Dakota* v. *Dole*, 483 US (1987).

Supreme Court of the United States, *Mistretta* v. *United States*, 488 US (1989).

Supreme Court of the United States, *Summit Health, Ltd.* v. *Pinhas*, 500 US (1991).

Supreme Court of the United States, *New York* v. *United States*, 505 US (1992).

Supreme Court of the United States, *United States* v. *Lopez*, 514 US (1995).

Supreme Court of the United States, *Loving* v. *United States*, 517 US (1996).

Supreme Court of the United States, *United States* v. *Morrison*, 529 US (2000).

Supreme Court of the United States, *Lawrence et al.* v. *Texas*, 539 US (2003).

Supreme Court of the United States, *Gonzalez, Attorney General, et al.* v. *Raich et al.*, 545 US (2005).

Supreme Court of the United States, *Kelo et al.* v. *City of New London et al.*, 545 US (2005).

Supreme Court of the United States, *Gonzalez, Attorney General, et al.* v. *Oregon, et al.*, 546 US (2006).

Ten, C.L. (1995), 'Constitutionalism and the rule of law', in Robert E. Goodin and Philip Pettit (eds), *A Companion to Contemporary Political Philosophy*, Cambridge, MA: Blackwell Publishers, Ltd, pp. 394–403.

Thaler, R.H. (2000), 'From *homo economicus* to *homo sapiens*', *Journal of Economic Perspectives*, **14**(1), 133–41.

Tollison, Robert D. (2001), 'Introduction', in Geoffrey Brennan, Hartmut Kliemt and Robert D. Tollison (eds) (2001), *The Collected Works of James M. Buchanan,* vol. 16, Indianapolis: Liberty Fund, pp. XI–XIII.

Tradesmen of the Town of Boston (1788), 'Resolutions of the Tradesmen of the Town of Boston', in Bernard Bailyn (ed.) (1993), *The Debate on the Constitution, Part One*, New York: Literary Classics of the United States, Inc., pp. 717–19.

Tversky, A. and R.H. Thaler (1990), 'Preference reversals', *Journal of Economic Perspectives*, **4**(2), 201–11.

Uhlmann, Michael (2005), 'A note on administrative agencies', in David F. Forte and Matthew Spalding (eds), *The Heritage Guide to the Constitution*, Washington, DC: The Heritage Foundation, pp. 229–31.

US Congress, House Resolution 7130, Public Law 93-344 (1974), *Congressional Budget and Impoundment Control Act of 1974*, Washington, DC: US Government Printing Office.

US Congress, House Resolution 1424 (2008), *Financial Stability Plan*, Washington, DC: US Government Printing Office.

US Congress, House Resolution 1 (2009), *American Recovery and Reinvestment Act of 2009*, Washington, DC: US Government Printing Office.

US Congress, House Resolution 1105 (2009), *Omnibus Appropriations Act, 2009*, Washington, DC: US Government Printing Office.

US Congress, House Resolution 3200 (2009), *America's Affordable Health Choices Act of 2009*, Washington, DC: US Government Printing Office.

US Congress Joint Economic Committee (2002), *Compilation of Laws Pertaining to the Committee and the Rules of the Joint Economic Committee, Congress of the United States*, Washington, DC: US Government Printing Office.

US Government Printing Office (2009), *Table of Federal Register Issue Pages and Dates*, Washington, DC: US Government Printing Office.

US Senate Committee on the Judiciary (1981), *Balanced Budget – Tax Limitation Constitutional Amendment*, Washington, DC: US Government Printing Office.

Viscusi, W. Kip, Joseph E. Harrington, Jr. and John M. Vernon (2005), *Economics of Regulation and Antitrust, Fourth Edition*, Cambridge, MA: The MIT Press.

Waldron, J. (1987) 'Theoretical foundations of liberalism', *Philosophical Quarterly*, **37**(147), 122–50.

Waldron, J. (1995a), 'Introduction', in Jeremy Waldron (ed.) (1995), *Theories of Rights*, Oxford: Oxford University Press, pp. 1–20.

Waldron, J. (1995b), 'Rights', in Robert E. Goodin and Philip Pettit (eds), *A Companion to Contemporary Political Philosophy*, Cambridge, MA: Blackwell Publishers, Ltd, pp. 575–85.

Warke, T. (2000), 'Classical utilitarianism and the methodology of determinate choice, in economics and ethics', *Journal of Economic Methodology*, **7**(3), 373–94.

Washington, George (1791), 'Third Annual Message to Congress', in John Rhodehamel (ed.) (1997), *George Washington: Writings*, New York: Literary Classics of the United States, Inc., pp. 786–92.

Washington, George (1796a), 'Farewell Address', in John Rhodehamel (ed.) (1997), *George Washington: Writings*, New York: Literary Classics of the United States, Inc., pp. 962–77.

Washington, George (1796b), 'Letter to Thomas Jefferson', in John Rhodehamel (ed.) (1997), *George Washington: Writings*, New York: Literary Classics of the United States, Inc., pp. 951–4.

Webster, Noah (1787), 'An Examination Into the Leading Principles of the Federal Constitution', in Bernard Bailyn (ed.) (1993), *The Debate on the Constitution, Part One*, New York: Literary Classics of the United States, Inc., pp. 129–63.

Webster, Noah (1802), 'An Oration on the Anniversary of the Declaration of Independence', in Charles S. Hyneman and Donald S. Lutz (eds) (1983), *American Political Writing during the Founding Era: 1760–1805, Volume II*, Indianapolis: Liberty Press, pp. 1220–40.

Weisman, Jonathan and Greg Hitt (2009), 'Obama outlines plan to curb earmarks', *The Wall Street Journal*, 12 March.

Wilde, K.D., A.D. LeBaron and D. Israelsen (1985), 'Knowledge, uncertainty and behavior', *American Economic Association Papers and Proceedings*, **75**(2), 403–8.

Will, George (1983), *Statecraft as Soulcraft: What Government Does*, New York: Simon & Schuster, Inc.

Winter, S. (1964), 'Economic "natural selection" and the theory of the firm', *Yale Economic Essays*, **4**(1), 225–72.

Zywicki, Todd J. (2009), 'Chrysler and the rule of law', *The Wall Street Journal*, 13 May.

Index

A.L.A. Schechter Poultry Corp. v.
    United States 99
Aaron, H.J. 143
Adair v. *United States* 91–2
Adams, J. 53
adaptability, perfect 145
administrative agencies 38–9, 100,
    109–13, 177–8, 180
Administrative Procedures Act of 1946
    (APA) 110
affecting commerce standard 98–9,
    104–8, 172, 173
Agricultural Adjustment Act of 1933
    96–7
Agricultural Adjustment Act of 1938
    107
Agricultural Marketing Agreement Act
    of 1937 106
American Recovery and Reinvestment
    Act of 2009 (Stimulus Bill) 12–13,
    18, 163
Annual Budget 180
Anti-Federalists 55, 117
antitrust policies 150
Arizona v. *California* 110–11
arson 108
Asset Guarantee Program (AGP)
    4
Auto Supplier Support Program
    (ASSP) 5, 9
Auto Warranty Commitment Program
    5, 9
Automotive Industry Financing
    Program (AIFP) 4–5, 9
autonomous self 53, 95, 115, 123–5,
    138
auxiliary precautions 3–4, 8, 18, 38,
    46, 63, 65, 72, 77–8, 113, 115, 123,
    152, 156
    see also federalism; separation of
        powers

bailouts 1–10, 162–3
Bair, S. 8
balanced budget amendment 165, 180
bankruptcy laws, uniform 9
baseline tax system 40
Bayh, E. 14
benevolent despot 78, 81, 134–5, 148
Bentham, J. 130, 136
Berger, R. 67
Bill of Rights 47, 51–2, 66, 82, 116, 137
bonus tax bill 6
bounded rationality 144
bounties 56–8
Brennan, G. 135
Brig Aurora 110
Buchanan, J.M. 21–2, 27, 35–6, 72–3,
    75–6, 78–9, 80, 81, 82, 83, 124,
    135, 140, 141, 142, 147, 148, 169,
    180
budget process law 14–18, 163–4
    reconciliation process 15–18, 164
business development programs 33

Camerer, C. 144
Capital Assistance Program (CAP) 4
Capital Purchase Program (CPP) 4
Cardozo, Justice 97, 99
Casey, L.A. 175
Catalog of Federal Domestic Assistance
    (CDFA) 29
categorical imperative (moral law) 53–4
Chevron U.S.A. Inc. v. *Natural
    Resources Defense Council, Inc.*
    111–12
choice of technique 145–6
Chrysler bankruptcy 9
civic virtue 46–8, 54, 117
class-of-activities standard 108, 172,
    173
Code of Federal Regulations 37
cognitive limitations 143–4

Commerce Clause 95, 98–9, 104–9,
    151, 171–7
community bankers 7
compensation practices, rules for
    changing 8
competitive equilibria 131–2, 146–7
Congleton, R.D. 21–2, 27, 35–6, 76, 81,
    141, 169
Congressional Budget and
    Impoundment Control Act of
    1974 15–16, 39, 40
congressional budget process *see*
    budget process
consequentialism 59
Constitution 3, 50–51, 82, 116, 137,
    156, 157, 158
    auxiliary precautions *see* auxiliary
        precautions
    Commerce Clause 95, 98–9, 104–9,
        151, 171–7
    Fifth Amendment 91–2, 171
    Founders' vision 60–71
    Fourteenth Amendment 89–90, 92,
        93
    General Welfare Clause 95, 96–7,
        101–4, 151, 168
    Legislative Powers Clause 4, 6, 95,
        99–100, 109–13, 151, 177–8
    Necessary and Proper Clause 95,
        97–8, 101–4, 151, 161, 168–9
    Tenth Amendment 69, 96, 97, 174
constitutional amendments 82
    Founders' view and proposed 179–80
    possibility of amendment 60–61
constitutional imperative 121–2
constitutional order 140
constitutional political economy (CPE)
    approach 75–84
constitutive political position 118
contingent legislation 110
continuing resolutions 14, 180
contract
    regulation of many contracts 117–18
    rights 89–94, 117
contractarianism 72, 73
Controlled Substances Act 99
Coppage v. *State of Kansas* 92–3
Covel, S. 10
credit market stabilization activity
    19–20

credit programs 31–5, 170
crop insurance 35–7

Day, Justice 93
debt limit 20, 21, 164
defense spending, national 22–7,
    165
delegation of legislative power 38–9,
    100, 109–13, 177–8, 180
democratic institutions 122
democratic spirit 63
deposit insurance 22, 35–6
derivative political positions 127–9
Development Credit Authority 34
discretionary programs 22–7, 28–9
distributive justice 75, 88, 119, 123,
    130–32, 133–4
    see also redistribution
due process 92–3, 110
duty 59–60
Dworkin, R. 118, 119, 120, 123, 125–6,
    127–8, 129–30, 136, 138, 169

earmarks 15, 97, 163–4
Eastman, J.C. 101, 102
economic efficiency 76, 130–32, 133,
    141, 148, 157
economic indicators 26–7
economic man (*Homo economicus*)
    131, 142–3
economic market 127–9
economic nationalism 95–6
economic rights for hard times 138–9
economist's theory of the state *see*
    social welfare theory
education credit programs 33
efficiency
    economic 76, 130–32, 133, 141, 148,
        157
    political 40, 76, 130, 141, 156
efficiency frontier (welfare frontier)
    131–2, 141–7
Ely, R. 117–18
Emergency Economic Stabilization Act
    of 2008 1–10, 20–21, 162
Employment Act of 1946 25–6,
    150–52, 165
end-state theory of justice 75, 134
endorsement constraint 126
ends over means 122–5

Energy Improvement and Extension Act of 2008 1, 10–11, 162
Enhanced Heavily Indebted Poorest Countries Initiative 34
enumerated powers 22, 101, 102, 159–61, 180
Epstein, R. 6, 108, 112
equal political participation 18, 60, 64, 65–6, 121, 158, 180–81
equal respect 124
equal treatment 83, 116, 118, 125–9
ethical equilibria 131–2
   moral content of 133–4
Exchange Stabilization Fund 34
Export Credit Guarantee Programs (GSM programs) 34
Export-Import Bank 34
external preferences 120, 126, 129–30

factions/factious behavior 43–6, 56, 76
Fair Labor Standards Act of 1938 106
Farm Credit System (FCS) 33–4
Farm Service Agency (FSA) 33
federal activity 1–41, 151–2, 158–81
   bailouts, stimuli etc. 1–19, 162–4
   off-off-budget activity 19, 31–40, 170–81
   on- and off-budget activity 19, 20–31, 164–70
   thought experiment 158–62
Federal Agricultural Mortgage Corporation (Farmer Mac) 33–4
Federal Credit Reform Act of 1990 21
Federal Family Education Loan (FFEL) program 33
federal government role 67–70
Federal Home Loan Bank System 33
Federal Home Loan Mortgage Corporation (Freddie Mac) 33
Federal Housing Administration (FHA) 32
Federal National Mortgage Association (Fannie Mae) 33
Federal Register 37
federalism 18, 38, 46, 50, 80–81, 115, 152, 156
Fifth Amendment 91–2
   Takings Clause 171
Fleischacker, S. 43
flood insurance 35–7

forbidden inequalities 128, 139–40, 152
foreclosure mitigation plan 5, 9–10
Forte, D.A. 99
Founders 3–4, 42–87, 115, 121, 122–3, 125, 156–8
   Constitution 60–71
   moral and political philosophy 42–60
   political economy 71–84, 135
   view and present-day federal activity 156–82
      bailouts, stimuli etc. 162–4
      off-off-budget activity 170–81
      on- and off-budget activity 164–70
      thought experiment 158–62
Fourteenth Amendment 89–90, 92, 93
freedom 116
   from restraint 50
   wage labor and 89–94, 117–18
fundamental welfare theorems 32, 75, 129, 131–2, 140, 157, 170
Furubotn, E.G. 142, 147

General Services Administration (GSA) 29
General Theory of Second Best 149–50
general welfare 80, 102
General Welfare Clause 95, 96–7, 101–4, 151, 168
generality constraint (impartiality constraint) 21–2, 31, 36–7, 77–80, 82, 83, 180
genuine consent 117–18
Gibbons v. *Ogden* 104–5
golden rule 53
Gonzalez v. *Oregon* 99, 108, 173
Gonzalez v. *Raich* 99, 108, 173–4, 175, 176
good life 118
Goodin, R.E. 120–21
Gordon, R.J. 150
Government Assistance Almanac 29
government sponsored enterprises (GSEs) 31
Graaff, J. de V. 132, 135

Hall, K.L. 161
Hall, M.D. 161
Hamilton, A. 47, 50, 56–8, 60–61, 62, 68, 83, 89, 101, 158, 159, 180

Hampton, J. 72
Harlan, Justice 89, 90, 110–11
Hart, H.L.A. 137
Hayek, F.A. von 63, 125, 139
health-care reform bill 17
health-care reform debate 17, 167,
    175–6
Helvering v. *Davis* 96, 97, 101, 103,
    167
heteronomy 55, 73
highway funds 103
Hitt, G. 6
Hobbes, T. 43
Holmes, Justice 90, 92, 93
Homo economicus (economic man)
    131, 142–3
hospital privileges 108
housing credit programs 32–3
Hughes, Chief Justice 106

identity, social 143
ignorance, veil of 72, 73–4
impartial spectator 53–4
impartiality 6–7, 18, 44–6, 49, 55–6, 75,
    116, 121, 123, 130–31
impartiality constraint (generality
    constraint) 21–2, 31, 36–7, 77–80,
    82, 83, 180
in-period discrimination 35
independence of the judiciary 61–2
inequalities 116
    of bargaining power 93, 113
    forbidden 128, 139–40, 152
    required 128
    of wealth 95–6
insurance programs 35–7, 170
interdependencies 95–6, 172–3
intergenerational discrimination 21–2,
    35
Internal Revenue Service 179
international credit programs 34
International Monetary Fund 34
interstate commerce 91–2, 95, 98–9,
    104–9, 171–7, 180

Jackson, A. 116
Jefferson, T. 6–7, 12, 43, 54–5, 58–9,
    61, 65, 69–70, 80–81, 128, 158,
    159, 167
just constitution 77

justice 6–7, 55–6
    distributive 75, 88, 119, 123, 130–32,
        133–4
    end of government 48–9
    as impartiality *see* impartiality
    procedural 60, 74, 88, 123
    social 80, 119, 133–4, 136–40
    social welfare theory of 133–5
    time-slice theory of 75, 134

Kansas statute of 1903 92–3
Kant, I. 53–4, 55, 72, 73
Kelo et al. v. *City of New London* 171
Kent, J. 48
Kurland, P.B. 116
Kymlicka, W. 74

labor law 89–93, 117–18
labor organization membership 91–2
Lancaster, K. 149, 150
legislative encroachments 4, 70–71,
    151–2, 168
Legislative Powers Clause 4, 6, 95,
    99–100, 109–13, 151, 177–8
legislative process, speed of 12–13,
    64–5, 180
Lerner, R. 116
Levy, R.A. 99, 101, 102, 109, 167–8
liberty 49–51, 63–4
likes
    and wants 144–5
    see also preferences
Lilly, S. 13, 15
limited constitution 68, 111
limited government 8, 22, 68, 88,
    111
Lipsey, R. 149, 150
local governments *see* states' powers/
    responsibilities
Lochner v. *New York* 89–91
Locke, J. 43, 136
Loving v. *United States* 109–10
Lucchetti, A. 6
lump-sum taxes and subsidies 129

MacDonald, M. 137
macroeconomics 150–52
Madison, J. 6–7, 22, 40, 42, 43–6,
    47, 51–2, 56, 60, 61, 67–8, 68–9,
    70–71, 81, 89, 95, 96, 111, 118–19,

124, 152, 157, 158, 159, 167, 168, 175, 179, 181
majoritarian cycling 36, 76–7
majoritarian democracy 30, 66, 76–7, 79, 88, 169
majority rule 64, 66
Making Home Affordable (MHA) program 5, 9–10
mandatory programs 22, 23–4, 27–31, 166–8
Mann, T. 13, 15, 158, 163
manufacturing 56–8, 105
market failures 31–2, 39, 75, 112–13
Marshall, Chief Justice 104–5, 109, 110
McClintock, S. 48
McCulloch v. *Maryland* 97, 176
McDonald, F. 163
McKenna, Justice 91–2
means, ends over 122–5
Means Tested Entitlements 22, 23, 27, 28, 166–8
Medicaid 27
Medicare 27, 168
Medicare prescription drug bill of 2003 13
Mellor, W. 99, 101, 102, 109, 167–8
milk prices 106–7
minimum drinking age 103
mining 105
minor transactions 106
Mistretta v. *United States* 111
modern liberalism 42, 88, 115–55, 156–7, 165–6
    ends over means 122–5
    new political morality 125–30
    see also social welfare theory; utilitarianism
Montesquieu, C. 43, 48, 54
moral community 124, 138
moral equivalence of persons 3, 7, 12, 30–31, 52, 53–4, 59–60, 64, 73, 88, 115, 121, 125, 156
moral norms, promulgation of 83
moral philosophy
    Founders' 42–60
    modern liberalism 125–30
moral sense 52–5
mortgage modification program 5, 9–10
Muller, J.Z. 52

national defense spending 22–7, 165
National Flood Insurance Program 36
National Labor Relations Act of 1935 98, 106
natural rights 136–7
naturalistic fallacy 136
Necessary and Proper Clause 95, 97–8, 101–4, 151, 161, 168–9
necessitous men 117, 138
'New' Supreme Court *see* Supreme Court
New York v. *United States* 171
New York State labor law 89–91
nirvana approach 140–52
NLRB v. *Jones and Laughlin Steel Corporation* 98, 106
non-budgetary activities *see* off-off-budget activity
non-defense outlays 22–7
Non-delegation Clause *see* Legislative Powers Clause
Nozick, R. 75, 134

Obama, B. 17
O'Connor, Justice 103–4, 171, 174, 175, 176
off-budget activity 19, 20–31
    Founders' view and 164–70
off-off-budget activity 19, 31–40
    Founders' view and 170–81
Office of Information and Regulatory Affairs 38
Office of Management and Budget (OMB) 19, 26, 31–2, 39–40
    'Long-Run Budget Projections' 28–9
'Old' Supreme Court *see* Supreme Court
Omnibus Appropriations Act of 2009 14–15, 163
omnibus appropriations bills 14–15, 163, 180
omniscient being – observing economist construal 78, 134–5, 148–9
on-budget activity 19, 20–31
    Founders' view and 164–70
original position 73–4
Ornstein, N. 13, 15, 158, 163
Overseas Private Investment Corporation (OPIC) 34

pace of legislation 12–13, 64–5, 180
Paretian conditions 131, 149
partial equilibrium welfare economics
    149–50
path-dependencies 142
patriotism 47
Peckham, Justice 89
Pension Benefit Guaranty Corporation
    (PBGC) 36
pension guarantees 35–6
perfect adaptability 145
Pitney, Justice 92–3
policy goals 25–6, 110–11, 165–6
policy judgment 100, 111–12
political distribution, general theory
    of 127
political economy, Founders' 71–84,
    135
political efficiency 40, 76, 130, 141, 156
political philosophy
    Founders' 42–60
    modern liberalism 125–30
Polk, J.K. 102
Pound, R. 117
preferences 120–21, 129–30, 133,
    142–3, 152
    external 120, 126, 129–30
    social 148
Price, T. 12
procedural imperative 72–3
procedural justice 60, 74, 88, 123
production function 145–6
Progressive movement 95–6, 117
progressive taxation 30, 169–70
property rights 89–94
proportional expenditure tax 31, 40,
    170, 179
Public-Private Investment Program
    (PPIP) 5
public use 171
public welfare 80

Rakove, J. 51–2
rational basis test 107–8, 173–4
Rawls, J. 31, 60, 63–4, 73–4, 77, 120,
    121, 134, 140, 158
reconciliation, budget 15–18, 164
redistribution 75, 118, 119, 128–9,
    169–70
    see also distributive justice

'regular order' 13, 158, 163, 164
regulation 37–9, 150
Regulatory Right-to-Know Act of
    2001 38
regulatory state 99–100
    see also administrative agencies
Rehnquist, Chief Justice 103
rent seeking 7–8, 66, 76
Report to Congress on regulatory
    benefits and costs 38
representative democracy 127–8
required inequalities 128
respect for the moral law 53–4, 63, 82,
    156
Richter, R. 142
rights 43, 51, 123
    Bill of Rights 47, 51–2, 66, 82, 116,
        137
    modern liberalism 125–6, 129–30,
        132–3, 152, 157
    rights and social justice 136–40
    'Old' Supreme Court and contract
        and property rights 89–94
Rivkin, D.B. 175
Roberts, Justice 96
rough equality, principle of 127–8
rule of law 63–4
rule-making authority 110–13, 177–8,
    180
rule-utilitarianism 121–2
rules of conduct 125
rural development programs 33–4
Rural Housing Service (RHS) 33
Rush, B. 46
Russell v. *United States* 108

Salanié, B. 150
Sandel, M.J. 90, 93, 94, 116, 117, 118,
    137–8
second mortgages 9–10
self-government 18, 47, 115–16, 137–8
self-interest 54–5, 79
Sen, A. 143, 148, 153
Sentencing Commission 111
separation of powers 18, 38, 46, 50,
    109–10, 115, 152, 156
Simon, H.A. 143
Simon, R. 10
Small Business Administration (SBA)
    33

Smith, A. 43–6, 52–3, 54
social good 80
social identity 143
social indicators 26–7
social justice 80, 119, 133–4, 136–40
social order 62–3
social preference 148
Social Security 22, 23, 27, 28, 168
Social Security Act 97
social welfare function 141, 147–52
social welfare theory 42, 74–5, 81, 119,
    128–52, 156–7
  moral and political problems 132–5
  nirvana approach 140–52
  normative use of 130–32
  rights and social justice 136–40
  see also utilitarianism
South Dakota v. *Dole* 103–4
Special Inspector General for the
    Troubled Asset Relief Program
    (SIGTARP) 2–3, 4, 6
Spors, K.K. 10
standards 100, 110–11, 177, 178
  ambiguous 112
states' powers/responsibilities 37, 161,
    167–8, 170–71, 174–5
  Founders' vision 67–70, 80–81
  modern liberalism 126–7
  Supreme Court and 89, 93–4, 101–2
stealth legislation 15, 163
Stevens, Justice 173–4
Stimulus Bill 12–13, 18, 163
Stone, Chief Justice 106
Stone, T. 49–50
strict scrutiny standard 107–8
subsidies 56–8, 129
Summit Health, Ltd v. *Pinhas* 108
Supreme Court 38, 67–8, 70–71, 151,
    157, 166, 168
  'New' 95–114, 118
    Commerce Clause 98–9, 104–9,
        171–7
    General Welfare Clause 96–7,
        101–4
    Legislative Powers Clause 99–100,
        109–13, 177–8
    Necessary and Proper Clause
        97–8, 101–4
    overview 96–101
  'Old' 88–94, 117

Adair v. *United States* 91–2
Coppage v. *State of Kansas* 92–3
Lochner v. *New York* 89–91
Systematically Significant Failing
    Institutions Program (SSFI) 4

Targeted Investment Program (TIP)
    4
tax expenditures 39–40, 168, 178–9
Tax Extenders and Alternative
    Minimum Tax Relief Act of 2008
    1, 11–12, 162
taxation 30–31, 101–2, 168–70
  Energy Improvement and Extension
      Act of 2008 10–11
  progressivity 30, 169–70
Tenth Amendment 69, 96, 97, 174
Term Asset-Backed Securities Loan
    Facility (TALF) 5, 10
Thomas, Justice 99, 174, 176
thought experiment 158–62
time-slice theory of justice 75, 134
transcendental autonomous self 53, 95,
    115, 123–5, 138
transfer programs 27–8, 166–8
Treasury 4, 8–9, 162
Troubled Asset Relief Program
    (TARP) 1–10, 18, 19, 20–21,
    162–3
Tullock, G. 78–9, 180
two-person perspective 54

Uhlmann, M. 109, 113, 177
*Unified Agenda of Federal Regulatory
    and Deregulatory Actions* 38
Unified Budget 19, 20–31, 164–70
uniform bankruptcy laws 9
United States v. *Butler* 96–7, 101, 103
United States v. *Darby* 106, 171
United States v. *E.C. Knight Co.* 98
United States v. *Lopez* 99, 108, 173
United States v. *Morrison* 99, 108, 173
United States v. *Shreveport Grain and
    Elevator Co.* 100
United States v. *Wrightwood Dairy Co.*
    106–7
United States Agency for International
    Development (USAID)
    Development Credit Authority
    34

United States Department of
    Agriculture (USDA) 33
    Export Credit Guarantee Programs
      34
universality 17–18
Unlocking Credit for Small Businesses
    Program (UCSB) 5–6, 10
utilitarianism 59, 73, 119–22, 130
    see also modern liberalism; social
      welfare theory
utility domains 147–8

values 142–3
veil of ignorance 72, 73–4
Veterans Affairs, Department of 32–3
virtue 46–8, 52–3, 54, 117, 124
Viscusi, W.K. 150

wage labor 89–93, 117–18
Waldron, J. 136
wants
    likes and 144–5
    see also preferences
Washington, G. 47, 60, 181
Wayman v. *Southard* 100, 109, 110
Webster, N. 48, 50
welfare frontier (efficiency frontier)
    131–2, 141–7
wheat prices 107
Wickard v. *Filburn* 98, 99, 107, 173
William D. Ford Federal Direct
    Student Loan Program 33
Wilson, J. 18, 61–2, 64–5, 97, 159–61

Zywicki, T.J. 9